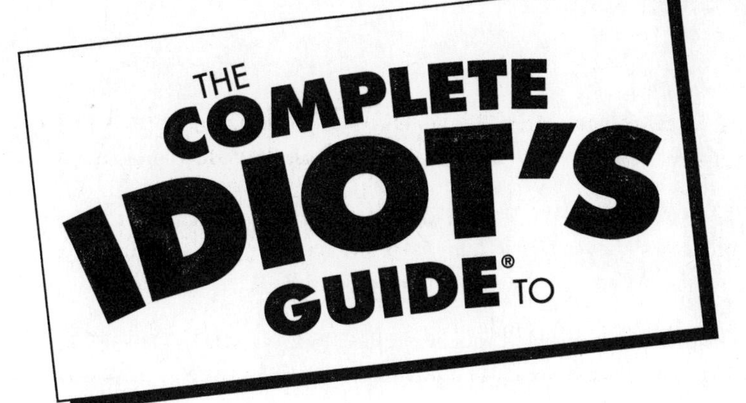

Motorcycles

Third Edition

by the Editors of Motorcyclist™ *Magazine with Darwin Holmstrom and Charles Everitt*

A member of Penguin Group (USA) Inc.

ALPHA BOOKS

Published by the Penguin Group

Penguin Group (USA) Inc., 375 Hudson Street, New York, New York 10014, U.S.A.

Penguin Group (Canada), 10 Alcorn Avenue, Toronto, Ontario, Canada M4V 3B2 (a division of Pearson Penguin Canada Inc.)

Penguin Books Ltd, 80 Strand, London WC2R 0RL, England

Penguin Ireland, 25 St Stephen's Green, Dublin 2, Ireland (a division of Penguin Books Ltd)

Penguin Group (Australia), 250 Camberwell Road, Camberwell, Victoria 3124, Australia (a division of Pearson Australia Group Pty Ltd)

Penguin Books India Pvt Ltd, 11 Community Centre, Panchsheel Park, New Delhi—110 017, India

Penguin Group (NZ), cnr Airborne and Rosedale Roads, Albany, Auckland 1310, New Zealand (a division of Pearson New Zealand Ltd)

Penguin Books (South Africa) (Pty) Ltd, 24 Sturdee Avenue, Rosebank, Johannesburg 2196, South Africa

Penguin Books Ltd, Registered Offices: 80 Strand, London WC2R 0RL, England

International Standard Book Number: 1-59257-303-7
Library of Congress Catalog Card Number: 2004113217

06 05 8 7 6 5 4 3

Interpretation of the printing code: The rightmost number of the first series of numbers is the year of the book's printing; the rightmost number of the second series of numbers is the number of the book's printing. For example, a printing code of 04-1 shows that the first printing occurred in 2004.

Printed in the United States of America

Publisher: *Marie Butler-Knight*
Product Manager: *Phil Kitchel*
Senior Managing Editor: *Jennifer Chisholm*
Senior Acquisitions Editor: *Mike Sanders*
Development Editor: *Jennifer Moore*
Senior Production Editor: *Billy Fields*
Copy Editor: *Krista Hansing*
Cartoonist: *Richard King*
Cover/Book Designer: *Trina Wurst*
Indexer: *Heather McNeil*
Layout: *Ayanna Lacey*

Contents at a Glance

Contents

Appendixes

Foreword

I have these really vivid visual images of bikes from when I was very young. I remember when I was about 5 years old, my aunt was going with a guy who had a bike. He came over to the house with his Harley. It had the two-tone tinted windshield like they had in the '50s, and on the bottom part of the windshield there was a sticker of a girl in a two-piece bathing suit. And I remember my mother going, "Get away from there!" And I said, "I'm not looking at the girl, I'm looking at the bike." And she said, "I know what you're looking at. Get out of there." "I'm not, I want to look at the bike." So I remember my mother having a huge fit over this pornographic motorcycle!

The first bike I ever got was a Honda 350 back in 1971. I bought it from a Harley-Davidson dealer in Everett, Massachusetts. I remember I went down and just bought it. You didn't have to have a license in those days. You didn't even have to know how to ride. You bought a motorcycle like you bought an air rifle. The salesman said, "Hey, okay, good luck," and you were off.

I remember getting on the freeway, not knowing what I was doing. I turned my head to see if a car was coming, and my glasses blew off. So now I'm on something I've never ridden, in the rain, with no helmet, of course, and I can't see. But I still remember thinking, "This is fun!"

Another time I was on that bike, still not very familiar with it, I got caught in some rain grooves. The tires just wanted to follow the grooves, you know? I thought, "How do I get out of this?" I remember just sailing past my exit and thinking that maybe I'd run out of gas or something. I had no idea what to do. That's why I think training is important. Back then, I learned by *almost* having accidents.

Riders today shouldn't have to learn the way I did. My advice to newcomers to motorcycling is this:

- Take a motorcycle safety course. That's the first thing.
- Lie down on the ground and have a friend put the bike gently on top of you. (Just kidding, folks—don't try this at home.) Okay, now magnify that feeling by a thousand because that's what it's like when you fall off a bike. Everybody falls off at some point, and you have to be willing to accept that.
- Never take the bike when you're in a hurry because that's when you'll have an accident. If work is 10 minutes away and I got up an hour early, I'll take the bike. If work is 10 minutes away and I've got to be there in 10 minutes, I'll take the car.

The motorcycling world is different now than when I got started. It's less cohesive than it used to be. The simplest poll to take is to ride down the street and wave, and see how many riders wave back. I'm probably the last generation of guys who waves at everybody. Owning a motorcycle used to be a lifestyle. Now it's more a lifestyle accessory, like a cellphone or a fanny pack.

Today people have a lot more money to spend, and they're not learning how to ride. I'm amazed at the number of people who just don't know how to ride. It's like you just buy this rocket ship that you sit on. But you have to prepare for motorcycling like it's a sport—because it is.

The editors at *Motorcyclist*™, Darwin Holmstrom, and Charles Everitt have pulled together a lot of great advice and information on the sport of motorcycling. As both an idiot and a motorcyclist, I found this book very helpful.

—Jay Leno

Motorcycle enthusiast, comedian, and host of *The Tonight Show*

Introduction

Motorcycles represent different things to different people. For some folks, they represent basic transportation. To others, they represent the exhilaration of power and speed. To the humorless, they represent a societal irritation. To me, motorcycles represent pure freedom.

Growing up on an isolated farm in northern Minnesota, I had a rather lonely childhood. Our nearest neighbor was several miles away, and I could go weeks or even months without seeing another kid once school let out for the summer. That changed during my eleventh summer, when I got my first motorcycle. My life has never been the same.

That was more than 25 years ago, and since then I've traveled hundreds of thousands of miles on a dozen different motorcycles. I've visited every contiguous state west of the Mississippi and a bunch to the east. I've lived in different cities and held different jobs, but the one thing that has remained constant is my devotion to the sport of motorcycling. As I write, the exhaust pipes on my motorcycle are cooling in my garage, having just returned from a 150-mile ride. (I ride year-round, which is no small feat, considering I live in Minnesota.)

I never feel more alive than when I'm riding a bike. For me, traveling in a car is too much like watching television: I feel as if I'm viewing my surroundings through the end of a glass tube. When I'm on a bike, I feel as though I am actually there, experiencing the world. Not only do I see my surroundings, but I feel them, smell them, and taste them. I feel a part of something larger, something complete, instead of feeling like an uninterested voyeur.

I derive great comfort from that feeling. Sometimes when I haven't ridden for a while, I start to feel disconnected. I don't notice it while it's happening, but when I finally get back out on the road, when I run my bike through the gears and watch the city disappear in my rearview mirror, I realize how out of touch with myself I've been. When I start to feel that way, I know it's time to go for a ride.

Because the sport of motorcycling has brought me so much pleasure and satisfaction, I want to share this activity with others; my goal is to bring as many people into the motorcycling community as I can. But it is not a community to be entered into lightly. As rewarding as motorcycling is, it comes with risks. This is especially true for new riders. Your chances of getting in trouble decrease as you become more experienced.

But motorcycling can be a safe sport, even when you are just starting out. The key is proper training. Such training hasn't always been easy to obtain. Back when I was learning to ride, I had absolutely no guidance. The dealer who sold me my first bike explained how to shift the gears and then sent me on my way. That was the extent of my training.

Times have changed. Thanks to the work of such organizations as the Motorcycle Safety Foundation (MSF), rider training is available in most parts of the United States. In this book, I've gathered information from the best sources and combined it with my own experience to create what I hope will be one of the best books available for a beginning rider.

I've also included a lot of practical and fun information unavailable anywhere else to help make this book the most complete beginner's resource you can buy. In addition to basic and advanced riding techniques and general motorcycle maintenance, I've covered the history of motorcycling, the types of bikes available, and the general workings of a bike.

In this book, you'll learn how to buy a bike. You'll learn about motorcycle racing and how you can become a racer. I'll show you what accessories will make your motorcycle more enjoyable to ride and where you can find those accessories. Perhaps most important, I'll teach you about the motorcycling community itself.

And, of course, there are plenty of pictures. If you're anything like me, you enjoy looking at motorcycles almost as much as riding them.

How to Use This Book

This book follows a linear, step-by-step structure and takes you through the entire motorcycle experience from start to finish. This book is structured this way to help you minimize the risks associated with motorcycling, to help make your entry into the sport safe and enjoyable.

I've divided the book into five parts, each designed to take you to a new level of enjoyment in a safe, orderly fashion.

Part 1, "Biker Basics," sets the stage for the adventure you are about to embark on, providing a general overview of why we ride, the history of motorcycling, and the types of bikes available.

Part 2, "So You Want to Buy a Bike?" helps you identify what type of motorcycle you need and teaches you how to buy your first motorcycle. You get detailed discussions about the parts of a motorcycle and, more important, how those parts relate to you, the rider.

Part 3, "On the Road," is probably the most important part of this book. It helps you actually get out and ride. This is where you put your knowledge to the test, where theory translates into reality.

Part 4, "Living with a Motorcycle," condenses the entire spectrum of the motorcycle-ownership experience into chapters that cover maintenance, repair, customization, and collecting.

Part 5, "The Motorcycling Community," provides an overview of the world you are getting into. When you buy a motorcycle, you are not just buying an object; you're investing in a lifestyle. This part discusses the many places in which you'll meet fellow motorcycle enthusiasts, including motorcycle clubs, races, and rallies.

I've also included five appendixes that you'll find useful. Appendix A lists all the new streetbikes for sale in the United States, along with the bikes that are best suited for beginners and the bikes I believe are best buys. Appendix B features a comprehensive list of used bikes that make ideal first motorcycles. Appendix C highlights useful motorcycle-related resources, and Appendix D is a glossary of the terms you'll encounter in this book.

Extras

Throughout this book you'll find tips and information that will help you ride better and safer without looking like a dork in the process. This information is highlighted in sidebars:

Motorcycology

Tips and inside information providing insights into safe, enjoyable motorcycling.

Motorcycle Moments

Anecdotes of historical and personal moments in the history of motorcycling.

Steer Clear

Advice on practices and hazards to avoid if you want to keep the shiny side up, which means not falling down.

Cycle Babble

Definitions of technical motorcycling terms that pop up throughout the book.

A Note About the Third Edition

The Buddhists have a saying: "He who knows, doesn't know. He who knows he doesn't know, knows." Looking back at *The Complete Idiot's Guide to Motorcycles*, I realize I've forgotten more about motorcycling than I thought I knew when I originally wrote the book. Even though I've been riding now for 30 years, I still learn something new about the fascinating and complex activity of motorcycling each and every time I ride. And as I wrote in the original introduction, the more you know, the more rewarding riding your motorcycle will be.

Every activity entails a certain amount of risk, whether that activity is inline skating, swimming, working out on a treadmill, or riding a motorcycle. Even inactivity entails a certain amount of risk—just look at the number of couch potatoes who suffer from heart disease. But motorcycling probably entails a higher-than-average amount of risk.

I accept a certain amount of risk, but I also do everything in my power to keep that risk to a minimum. I always wear protective gear, even when I'm just running to the corner store for some ice cream. I keep a constant vigil over other traffic, and I do all my spirited riding as far from populated areas as possible. I read as much as I can about riding techniques, and I practice those techniques on a regular basis. And I always strive to stay alert and focused on my riding at all times.

I have crashed over the years, and I have been seriously injured, yet only once have I ever contemplated quitting riding. It was the day I learned *Motorcyclist*™ editor Greg McQuide had been killed in a motorcycle accident. I learned the news while at work, and after hearing about Greg, I didn't want to get on my bike to ride home. Then I thought about Greg, a man who lived life with more joy than just about anyone I have ever met. It occurred to me that Greg would feel terrible if he knew he had contributed to my decision to quit riding. He knew how much I love riding motorcycles, how much pleasure they give me. That ended my brief flirtation with abandoning the sport.

At the end of Sinclair Lewis's novel *Babbitt*, the title character reflects back on his life. Babbitt realizes his life had been a total waste because he had never done a single thing he wanted to do. Greg McQuide wouldn't have had that realization, and I hope it's not one I ever have. I intend to keep riding as long as I'm able. I will, however, continuously strive to be more focused and cautious when I ride. I think Greg would appreciate that.

Acknowledgments

I would like to thank all the people who helped with this book. Judy and Dan Kennedy at Whitehorse Press have been incredibly helpful, providing me with much information at the exact moment I needed it. It's as if they read my mind at times. I found their excellent book *The Motorcycling Safety Foundation's Guide to Motorcycling Excellence* to be the single most useful resource I used in writing this book. Whitehorse's *Street Smart* video series also proved to be an essential source of information.

I would also like to thank the Motorcycle Safety Foundation itself, partly because, without the groundbreaking work it has done in the field of motorcycle safety, this book could not have been written, and partly because of all the lives it has saved.

I received a great deal of last-minute help getting items I needed for photo shoots from several people and companies, especially Ron Harper at Chase Harper, Ann Willey at National Cycle, and Fred Wyse at Vanson. Over the years, I have used products from all three companies, which is why I chose them for the photos—I know they are of the highest quality. It was nice to discover that the folks making those products are of the same high quality.

I want to thank the photographers who supplied me with last-minute photography: Brian J. Nelson, Timothy Remus, and Rick Menapace. I'd also like to thank the people who helped with the photo shoot: Jennifer and Dave Berger and Ed Ostoj.

Dan Keenen at Dynojet Research helped me put some technical information into terms anyone can understand, for which I am grateful. I'd also like to thank all the other individuals and groups who helped me write this book.

I'd like to thank all the motorcycle journalists who inspired me to not only ride, but to write about my experiences. The work of Phil Schilling, Cook Neilson, John Burns, Gordon Jennings, Jamie Elvidge, Art Friedman, Kevin Cameron, Peter Egan, Mark Cook, David Edwards, Greg McQuide, Ed Hertfelder, Andy Cherney, Clement Salvadori, Steven Thompson, Andrew Trevitt, Matthew Miles, Jon Thompson, Lee Parks, Steve Anderson, Mark Hoyer, Fred Rau, Evans Brasfield, Bob Carpenter, Kent Kunitsugu, Don Canet, and countless others helped me get through many long winters in the Northern Plains. I'd like to give a special thanks to those journalists who write about safety issues, writers such as David Hough and Lawrence Grodsky. Not only have they helped me learn what I needed to know to write this book, but they also may have saved my life a time or two.

I'd also like to thank my wife, Patricia, whose support (and tolerance) helped make this book possible.

I'd especially like to thank *Motorcyclist*™ editor Mitch Boehm, who connected me with this project.

This book is dedicated to the memory of Greg McQuide, *Motorcyclist*™ associate editor and eternal FNG. Greg was one of the finest people with whom I have ever had the opportunity to work, and I suspect he is one of the very best editors in heaven.

Trademarks

Part 1

Biker Basics

Congratulations! As a beginning biker, you are about to embark on an adventure that will change your life. No other hobby will affect you at such a fundamental level as motorcycling. It will start subtly: at work, you'll find yourself daydreaming about going for a ride while you stare at the gibberish on your computer screen; in meetings, you'll look right through your boss and instead see the road outside the window. In your mind, you'll be riding on that road. Before you know it, you'll have a pet name for your motorcycle, which, of course, you'll tattoo on some hidden part of your body.

In other words, you will become a biker.

You are about to enter the community of motorcyclists. In this part of the book, you'll learn about that community, its history, and all it has to offer you—including an introduction to the joys of motorcycling.

Chapter 1

The Motorcycle Mystique

In This Chapter

- Why motorcyclists love to ride
- Motorcycles as chicken soup for your soul
- The cultural impact of motorcycles
- How motorcycle films have shaped generations of motorcyclists
- The advantages of owning a motorcycle

Perhaps one word best sums up the appeal of motorcycles: *fun.* Fun is what I had the first time I rode my neighbor's minibike nearly three decades ago. It's what I had this morning when I took my bike out for a ride.

But it's a complex fun, composed of many facets. Part of the pleasure of riding comes from the freedom and mobility the machine gives you. The exhilaration you feel as you power effortlessly up to cruising speed provides a portion of the fun. Part of your enjoyment comes from developing your riding skills—your ability to control the beast.

In this chapter, I'll show you why motorcycle riding can be such a rewarding, exhilarating, and liberating experience.

The Thrill of the Open Road

The sun creeps over the treetops, its warm rays driving the chill from your limbs as you open the garage door and wheel your motorcycle out onto the driveway. You prop up the bike and check to make certain everything is okay, which it will be because you take good care of your machine. You don your helmet and jacket and pull on your gloves, and then start your engine. The beast jumps to life and then settles into a lumpy, powerful idle. You look over the bike one last time, and then mount up and ride away. Now the fun begins.

At about the same time, your neighbor, co-worker, friend, or family member is unloading his—or her—dirtbike at a local off-road park. He goes through the same rituals, giving the machine a thorough preflight inspection, donning protective gear, and then mounting up, snicking the machine into gear, and riding away. Now the fun begins.

You take it easy at first, waiting for your tires to warm. You shift through the gears, feeling the satisfying mesh of the cogs, and breathe in the cool, clean morning air. The vibration through the handlebars and footpegs feels reassuring, making you aware of your machine's mechanical presence.

As you ease out onto the practice track, looking for oncoming riders, you do a warm-up lap. With each lap, you increase your speed, getting air over the jumps. The bike responds perfectly to every weight shift, to every control input.

As your tires warm, you start accelerating harder through each curve. You snake through a series of S-curves, settling into a rhythm among you, the road, and your bike, engaged in a dance as elegant as any ballet. This is what it's all about.

As your muscles warm, you start riding harder, hitting the triple section perfectly, and taking inside lines where others are taking the longer, slower outside one. You and your bike find the track's rhythm, one that's less of a ballet and more of a break dance. This is what it's all about.

It doesn't matter whether you're riding a cutting-edge sportbike, a heavyweight cruiser, a big touring bike, or a powerful but agile dirtbike; the thrill of the ride is what draws you out again and again. Whatever emotional baggage you may have accumulated, you leave behind on the open road. When you're participating in a dance with your bike and the road, it doesn't matter that your boss is a pointy-headed sociopath, that your spouse shouts at you, or that your kids act like juvenile delinquents. There's no room for such worries on a bike because the activity at hand requires your total, undivided attention.

Bikes Are Beautiful

Most of us find motorcycles themselves gratifying—objects of art with an innate beauty that fills some need within us.

Cycle Babble

While it's not exactly a technical term, often you will hear the word **gearhead** used when describing a motorcyclist. Gearhead refers to a person with a strong interest in all things mechanical.

Motorcyclists tend to be *gearheads*. We love looking at our motorcycles almost as much as we love riding them. (In fact, some folks seem to be more enamored of viewing their machines than they are of riding them; legions of people trailer their motorcycles to different events around the country instead of riding them.)

Motorcycles possess a raw mechanical beauty. You'll be seeing all kinds of beautiful bikes throughout this book, but for starters, I think no bike better illustrates this visceral look than Harley-Davidson's Sportster. While Sportsters are Harley's smallest bikes, they are by no means small. They're midsize bikes, weighing around 525 pounds with a full tank of gas. Visually, the 1998 model is little changed from the original Sportster introduced in 1957, and many people agree that that's a good thing.

Harley's Sportsters, such as this XL 1200R Roadster, represent the elemental motorcycle. They consist of an engine, a couple of tires, and a gas tank—you'll find virtually nothing superfluous here.

(Photograph by Kevin Wing)

Until 2004, Sportsters were practically dinosaurs in every respect: They weren't very powerful, they were uncomfortable, they didn't handle exceptionally well, and they shook like unbalanced washing machines. Yet Harley sold as many of them as it could build. The latest Sportsters, with their rubber-mounted engines, belong firmly in the present. Yet they retain what I believe is an honest, brutal appearance that, to many eyes, is how a motorcycle should look. But now riders no longer have to overlook or correct a Sportster's flaws just to ride the archetypal motorcycle.

The looks of most Harleys, not just Sportsters, elicit strong, mostly favorable responses from motorcyclists and nonmotorcyclists alike. No other motorcycle company has had its products elevated to near-art status the way Harley-Davidson has.

As you'll see in Chapter 18, the customized machines of such builders as Arlen Ness, Mallard Teal, and Donnie Smith often resemble metallic sculptures more than motorcycles. A visit to any custom-bike show can take on the trappings of a visit to a museum.

All of this provides a good example of how important the look of a motorcycle is. That's as true of a Yamaha, Triumph, Laverda, or BMW as it is of a Harley. Motorcyclists love the way bikes look, and for every bike, there is someone who loves its appearance.

I learned this the hard way. A while back, in an article on motorcycle style, I poked fun at a bike that was generally accepted as being one of the uglier machines to have been produced during the past 20 years. I wrote that these motorcycles were probably very nice bikes, but they were so butt-ugly that no one ever found out because no one would be seen on one. I thought this was a fair assessment, since the bike had been a sales disaster.

Motorcycology

The demise of an entire motorcycle company can partly be traced to its producing one motorcycle that the public found visually unappealing. BSA attempted to enter the modern motorcycle market by producing a three-cylinder motorcycle, the BSA Rocket 3. The bike showed promise, but its styling, created by an industrial design firm with no experience in the motorcycle market, received such a dismal public reception that the resulting low sales caused BSA to implode.

Fair or not, at least one reader took issue with my critique and wrote in suggesting that my head was deeply embedded in a place that defied all laws of physics. The man owned one such "ugly motorcycle," and it had given him more than 100,000 miles of enjoyment. I felt bad about that situation, not because the reader questioned my hygienic habits and insulted my ancestors, but because I had belittled a motorcycle that obviously meant a great deal to him.

The Tao of Two Wheels

Some time ago, a colleague of mine, a reporter who covered religious topics at a newspaper, asked me why I didn't go to church. I told her I did go to church every day I went out riding my motorcycle.

For many motorcyclists, the ceremony of going for a ride provides the same spiritual sustenance other people find through the ceremonies conducted by organized religions. The similarities are striking. We wear our leathers and riding suits as vestments, we have a prescribed ritual for starting our engines, and our favorite roads compose our liturgy.

The very nature of riding a motorcycle forces the rider into a spiritual state. Think of it this way: most religious systems encourage some form of meditative technique. Christians have prayer. Some Native Americans meditate inside sweat lodges, and Eastern spiritual systems advocate elaborate chanting techniques. All these methods have as their common general goal the transcendence of the self or ego in order to get in touch with some greater force.

Motorcycling forces riders to transcend their egos—to empty themselves and exist in the world around them. The consequences of not being totally aware of their actions and environment, of becoming distracted by the baggage of their everyday lives, are too great. When you're out in the world on a bike, you must be completely in the moment, completely aware of your surroundings, or you may find yourself meeting your concept of God earlier than you might have hoped.

But when everything is working, when you and your bike are totally in sync and the road rushing under your feet feels like an extension of your body—at those times, you get in touch with divinity.

Biker Chic

Not all that long ago, motorcycles were considered the domain of leather-clad hoodlums—guys you didn't want your daughter to be seen with. But that stereotype has always been inaccurate, and most people now realize that.

Motorcycling began to gain social acceptance in the 1960s, when the Japanese began exporting small, unintimidating motorcycles to the United States, but only in recent years has motorcycling been elevated to the status of high fashion.

Motorcycle Moments

Although most people realize that motorcyclists are respected members of society, a few holdouts still cling to the image of the outlaw biker. During the summer of 1997, the BMW Riders Association held a rally at Fontana Village in Graham County, North Carolina. Citing Graham County Sheriff's Office reports that 14,000 outlaw bikers were about to invade the county, law-enforcement agencies from across the state descended on the rally. They set up road blocks, searched motorcycles for drugs and weapons, and generally harassed rally-goers. Apparently, intelligence gatherers failed to inform officials that BMW riders tend to be the most conservative segment of the motorcycling community and that there probably aren't 14,000 outlaw bikers left in the entire country.

Celebrities have always ridden motorcycles. Clark Gable terrorized Los Angeles on his Ariel Square Four. Marlon Brando used his own personal motorcycle in the film *The Wild One*. James Dean rode bikes from the time he was in high school. Steve McQueen's real-life racing antics made the jump scene in *The Great Escape* look feeble.

But these were Hollywood's bad boys—sexy rebels who knew no fear. You wouldn't find a nice woman like Donna Reed or a respectable fellow like Jimmy Stewart straddling a motorcycle.

Sometime during the 1980s, that changed. This shift in our collective perception began slowly. Photos of celebrity CEO Malcolm Forbes touring the world on his Harley-Davidson appeared in mainstream magazines, and Juan Carlos, the King of Spain, could be found touring his domain on a Harley. And, of course, Hollywood's latest string of bad boys—people such as Mickey Rourke, Sylvester Stallone, Bruce Willis, and Arnold Schwarzenegger—came out of the closet and proclaimed themselves bikers.

But it didn't stop there. Nice, respectable folks such as Jay Leno and Mary Hart let the world know they were motorcyclists. Country boy Lyle Lovett began appearing on magazine covers aboard his hot-rod Ducati. Rosie O'Donnell seldom appeared in the tabloids without her Suzuki Intruder. Ewen "Obi-Wan" McGregor took months off from his lucrative film career to take the trip-of-a-lifetime adventure tour. Mark-Paul Gosselaar of *NYPD Blue* likes to ride motocross. And Anthony Quinn's son Francesco has been riding since the tender age of 4.

Now motorcycles are must-have fashion accessories for celebrities and celebrity wannabes, much like nipple rings were *de rigueur* for Seattle grunge rockers in the early 1990s.

The Art of Motorcycles

Although the motorcycle-as-nipple-ring is a fairly recent development, bikes have always had a strong influence on popular culture. In turn, popular culture has played a strong role in developing the motorcycle community.

The appeal of motorcycles to actors is no coincidence. Because riding a bike is a high-profile activity, motorcycles have always been an excellent method for studios to showcase and draw attention to their stars.

The history of motorcycles in film is as old as the history of motion pictures itself. Motorcycles appeared in some of the earliest silent films, including *Mabel at the Wheel* (1914), in which Charlie Chaplin drops Mabel off the back of his motorcycle and into a mud puddle.

Films about motorcycle riders appeared early on, including in *No Limit* (1935), in which English actor George Formby played a motorcycle-riding hero battling a gang of biker toughs.

While motorcycles played many roles in Hollywood films, the medium of film played an even more influential role in shaping motorcycle culture. As motorcycle films became more popular, increasing numbers of riders tried to emulate their screen heroes. When Marlon Brando portrayed Johnny in *The Wild One*, he portrayed a very atypical motorcyclist. After a generation of bikers grew up with Brando's Johnny as a role model, though, the image of the leather-clad motorcycle-riding hood, while still an aberration, became much more common.

Because of the influence of films, portrayals of motorcyclists became self-fulfilling prophesies. The myriad outlaw biker B-movies Hollywood cranked out during the 1960s and 1970s spawned a subculture of motorcyclists who modeled themselves on the bikers in those films. When Peter Fonda portrayed the philosophical Wyatt in *Easy Rider*, he gave birth to the real-life hippie poet-biker stereotype. When Arnold Schwarzenegger came back as promised in *Terminator 2: Judgment Day*, he did so on a Harley Fat Boy. Soon a Harley and a cigar were the fashion accessories of the 1990s.

From a Wild One to an Easy Rider

The films *The Wild One* and *Easy Rider* marked the beginning and the end of Hollywood's most influential period on motorcycling and are the two most important motorcycle films ever made.

The Wild One became the archetypal biker flick because it was the first to portray the unique breed of bikers that sprang up in post–World War II America.

Motorcycle Moments

The event that inspired the film *The Wild One,* the so-called Hollister Invasion, was actually more of a nonevent. On the Fourth of July of 1947, about 3,500 motorcyclists rode to Hollister, California (a town of about 4,500), to attend an American Motorcycle Association (AMA) race meeting. Another 500 or so riders showed up just to have a little fun. A few bikers got a bit out of hand, and by noon the next day, 29 of them had been cited for drunkenness, indecent exposure, and traffic violations. The real importance of the event involved its press coverage: Newspapers ran hyperbolic tales of anarchy and debauchery as thousands of bikers ran amuck, and *Life* magazine printed an infamous photo of a beer-guzzling rider stretched out on his customized Harley amid a pile of beer bottles. (The photo was staged by the *Life* photographer.) The myth of the outlaw biker was born.

According to legend, the term *onepercenter,* used to describe outlaw bikers, was created after the Hollister Invasion, when an AMA official blamed the trouble on the 1 percent of motorcyclists who belonged to the outlaw contingent.

This film initiated a decades-long period of mistrust between motorcyclists and the general public. Johnny and his buddies seem pretty tame by today's standards; compared to bikers portrayed in later flicks, they're about as nice a bunch of boys as you'll ever meet. But back in 1953, Johnny represented the antichrist to Middle America.

The Wild One gave birth to a new genre: the B biker movie. In the 1950s and 1960s, Hollywood cranked out a pile of low-budget biker flicks. Each of these films tried to outdo the others in portraying the wild outlaw biker. *Easy Rider,* starring Peter Fonda, Dennis Hopper, and Jack Nicholson (in his first major film role), shattered that stereotype. Directed by Dennis Hopper, the movie changed everything. No longer was the antihero biker a confused Neanderthal, mindlessly lashing out at whatever got in his way. Instead, *Easy Rider* presented the biker as a sensitive, thoughtful enigma.

With the film Easy Rider, *actors Dennis Hopper and Peter Fonda turned the Hollywood biker image upside down.*

(Photo courtesy Motorcyclist™ *magazine)*

The financial success of *Easy Rider* ensured another host of imitators, but the biker-flick genre's success was short-lived. The problem seemed to be that there was no new ground to break: *Easy Rider* was such an encompassing film that all following flicks were pale imitations by comparison.

Motorcycle Moments

Although Peter Fonda was an accomplished motorcyclist before he filmed *Easy Rider,* co-star Dennis Hopper was anything but. Before he made the film, Hopper's motorcycle experience was confined to a scooter he had owned in the 1950s—and he had crashed that machine in a rather spectacular fashion. After finishing the film, Hopper admitted to having been scared silly by his Harley.

Easy Rider: The Convenience of Bikes

Given the influence motorcycles have had on film and on our general culture, it's easy to argue the more esoteric appeal of motorcycling, but the sport has some practical benefits as well.

The relatively low price of motorcycles makes them attractive as practical transportation. While prices have risen dramatically during the past couple of decades, for the most part, bikes are still much less expensive than cars. You can buy a motorcycle in "like-new" condition in the $2,500 price range. For that money, you can pick up a bike that will deliver years or even decades of trouble-free transportation. Try finding a car for the same amount that isn't ready for the crusher.

In congested urban areas, the small size and mobility of a motorcycle provide real advantages over a car. An experienced rider can zip through traffic, and in places where the practice is legal (such as California), you can ride between lanes on the freeways (a practice known as *lane splitting*).

Cycle Babble

Lane splitting refers to the practice of riding between lanes of traffic on a freeway. While this practice may sound dangerous, studies indicate that it might actually be safer than idling along in a traffic jam.

And with a motorcycle, you will never have to worry about a parking spot. You can always find a space to back into because you'll require only a fraction of the space a car requires.

Another practical benefit of motorcycles is their fuel efficiency. Even the biggest touring bike or fastest sportbike gets as many miles to the gallon as most econocars, and when ridden prudently, a smaller motorcycle can get 60 miles to the gallon or better. My wife once got 79 miles to the gallon on a small motorcycle she rode through the mountains of Colorado.

If global climate change really is caused by the burning of fossil fuels, as the majority of respected scientists believe it is, we may soon be facing the prospect of ever more dramatically increased fuel prices. While this does not bode well for motorsports in general, because of the fuel-efficient nature of motorcycles, we could be poised for a new boom of motorcycles as a form of practical transportation. This has been the case for years in Europe.

The Least You Need to Know

- You get from motorcycling what you put into it.
- Like meditation, motorcycling requires your undivided attention.
- Biker flicks have shaped motorcycle culture as much as motorcycle culture has shaped biker flicks.
- Motorcycles can be practical as well as fun.

Chapter 2

A Brief History of Bikes

In This Chapter

- How motorcycling developed from cheap transportation into a passionate hobby
- The myth of the outlaw biker
- How the baby boomers changed the face of motorcycling
- Harley-Davidson's role in today's motorcycle market

Motorcycling offers more pleasure than any other activity a person can engage in (well, okay, not *any* other activity, but almost). It also extracts a high penalty for making mistakes. If you're going to be a motorcyclist, you'll need as much knowledge as you can get to survive out there, and a solid understanding of the history of the sport is part of that knowledge.

But knowing how we got here from there serves as an ego boost as well. Motorcyclists are gearheads, people with an almost unnatural attraction to things mechanical. Like every other group, we have our inside secrets, status symbols that tell whether a person is a hardcore rider or just another dork with a motorcycle. Few of these clues scream "Dork!" as loudly as a rider poorly versed in the history of motorcycles. In this chapter, I'll give you the inside info you'll need to become a true motorcyclist.

Humble Beginnings

Almost as soon as the modern bicycle appeared toward the end of the nineteenth century, some inspired individual decided to strap an internal-combustion motor to the contraption. By the turn of the century, a variety of motorized bicycles was available to the general public.

The motorized-bicycle experiments of two young men, William S. Harley and Arthur Davidson, proved to be more influential to American motorcycling than all the rest combined.

The pair realized their experiments had commercial potential, and along with Arthur's brothers, Walter and William, they formed the Harley-Davidson Motor Company in 1903 to manufacture motorized bicycles. From this humble beginning sprang the longest continuously running motorcycle-manufacturing firm in the world, affectionately known as The Motor Company.

But Mr. Harley and the Davidson boys weren't the only people conducting such experiments.

Motorcycle Moments

Gottlieb Daimler, the German inventor who produced the first functional four-stroke engine, may well have created the first gasoline-powered motorcycle. After his early experiments using an engine to power a four-wheeled horseless carriage produced less than satisfactory results (probably due to the whopping 0.5 horsepower the motor cranked out), Daimler built his *Einspur,* or single-tracked test vehicle, in 1885. Although crude, this vehicle incorporated many features still found on motorcycles today, such as a cradle frame and twist-grip controls on the handlebars.

But even that wasn't the first motorcycle. The Smithsonian Institute's National Museum of American History displays a two-wheeled powered vehicle built in about 1868 by Sylvester H. Roper, a Massachusetts resident. The main difference between Roper's and Daimler's machines was Roper's use of a steam engine.

In 1902, one year before the formation of The Motor Company, a German engineer named Maurice (Mauritz) Johann Schulte designed a motorcycle, the first to be produced by Triumph Cycle Co., Ltd., of England. This machine was still very much a motorized bicycle with a Belgian-produced engine fitted to its frame.

The early years of the twentieth century saw hundreds of similar companies form. The low power output of the engines available at the time made them better suited to power small, two-wheeled vehicles than larger, carriage-type machines, and motorcycles thrived as forms of personal transportation. Plus, cars were still too expensive for most people to own; motorcycles were cheaper and more plentiful.

Like all technology of that time, motorcycle development proceeded at a frantic pace. Soon the early motorized bicycles were supplanted by machines designed from the start to be operated by some form of engine. By the end of World War I, most of the technical innovations we see today had been tried with varying degrees of success. Because other technologies, such as metallurgy—the study of metals—hadn't kept pace with such innovations, by the 1920s, motorcycle designers had settled on relatively simple designs. The brilliant ideas of those early designers proved to be ahead of their time, and many would have to wait until the 1970s or 1980s to finally find acceptance.

Although the sport of motorcycling thrived initially, the same technological advances that drove its success led to the first of the sport's many crises. As internal-combustion engines became more powerful and efficient, they became more practical as power sources for horseless carriages. And with the advent of affordable automobiles such as Henry Ford's Model T in 1913, average people could afford to buy cars. Clearly, it was easier to haul the entire family to church in an automobile; you could only haul three or four family members on a motorcycle, and then only if it was equipped with a *sidecar*. By the end of World War I, many of the companies manufacturing motorcycles had either gone out of business or switched to the manufacture of some other product. Motorcycles might have become extinct except for some clever marketing moves on the part of the remaining manufacturers.

Cycle Babble

Sidecars are small carriages attached to the side of a motorcycle to provide extra carrying capacity and extra stability in low-speed, low-traction conditions. Sidecars usually consist of a tubelike cockpit area resting on a frame that attaches to the motorcycle on one side and is held aloft by a wheel on the opposite side.

Motorcycling survived by positioning itself as a sport, a leisure activity, rather than trying to compete with automobiles as practical transportation. The move made sense. People had been racing motorcycles all along; promoting riding in general as a sport was a logical extension of that activity.

This market positioning helped motorcycling survive its second great crisis: the Great Depression. This worldwide economic disaster finished off many of the remaining motorcycle-manufacturing firms that had survived the advent of the inexpensive, reliable automobile, and, again, those companies that survived did so by promoting motorcycling as a sport.

The Wild Ones: The Outlaws' Conveyance

Motorcycling in America entered the modern era following World War II. Important technological advances had been made before the war, but most people were too busy struggling to survive the Depression to pay much attention.

World War II changed all that. After the war, a lot of restless people came back from Europe and Asia, people not content to go back to the way things were. They could afford transportation, and they had an elaborate new highway system to explore. Many of them decided to explore those new roads via motorcycles.

As you saw in the previous chapter, the film *The Wild One* played an important role in the formation of the postwar motorcycling community. It was a difficult time for many Americans. We'd won the war, but afterward, nothing seemed quite the same. To the general public, Johnny, Marlon Brando's character in the film, represented everything that was wrong with the country. Like Communism, the stereotype of the outlaw biker became a focal point for their fears.

When Marlon Brando roared into small-town America in The Wild One, *he used his own motorcycle, a 650-cc Triumph Thunderbird very much like this 1953 example.*

(Photo © 1998 Timothy Remus)

But not everyone feared Johnny. Some people wanted more out of life than the latest automatic appliances in the kitchen and a new Plymouth sedan parked in the driveway. For them, Johnny represented an escape from the mind-numbing conformity of McCarthy-era America. In Johnny, Brando created a role model for these disaffected young people—a figure who jelled in America's psyche as the archetypal outlaw biker.

The Japanese Invasion

Throughout the 1950s, motorcycling remained the domain of extreme gearheads and onepercenters (outlaws). Nice people didn't ride a bike. Nice people didn't even associate with those who did ride, whether they were upstanding members of the American Motorcycle Association (AMA) or hardcore outlaws.

The reason for this involved more than just the perceived danger of the sport or of motorcyclists' outlaw image. There were practical reasons for the marginality of motorcycling as well.

Part of the problem was that the machines themselves demanded a great deal from their owners. The technological advancements of motorcycling hadn't kept pace with those of automobiles. By the 1950s, cars were relatively reliable, easily maintained devices, and the experience of owning one wasn't all that different than it is today.

Bikes were another story.

The reason only gearheads owned motorcycles back then was that you *had* to be a gearhead to own one. There was nothing easy about riding a bike. Even starting the beast was a traumatic experience in those pre-electric-start days. Glance at the starting procedure of a mid-1950s Triumph as outlined in its owner's manual, and you'll be instructed to tickle carburetors, retard the spark, and align the piston according to the phase of the moon. Once you'd accomplished all this, it was time to kick the starting lever. If all was in sync and the gods were smiling on you, the machine would start without backfiring and smashing your ankle into hundreds of tiny bone shards (which happened more frequently than you might imagine).

And all this just to *start* the bike. Keeping it running was just as difficult. Riders who put a lot of miles on their machines knew the inner workings of their bikes intimately. They saw them frequently, sometimes even when they hadn't intended to: more than one rider saw pistons, valves, and connecting rods flying from their engines as they exploded like grenades between the riders' legs.

You Meet the Nicest People on a Honda

Part of the reason for the stagnation in motorcycle design at this time was lack of competition. The Indian Motorcycle Company (the first American motorcycle company, preceding Harley-Davidson by two years) had quit building motorcycles by the mid-1950s; even before it gave up the ghost, it had long ceased being competitive with Harley-Davidson. The British manufacturers had to keep up with only one another, and as long as none of them raised the stakes too high, none of them had to try too hard. There were interesting developments taking place in other European countries, but those countries were still in such turmoil from the war that manufacturers there concentrated on producing cheap transportation for their own people and weren't interested in exporting motorcycles to the rest of the world.

That was soon to change. In only a few years, these complacent manufacturers found themselves up against some very serious competition from a most unlikely source: Japan.

Like Italy and Germany, Japan was in ruins following World War II. Japan's manufacturing infrastructure had been even more severely devastated. After the war, Japan had to start from scratch. The Japanese rose to the challenge, and rather than rebuilding the past, they looked to the future for their inspiration.

Motorcycle Moments

While most early Japanese motorcycles were small bikes, the bikes manufactured by the Rikuo company were big exceptions. That company manufactured large V-twin Harley-Davidson replicas, built under a licensing agreement with The Motor Company. Soon Rikuo was improving on the Harley design, introducing telescopic forks in 1948, a year before Harley introduced the innovation. This was followed by the introduction of a foot-operated gearshift (Harley still used a cumbersome, hand-operated system) and automatic spark advance (for easier starting). By this time, Rikuo believed it had modified its design to the point that it no longer had to pay for the license agreement. Harley disagreed and made its displeasure known to the Japanese government, which, in turn, withdrew its orders for police bikes from Rikuo, forcing the company out of business.

As in European countries, Japan's postwar motorcycle industry emerged to service society's need for cheap transportation. That industry had a humble beginning, with many manufacturers building clones of bikes from other countries.

Americans had little use for the more or less overgrown mopeds coming out of Japan, nor did any other country for quite a few years. But by the late 1950s, Japanese motorcycles began to make their way into Europe and then into the United States. By this time, Japanese bikes had evolved into distinctive, original machines with innovations that made riders take note. These were elegant, reliable, nimble, and fast bikes—and cheap, to boot.

The innovation people most took note of was the inclusion of electric starters on many of these machines. No longer did riders need the legs of mules to kick-start their bikes; they simply pushed a button and rode off.

Unlike other manufacturers, the Japanese realized the sales potential of motorcycles that were convenient to use, and no Japanese company capitalized on convenience as a selling point as well as Honda. In an ad campaign designed to highlight the utility of its machines, Honda set the sport of motorcycling on the path toward respectability.

Motorcycology

Before becoming a manufacturer of motorcycles, Soichiro Honda, the founder of Honda, operated a series of businesses that were less than successful. In fact, he once described his life as "Nothing but mistakes, a series of failures, a series of regrets." But he credited those failures for his success. "Success can be achieved only through repeated failure and introspection. In fact, success represents 1 percent of your work and results from the 99 percent that is called failure."

That campaign was the famous "You meet the nicest people on a Honda" series of ads, and it singlehandedly undid much of the damage done to the image of motorcycling by films such as *The Wild One.* The ads, which featured "normal" people doing nonoutlaw-type things on Honda motorcycles, appeared in 1961 and were so effective that they made the sport of motorcycling seem acceptable to society as a whole. The ads had such a powerful effect that for years afterward, the word *Honda* became synonymous with small motorcycles, much like the name *Xerox* is used as a verb meaning "to photocopy."

This Honda ad proved so effective at getting people to buy motorcycles that it's still studied in advertising classes today.

(Photo courtesy Vreeke and Associates)

The Japanese Hit the Big Time

Because the Japanese were producing only small motorcycles and not "real" bikes, the other major manufacturers didn't consider them a serious threat and paid little attention to them. That proved to be a mistake—a fatal mistake for many of the more marginal manufacturers—because the Japanese were deadly serious.

As the 1960s progressed, the bikes coming from Japan increased in size and capabilities, but the other manufacturers still paid them little heed. By 1965, when Honda introduced its CB450 Super Sport, the competition had wised up. This bike, known as the Black Bomber for its racy black bodywork, handled like a European machine and could outrun a stock Harley-Davidson with more than twice its engine displacement.

Finally, Japan's competitors realized what they were up against and found the motivation to respond to the threat. The British manufacturers BSA and Triumph began to jointly develop a large-displacement multicylinder machine in an attempt to preserve their advantage in sporting bikes, and Harley grafted an electric starter onto its big-twin engine in an attempt to provide Japanese-style convenience.

Both these projects proved to be too little too late. By the time the British unveiled their triples, which were flawed machines with styling only a mother or designer could love, Honda had unveiled its big gun: the four-cylinder CB750 Four.

Perhaps the most significant motorcycle in history, the 1969 Honda CB750 Four changed the face of motorcycling.

(Photo courtesy Vreeke and Associates)

It's impossible to overstate the impact this bike had on the motorcycling world.

What Honda did by introducing the CB750 was the equivalent of a car company producing a high-quality sports car equal to or better than the best machines produced by Porsche or Mercedes, and then selling it for the price of a Hyundai. Here was a machine capable of outrunning any mass-produced motorcycle on the road and able to do so all day long without any mechanical problems. Plus, people could afford it.

Given the success of the big Honda, it was only a matter of time before other Japanese manufacturers followed suit and produced big bikes of their own. Kawasaki jumped into the four-cylinder arena with its mighty Z1, and after a couple of false starts, Suzuki also joined the fray, followed by Yamaha.

These big-bore motorcycles devastated the competition. For the British, hampered by management unable to let go of pre–World War II motorcycle designs, the competition proved to be too much. Harley-Davidson managed to survive, partly due to the fanatical loyalty of its customers, but entered into a long period of decline. For a while in the 1970s, it looked like the Japanese would be the only people left in the motorcycling business.

Baby Boomers on (Two) Wheels

The success of the Japanese manufacturers in the United States provides one of history's best examples of being in the right place at the right time. The Japanese caught a wave caused by the baby-boom generation, and this massive influx of young people provided the fuel to propel the Japanese invasion.

Although some restless individuals returning from the war spent their newfound wealth on motorcycles and raising hell, most used that money to pursue the American dream—a dream that included raising a family. And raise families they did, prolifically, creating a new generation so large that their whims would dictate trends for the rest of their lives and shape our culture for generations to come. The impact of the so-called baby-boom generation will be felt long after the last baby boomer has moved on to that great salvage yard in the sky.

The Boomer Boom

Just as the first small Japanese motorcycles began to appear on the West Coast, the first wave of baby boomers was getting its collective driver's license. It didn't take an advanced degree in economics to see the profit potential of providing these kids, products of unprecedented affluence, with fun, affordable, and reliable motorcycles.

The maturation of the Japanese motorcycle industry mirrors the maturation of the baby-boom generation. As these kids grew in size, so grew the Japanese bikes. By the 1970s, most baby boomers were entering adulthood. They roamed farther, rode faster, and were physically larger than when Mr. Honda started importing his small

Super Cub and Dream motorcycles into the country. They no longer needed small, inexpensive motorcycles to ride to football practice or down to the beach. What they needed were full-size motorcycles with enough power to satisfy their adventurous spirits, bikes comfortable enough for cross-country trips. And the Japanese were happy to oblige.

By this time, these young people had become accustomed to the convenience and reliability of Japanese motorcycles. Harley-Davidsons of the 1970s were only incrementally improved over those built during the 1930s. Compounding these problems, American Machine and Foundry (AMF), Harley's parent company at that time, was more interested in turning a quick buck than in doing long-term development. Even Willie G. Davidson, a direct descendant of one of the company's founders, Arthur Davidson, admits that their bikes suffered quality-control problems during this period as a result of AMF's desire to get as many bikes as possible to the market.

Motorcycology

While the Italians produced mechanically brilliant motorcycles during the 1960s and 1970s, cosmetically they left much to be desired. The bikes were beautiful from a distance, but upon closer inspection, the quality of paint and bodywork was abysmal. One well-known example of this was *Cycle* magazine's 1974 Ducati 750SS test bike, which came with an actual fly embedded in the fiberglass of the fuel tank.

Problems were even worse over in England. During the 1950s and 1960s, the British bike industry was run in large part by the same people who had brought the industry to prominence in the 1930s and 1940s. These people tended to oppose even the slightest change.

The result was that the British motorcycle industry was in complete disarray and unable to cash in on the demographic trends taking place in the United States. It couldn't even develop a reliable electric-starting system that didn't explode through the engine cases on every ninth or tenth starting attempt.

For the bulk of this massive new generation of Americans, British or American motorcycles were not an option. The German firm BMW produced spectacular bikes that were as reliable and convenient as Japanese machines, but they cost more and weren't as widely marketed in the United States. The Italians also produced motorcycles that were in many ways equal to or superior to the Japanese bikes, but these, too, came at a premium price. Add to this the peculiar Italian penchant for designing and developing spectacular machinery but then showing near-total disinterest in producing or marketing those same bikes, and the Italians were an even smaller blip than the Germans on the radar of most motorcyclists. For most riders, the only real option was to buy Japanese.

The Bust

Whenever something is going well, those profiting from it convince themselves that it will go well forever. That's just human nature. The Japanese manufacturers imagined that their lock on the American motorcycle market was secure. But they were wrong.

In hindsight, it makes sense. As the baby boomers grew older, many of them lost interest in the adventuresome activities they engaged in during their youth. Even if they were still interested in pursuing sports such as motorcycling, their lives were changing in ways that limited the available time they had to do so. After they graduated from college, their careers began demanding ever-increasing amounts of their time. And when they started families, those families cut into both the free time they had to ride and the amount of cash available to spend on adult toys such as motorcycles.

You would think the motorcycle manufacturers would have seen this trend coming, but they didn't. By the time the tail end of the baby-boom generation entered the workforce in the early to mid-1980s, a time when the manufacturers could have logically expected a market downturn, the Japanese had increased production to record levels. And when the bust hit, American distributors found themselves with warehouses filled with unsold Japanese motorcycles.

Throughout most of the 1980s, the American distributors concentrated on eliminating this surplus, selling three-, four-, and even five-year-old carryover bikes at a fraction of their original cost. The cost of carrying these machines for nearly half a decade drove many dealers out of business, and the lost profits from having to sell the motorcycles below cost almost bankrupted at least one of the Japanese manufacturers.

Manufacturers are still feeling the effects of this debacle. Those few people who had bought motorcycles at list price during the early 1980s were not too pleased to come back to trade those machines a year or two down the road and see the exact same bikes sitting on showroom floors priced at less than half of what they had paid. Not only was this insulting, but it made it extraordinarily difficult for them to sell their own used bikes.

Motorcycle Moments

While the 1980s surplus of unsold motorcycles proved an expensive mistake for the sellers of those bikes, bargain hunters had a field day. In 1985, I purchased a brand-new carryover 1982 Yamaha Seca 650, a bike that listed for $3,200 new in 1982, for $1,399 right out of the crate. Many riders still use those bargain bikes on a daily basis, racking up hundreds of thousands of miles on them.

The Risen Hog: The Resurrected Motorcycle Market

Once again, the future of the sport of motorcycling appeared uncertain, but help was coming. The cavalry was on its way, but this time it had chosen a most unlikely mount: Harley-Davidson motorcycles.

In 1981, a group of 13 senior Harley-Davidson executives purchased Harley-Davidson from AMF. Work commenced on a new engine, and the introduction of that engine, known as the Evolution, opened up an entirely new market for Harley-Davidson.

Before 1981, Harleys were still motorcycles of the old school, meaning that to own one, you had to have the mechanical acumen to overhaul the beast on the side of the road in the middle of the night with nothing but a Zippo lighter, an adjustable wrench, and an intimate familiarity with the motorcycle's internals to guide you. Harleys just were not practical, reliable machines for the majority of riders.

The Evolution, or Evo, engine ended that sorry state of affairs and proved to be a reliable, long-life engine. For the first time, an owner didn't have to be a grease monkey to ride a Harley.

Harley's image as an unreliable Stone Age artifact prevented the new machine from gaining immediate marketplace acceptance. To get a bit of breathing room, Harley petitioned the Reagan administration to impose a temporary tariff on imported motorcycles with engine displacements over 700 cc.

Cycle Babble

Harley's Big Twin engines have always had names. Before the introduction of the Evolution, or Evo, these names related to the engine's appearance. The first overhead-valve Big Twin, introduced in 1936, was called the *Knucklehead* because the valve covers included large nuts that looked like knuckles. This was followed by the *Panhead* in 1948, so named because the valve covers looked like upside-down cake pans. The *Shovelhead*, introduced in 1966, had valve covers that looked like shovels. With the introduction of the Twin Cam in 1999, the trend away from identification via the head style continued, but the liquid-cooled V-Rod resurrected the old naming system. Already the Harley faithful have been calling the new engine the "Waterhead."

In the end, Harley's successful comeback proved to be a blessing for everyone and contributed much to the rebounding of the industry as a whole. So successful was the new Evo engine that Harley asked the federal government to remove the tariff a year before it was originally scheduled to be lifted. By the early 1990s, Harley was selling every motorcycle it could make, with people waiting months and even years to be able to purchase one. By the summer of 2001, Harley surpassed Honda in total U.S. sales for the first time since the 1960s.

As you saw in Chapter 1, Harley's newfound success permeated every aspect of American culture. Soon you could buy everything from official Harley-Davidson underwear to Harley-Davidson toilet-seat covers and Harley-Davidson cigarettes.

Ironically, the one thing that was tough to find was an actual Harley-Davidson motorcycle. Weary of the quality-control problems it had during the AMF days, Harley was careful not to expand its production beyond its capabilities.

As Harley's increasing popularity fueled a new interest in motorcycles, the lack of available Harley-Davidsons created a vacuum. Once again, the Japanese stepped up to fill this vacuum.

And once again, the baby boomers were the driving force behind this new interest in motorcycling. These were the same people who had bought all those little Hondas in the 1960s, who had terrorized the highways on thundering Kawasakis in the 1970s, and who had spent the 1980s raising kids and making money.

Now their kids were grown up, and they once again found themselves with some free time and money on their hands. They missed the fun they used to have on their motorcycles, so they got back into the sport.

For some time, motorcycling's popularity has been increasing. Sales for the four Japanese manufacturers—Honda, Yamaha, Kawasaki, and Suzuki—have been on the rise since 1992, Harley-Davidson sells every bike it can build, and the European manufacturers are experiencing unprecedented popularity in the United States. BMW, Ducati, and Moto Guzzi are a larger part of the American market than they ever were in the past. Triumph began producing bikes in 1991, after being out of action for nearly a decade. Even MZ, an Eastern European manufacturer, has begun importing bikes to the United States.

We even have some homegrown competition for Harley-Davidson, for the first time since the first demise of Indian. Polaris, an American manufacturer of snowmobiles and all-terrain vehicles, introduced a large cruiser-type bike in 1998 and offers a four-bike lineup for 2004.

Today's motorcyclists can select from a larger variety of motorcycles than ever before, and every one of these motorcycles provides levels of reliability and performance that were unimaginable 30 years ago. There has never been a better time to be a motorcyclist.

The Least You Need to Know

- Motorcycles have been around nearly as long as the modern safety bicycle.
- The Japanese took the sport of motorcycling to new heights of popularity with their small, unintimidating, reliable, and fun machines.
- The fate of motorcycling since World War II has mirrored the fate of the baby-boom generation.
- The rebirth of Harley-Davidson following the introduction of the Evolution engine proved so strong that it helped pull the entire motorcycle industry out of an economic slump.
- Today's motorcycle buyers have more choices than at any other time since the first part of the twentieth century.

Chapter 3

Street Squid or Dirt Donk? Types of Motorcycles

In This Chapter

- The difference between types of motorcycles
- Doing it in the dirt: types of dirtbikes and dual-sport bikes
- Which street standards are endangered species
- Cruisers: the ultimate American bikes
- Touring machines

Unlike motorcycles of the past, modern bikes are convenient transportation devices. You no longer need to have legs strong enough to kick bricks out of walls or the ability to grind valves in a parking lot to ride them. But for that convenience, we had to give up something. We gave up simplicity.

Back in the bad old days, one bike pretty much served every purpose. You could buy a BSA Gold Star, for example, and use it as everyday transportation on public roads. That bike could be adapted to dirt use, too—just remove the front fender, change the tires, and bolt on a higher pipe. And should you want to go racing, with a little work on the engine, your Gold Star could be competitive on any track in the world.

This was true of just about any motorcycle made.

Life was much simpler then. Today a new rider is confronted with a disorienting variety of motorcycle types to pick from. In this chapter, I'll show you the different types of bikes and how to choose the best type for you.

Split Personalities: Dual-Sports

Many riders want to travel off the beaten path, but at the same time, they need a motorcycle they can legally drive on public roads to get to that unbeaten path. Motorcycle manufacturers have long recognized this need; that's why they make dual-sports. During the 1960s and 1970s, every maker, from Yamaha to Ducati, offered *dual-purpose motorcycles*—bikes that went by names such as Yamaha's Enduro.

Cycle Babble

Dual-sport motorcycles (sometimes called *dual-purpose* bikes) are street-legal motorcycles with varying degrees of off-road capabilities.

These bikes were primarily road bikes with some off-road capabilities thrown in. They were a blast to ride down logging roads, and they made great commuter bikes.

As the baby boomers aged, they lost interest in these versatile and fun machines, and their popularity declined. But the breed has gained popularity once again. Each of the big four Japanese companies, as well as several European firms, manufactures some form of dual-sport, as they are now called. Some examples are as follows:

- Honda makes the XR650L, probably the most off-road-worthy of the big dual-sports coming out of Japan.
- Kawasaki builds its KLR650, an excellent lightweight street bike that will get you down some trails, provided that the going doesn't get too hairy.
- Splitting the difference is Suzuki's DR650SE, which is generally a better street-bike than the Honda and a better dirtbike than the Kawasaki.
- BMW's main entry in the dual-sport market is its gigantic R1150GS (which will be discussed shortly). But BMW also builds the terrific F650, which, while not technically a dual-sport, is at least as capable off-road as Kawasaki's KLR650.
- KTM, a small European manufacturer, makes the 950 Adventure, a worthy (but pricey) entry into this category.

- Aprilia, an Italian maker, offers its ETV1000 Caponard, with a 998 V-twin and an advertised dry weight of 474 pounds. That's almost 100 pounds lighter than the BMW—but almost 100 pounds heavier than the KTM.
- Triumph's dual-sport entry is the Tiger. Unlike most of the twin-cylinder competition, the Tiger utilizes a transverse three-cylinder engine.

Any of these bikes makes an ideal first motorcycle. In addition to having varying degrees of dirt-worthiness, each makes a nimble, forgiving streetbike. They're all fantastic city bikes. Their light weight and easy handling make them excellent bikes for a learner, but their all-around capability means a rider won't outgrow them after learning to ride. (If you want to check out these and other dual-sports, see Appendix A.)

Not only is Kawasaki's KLR650 the lowest priced of all the big dual-sports, but it's also a terrific all-around motorcycle.

(Photo courtesy Motorcyclist™ *magazine)*

The only drawback these bikes have is that they're tall machines. Part of the reason they work so well both on and off the road is that they have long-travel suspensions, which place the seat high off the pavement. While this lets riders see traffic, it also presents some challenges for those with shorter inseams.

Cycle Babble

The term **leviathan** originally referred to a biblical sea monster but has come to mean something of immense size and power, a good description of these big, multicylinder dual-sports, which can weigh almost twice as much as the largest single-cylinder dual-sports.

In the last decade or so, another type of dual-sport has appeared: the *leviathans*. These are large-displacement machines based on streetbikes. In a way, they're throwbacks to earlier times, when a single machine was used for all purposes.

BMW introduced the first of the leviathans in 1980, when it brought out the R80GS, an 800-cc twin-cylinder bike with high fenders and upswept exhaust pipes. This versatile bike proved popular, especially in Europe, but it might have remained an anomaly had it not been for one event: the Paris Dakar Rally.

The Paris Dakar Rally (currently called the Telefónica Dakar) is an off-road race across thousands of miles of desert along the west coast of Africa, and it is here the leviathans really shine. The event's popularity generated the production of Dakar-style replicas from most of the major motorcycle manufacturers.

These were bikes like the original R80GS: basically streetbikes with a bit of off-road equipment, but with bodywork resembling the Dakar racers—bikes such as the Ducati/Cagiva Elefant and Triumph Tiger. Honda has long made its V-twin Africa Twin 750, and Yamaha produced its own Dakar-style bike, the 750 V-twin Super Ténéré, but these were never imported into the United States.

Most single-cylinder dual-sports have modest off-road capabilities, but these leviathans are best suited to graded dirt roads; they are just too heavy for off-road work. You probably don't want to take them up a mountain trail, for instance. But these big buggers make very good streetbikes, in part because of their long-travel suspensions, relatively light weight (at least when compared to, say, a Harley-Davidson), and nimble handling. You could do worse than to buy one.

Cruisers: The American Bikes

Choppers, customs, cruisers—whichever term you use, you are referring to a distinctly American style of motorcycle. The American landscape, both social and geographical, shaped this style of motorcycle into its present form.

As mentioned in Chapter 2, many of the restless soldiers returning from Europe and Asia after World War II chose to explore the United States on motorcycles, but the motorcycles that were widely available didn't suit them all that well. Outlaw bikers called the big Harley-Davidson touring bikes of that time "garbage wagons" because they considered all the accessories and extras mounted on them garbage. In fact, Bylaw Number 11 of the original Hell's Angels charter states, "An Angel cannot wear the colors (club insignia) while riding on a garbage wagon." The first thing most outlaws did was chop off all superfluous parts, which to them was anything that didn't help the bike go faster: fenders, lights, front brakes, whatever. Hence, the term *chopper.*

Cycle Babble

A **chopper** once referred to a custom motorcycle that had all superfluous parts "chopped" off in order to make the bike faster. Today it refers to a type of custom that usually has an extended fork, no rear suspension, and high handlebars.

Choppers like these may look cool, but by altering the suspension components, owners also alter handling characteristics, often rendering the machines nearly impossible to ride.

(Photo © 1998 Darwin Holmstrom)

Choppers came to symbolize the outlaw motorcycle contingent, the infamous onepercenters. By the 1960s, these bikes had evolved into radical machines far removed from the intent of the original customized bikes, which was improved straight-line performance. Anyone seeking outright performance rode a Japanese or British bike. Harley had long since given up the pretense of producing sporting motorcycles.

People rode Harleys to look cool, and nothing looked cooler than a Harley chopper. The extended forks and modified frames of these motorcycles made them nearly impossible to ride, but the owners didn't seem to mind. Riding a motorcycle with unsafe handling characteristics seemed to be another way of letting society know the rider didn't care if he or she lived or died.

Over the years, such machines gained in popularity—even as they declined in practicality—but manufacturers seemed not to notice. It wasn't until the 1970s, after decades of watching American riders customize their bikes, that the manufacturers got into the act and began offering custom-styled bikes.

The birth of the factory custom can in large part be attributed to one man: Willie G. Davidson. Willie G., as he is known, worked in Harley's styling department, but he was also an avid motorcyclist who knew what people were doing to their bikes. One popular customizing technique was to take the fork off of a Sportster and graft it onto a stripped-down Big Twin frame, so Willie G. did just that at the factory. The result was the original Super Glide.

The Super Glide model, offered in 1971, wasn't a screaming success, due in part to a funky boatlike rear fender (known as the *Night Train* fender). The next year, Harley gave the bike a more conventional rear fender and sold thousands of Super Glides.

Harley wasn't the only company working on a custom-styled bike. The British manufacturer Norton also developed a cruiser in the early 1970s. Unfortunately, its cruiser, the ungainly High Rider, wasn't well received. The bike only contributed to the company's eventual demise.

Kawasaki was the first Japanese company to test the factory-chopper waters, introducing its KZ900LTD in 1976. The bike featured pull-back buckhorn handlebars, a teardrop-shape gas tank, a seat with a pronounced step between the rider and passenger portions, and a liberal dousing of chrome plating. These bikes forced the rider into a backward-leaning riding position (raising unbridled hell with his or her lower back), but otherwise, they were still functional, useful machines.

As the decade progressed, the Japanese stuck to this formula. This approach had a limited future; the real future of cruisers was being forged elsewhere, by Willie G.

Two of Willie G.'s creations, in particular, proved to be the models for today's cruisers: the Low Rider, introduced in 1977, and the Wide Glide of 1980. Study these bikes, and you'll see elements of every cruiser now produced. The bobbed fender of the Wide Glide can be found on cruisers from Honda, Suzuki, and Kawasaki. The kicked-out front end and sculpted fenders of the Low Rider hint at the shape of Yamaha's Road Stars. These two bikes are arguably the most influential factory customs of all time.

Harley-Davidson's original Super Glide, with its fiberglass Night Train rear fender, was a sales failure when introduced, but today original examples command a premium price.

(Photo © 1998 Darwin Holmstrom)

What of the Japanese? As the 1980s progressed, Japanese manufacturers got closer and closer to building motorcycles that looked like Harley-Davidsons. But they have taken cruiser styling in new directions, too. Honda now builds its Valkyrie, a massive six-cylinder cruiser. Yamaha's Royal Star looks as much like a classic Indian motorcycle as it does a Harley-Davidson. (See Appendix A to get a good look at these bikes.)

This segment of the market is thriving, and for good reason: cruisers are easy bikes to live with. Many of them are nearly maintenance free. They look good and, when outfitted with a windshield, are comfortable out on the road. They may not handle as well as sportbikes, or haul as much gear as touring bikes, but in many ways, they fulfill the role of a standard, all-around motorcycle. Many riders don't ride a motorcycle to get from point A to point B as quickly as possible. They just like to ride. If that describes you, you might be cruiser material.

Power Cruisers

An interesting thing happened as the twentieth century wound to a close. People began demanding more performance from all types of motorcycles. Sportbikes began to increase in popularity, and not just among younger riders. Longtime riders and those who had returned to the sport after an extended absence from riding began to appreciate the tremendous performance offered by modern sportbikes. Even cruiser buyers began wanting more power and better handling. In response, manufacturers resurrected the "power cruiser" category.

The original batch of power cruisers in the early 1980s tended to be multicylinder machines, usually V-fours. Honda started this trend with its Magnas, and Suzuki joined in with its ill-fated Madura series. Yamaha's V-four power cruiser proved so popular that the mighty V-Max is still with us in the twenty-first century. Kawasaki also got in the act, but it used an inline-four engine to power the Eliminator series, its combatant in the 1980s power cruiser wars. Today's crop of power cruisers uses V-twin engines almost exclusively. Honda brought out the original member of the current class with its mighty VTX1800, which cranks out more than 100 horsepower at the rear wheel. But Honda breaks with V-twin conformity with its six-cylinder Valkyrie and show-stopping Valkyrie Rune. Yamaha and Kawasaki also jumped on the power cruiser bandwagon. Yamaha chose to go the low-tech route, using the air-cooled pushrod engine from its Road Star series to power its Road Star Warrior power cruiser. Kawasaki's 2004 Vulcan 2000 puts out 97 ponies at the rear wheel. In a turn of events that hasn't occurred since the introduction of the Knucklehead in 1936, Harley now ranks among the undisputed technological leaders in this class. The liquid-cooled V-Rod engine cranks out 109 horsepower at the rear wheel. Triumph, on the other hand, wants to trump everyone with its 2.3-liter three-cylinder Rocket III.

Harley's Wide Glide was one of the most influential cruisers ever built. Just about every cruiser now being produced displays some elements of Wide Glide styling.

(Photo courtesy Motorcyclist™ *magazine)*

Sportbikes

If you aren't the laid-back, easy-rider type, you might be interested in something with a little more sporting capability. Well, you are definitely in the right place at the right time: the range of sporting motorcycles available has never been better.

Sportbikes are designed to handle well at high speeds. When British bikes began to appear in the United States in appreciable numbers following World War II, it became obvious that while Harleys may be faster in a straight line, the British models could run circles around a Harley when the road began to wind. This gave the British a reputation as producers of highly sporting motorcycles. The British managed to maintain this reputation until the early 1970s with bikes such as Norton's 850 Commando.

Cycle Babble

During the 1970s, the Japanese became so identified with four-cylinder, standard-style motorcycles that the term **Universal Japanese Motorcycle (UJM)** was coined to describe them.

When the Japanese began producing large four-cylinder motorcycles, these became the new leaders in straight-line performance. The term *Universal Japanese Motorcycles* (*UJM*) was coined to describe them.

While they were wicked fast, most UJMs of the 1970s didn't handle all that well, mostly because of inferior suspension components and flimsy frames. They outhandled Harleys (which tended to be about as nimble as a freight train), but they couldn't keep up with a properly functioning Norton Commando.

The real breakthrough in the development of sportbikes from Japan was Honda's 750-cc Interceptor, introduced for the 1983 model year. With its revolutionary V-four engine, this bike was Japan's best purpose-built sporting motorcycle yet.

The Interceptor revolutionized sportbikes. It started off a technology war between the Japanese manufacturers that continues to this day. Kawasaki brought out its original 900 Ninja, a bike in many ways as groundbreaking as the Interceptor. Yamaha introduced its five-valve FZ750, a bike so influential that Ferrari adopted some of its technology for its cars. And Suzuki blew the world away by introducing its GSX-R series, bikes that were little more than racers with headlights.

The Italians are another prominent force in the sportbike scene. When they started building large-displacement sportbikes in the 1970s, such as Moto Guzzi's V7 Sport and Ducati's 750SS, the Italians raised the ceiling on riders' expectations from their machines. While not initially exported in numbers large enough to become a real presence in the American market, these bikes influenced the direction sporting motorcycles would take.

Today's sportbikes cover nearly the entire spectrum. Yamaha's FZ6, while being a more capable sporting motorcycle than the pure race bikes of just a few years ago, is so comfortable and versatile that it could almost be considered a sport-tourer. Suzuki's latest iteration of the GSX-R formula, the GSX-R1000, has such high-performance limits that only a few experienced riders can ever approach them. The razor-sharp handling of Ducati's 999 is just slightly removed from that of the bike Neil Hodgson won the 2003 World Superbike Championship on. And the next generation of sportbikes looks like it will raise current standards even higher.

Pure-Dirt

The motorcycles manufactured for purely off-road use today tend toward the extreme end of the motorcycle spectrum. These are machines such as the screaming race bikes leaping through the air in arenas around the country during Supercross races.

These bikes usually don't make good beginner bikes. In fact, many of them are intended strictly as racing machines. Many *dirtbikes* have two-stroke engines, which means you have to mix oil into your gas before you fill your tank, which is a messy, time-consuming process (and inconvenient if you find yourself miles from home without a can in which to mix fuel).

Adding to this inconvenience is the fact that *pure-dirt* motorcycles aren't legal to ride on public roads.

Cycle Babble

Dirtbikes are machines intended for off-road use and aren't legal to ride on public roads. Sometimes the term **pure-dirt** is used to distinguish a dirtbike from a dual-sport motorcycle.

Racing dirtbikes also tend to have extremely abrupt power delivery, unleashing a whole bunch of horsepower in a most surprising fashion. Riders inexperienced in handling these machines commonly suffer from broken bones in their hands. This is because the power catches the rider by surprise, causing the bike to flip over backward, crushing his or her hands with the handlebars. I've seen it happen more than once.

Probably the biggest disadvantage of a pure-dirt motorcycle is that it's not legal to drive on public roads (hence the term *pure-dirt*). This means you'll have to transport the machine from your garage to the place you intend to ride—for example, in a pickup truck or a trailer. These bikes don't meet the emissions or noise requirements for street-legal vehicles, nor do they have the electrical equipment, such as turn signals and horns, required in most states. In some states, it is possible to manipulate the legal system enough to license an off-road bike for use on public roads, but by doing so, you might be setting yourself up for future legal problems.

Four-Strokes: The New Power Elites

Alternatives to two-stroke racing dirtbikes are available for those who want to do serious off-road riding: four-stroke trailbikes.

First we must clear a big misconception: four-stroke power never went out of style. However, until recently, these bikes have been disadvantaged by weight and starting, compared to the two-strokes. Today's four-stroke pure-dirtbikes start as easily as or even easier than their two-stroke siblings, produce a smoother power that is easier to manage, and, in some cases, weigh less. Case in point: The 450-cc four-strokes now produce horsepower numbers in the realm of the old open-class two-stroke 500s, in a less violent manner, while weighing the same.

The big breakthrough was when the high-performance production four-strokes got their weight under 250 pounds and began to start easily. This wrapped the smooth power into a lightweight, easy-to-start package that really pushed the four-stroke ahead of the two-strokes. Honda has long been a proponent of such motorcycles, and its XR series (not to be confused with the XR-L series) offers terrific alternatives, as does the CRF250X. Yamaha has also jumped on the four-stroke bandwagon with its WR250F and TT-R250.

With four-stroke dirtbikes, you don't have to premix fuel. Plus, they generally have smooth, easily controllable power. Some even feature electric start. Unless your ultimate goal is to race and you have some familiarity with off-road riding, these bikes may make a better choice than pure-dirt bikes for your first dirtbike.

Street Standards: A Renaissance

Because Japanese motorcycles were so influential to motorcyclists who entered the sport in the 1960s and 1970s, the look of these bikes became imprinted in our psyches as the way a motorcycle should look.

These were pretty basic bikes: Back then, function dictated form. The gas tank sat above the engine to allow the gas to run down into the carburetors. The way the human body bends pretty much dictated the placement of the rest of the parts.

As motorcycles became more specialized in the 1980s, the look of motorcycles changed. Motorcyclists were so excited by new developments that we didn't realize we were losing something in the process. Then one day in the late 1980s, we realized that the basic bike no longer existed. Motorcyclists began complaining about this situation, and soon the Japanese designed bikes that embodied the virtues of those older models.

Unfortunately, while the inclusion of the older styling features contributed to a retro look for these new machines, it also detracted from their overall versatility. Suzuki and Kawasaki were the first to come to the market with standard motorcycles. Kawasaki's entrance into this new/old market segment was the Zephyr 550, a four-cylinder UJM-type bike introduced for the 1990 model year. The bike didn't sell well in the United States, and very few of these machines found their way to the public highways; therefore, they were soon dropped from Kawasaki's lineup.

Motorcycle Moments

After failing to sell many Zephyrs, Kawasaki tried to capitalize on the appeal of its 1980 family of GPz sportbikes by bringing out the GPz1100 in 1995. This very good (and reasonably priced) motorcycle also failed to find buyers, probably because, as good as it was, it still wasn't any better than the original.

The VX800, Suzuki's entrant that the same year, did slightly better in the market. It was a competent, full-size machine that fulfilled the promise of the versatile standard. In fact, it's a bike I highly recommend, whether you're a beginner or a longtime motorcyclist. But it was never a sales dynamo and was imported to U.S. shores for only four years.

Neither Kawasaki nor Suzuki gave up on the concept of standard bikes after the lukewarm reception of their initial efforts. Kawasaki imported increasingly larger Zephyrs, but they came with increasingly larger price tags. None of the Zephyr series offered anything a rider couldn't find in a used GPz900 Ninja—and for a fraction of the Zephyr's price.

In an attempt to recapture the sales success it had enjoyed with its big GS series of the 1970s and 1980s, Suzuki brought out the GSX1100G, a big 1980s-style standard with a modern single-shock rear suspension. On paper, the Suzuki fulfilled every requirement those clamoring for standard bikes claimed to need from a bike.

But the GSX was even less successful than the VX, probably because of the bike's appearance. At the risk of offending loyal GSX riders, many people considered the bike to be goofy-looking. One magazine wag even suggested they take the coloring crayon away from the designer who conceived the machine. (For the record, I kind of like the bike's look, if you get rid of the screwy high-rise handlebars and clean up the busy-looking front end.)

Honda was the first Japanese manufacturer to find relative success in the standard bike market, with its Nighthawk 750. Here was a bike that offered the versatility UJMs were known for and looked good doing it. Perhaps the factor that contributed most to the bike's success was its low price. In this case, you really did get your money's worth.

These were, and still are, great values for the money. My wife bought one of these bikes as her first full-size motorcycle, and one of my greatest regrets is selling that bike.

While the Nighthawk was the first modern Japanese standard to hold its own in the marketplace, it never set any kind of sales records. It seemed the standard might once again disappear from the market, had a couple of manufacturers not rethought the concept.

First Yamaha introduced the Seca II 600. At first glance, this nimble, fun bike might not be considered a standard, since it included a small, frame-mounted *fairing*. But riders didn't care; the fairing just added to the bike's practicality. It seemed that being *naked* wasn't a prerequisite for a standard. Suzuki also realized this and brought out its Bandit series. These bikes are comfortable motorcycles that incorporate some of the best technology available, a useful fairing, and a reasonable price.

The success of the Bandit spawned a resurgence in the standard motorcycle. Kawasaki was first to respond, introducing its ZRX1100, a bike that earned the nickname "Eddie Lawson Replica" because it used a paint scheme reminiscent of the bikes Eddie Lawson campaigned on in AMA Superbike racing in

Cycle Babble

The devices mounted at the front of a motorcycle to protect the rider from the elements are called **fairings.** These range from simple Plexiglas shields mounted to the handlebars, to complex, encompassing body panels that enshroud the entire front half of the bike. Bikes without any type of fairing are known as **naked bikes.**

the early 1980s. Suzuki fought back with a dramatically improved version of its Bandits, in both 600-cc and 1200-cc forms, and Yamaha entered the standard wars with its FZ1 (Fazer outside the United States). This bike uses the potent engine from Yamaha's R1 open-class sportbike, mounted in a steel frame with an upright riding position. Yamaha marketed this bike as "an R1 for the real world."

To drive home the performance Yamaha was targeting with the FZ1, it used Eddie Lawson himself in the television ads. Lawson had achieved his greatest racing success at the international level aboard Yamaha motorcycles. Kawasaki didn't take this lying down and introduced a new bike for 2001, the ZRX1200, which was much better in every respect than the original ZRX1100. Finally Honda entered the market with a standard bike, the 919, based on its CBR900RR (Fireblade outside the United States).

The fierce competition in this category indicates that there is a strong market for standard-style streetbikes. If you're a fan of these types of bikes (which I am), this is a great time to be a motorcyclist.

Suzuki finally got the modern standard formula right with its successful Bandit series.

(Photo courtesy Motorcyclist™ *magazine)*

The Ultimate Behemoths: Touring Bikes

Another category of specialized motorcycle to appear over the last several decades is the purpose-built *touring bike,* a bike equipped for longer rides on the road.

Harley started this trend by offering a fairing and luggage as optional equipment on its Electra Glide back in the 1960s, but other companies were slow to pick up on the trend.

In the late 1970s, BMW introduced its first factory dresser, the R100RT, a bike that met with market success.

Cycle Babble

A **touring bike** is a bike equipped for longer rides, with fairings and lockable saddlebags. While early bikers looked on motorcycles equipped for touring with scorn, calling them *garbage wagons*, over time they began to see their appeal. They began to refer to garbage wagons as *baggers* and finally *dressers*, the term many Harley riders use today.

Honda had been producing a bike specifically for touring: the Gold Wing. In time, Honda began offering fairings and luggage as accessories, but these were still add-on parts, equipment for which the machines hadn't been specifically designed.

Other companies offered touring packages for their standard bikes, too, but there's a problem with this approach: accessories affect the handling of a machine, often adversely. Large fairings and luggage can really make a bike get squirrelly.

So Honda took up the challenge, producing its 1980 GL1100 Gold Wing Interstate, Japan's first turn-key touring bike designed from the ground up to have an integrated fairing and luggage.

Of course, the other Japanese manufacturers responded with purpose-built touring rigs of their own, but it seemed as if every effort they made only sent Honda back to the drawing board with a vengeance. This one-upmanship led to the Gold Wing GL1200 in 1984. This bike set new standards in function and comfort. The Gold Wing 1500, a six-cylinder behemoth introduced in 1988, blew away even its predecessor. The Gold Wing proved to be such a perfect touring machine that the other Japanese manufacturers simply gave up trying to compete in that market segment.

The success of the Gold Wing meant that the ultimate behemoth class of touring bikes saw relatively little change for more than a decade, but eventually things began moving on the touring front again. All it took was a little competition, this time from BMW. In 1999, BMW introduced its K1200LT, and for the first time in more than 10 years, Honda's mighty six-cylinder Gold Wing began losing magazine comparison tests against its heavy-touring market competition. Honda responded by introducing the GL1800 Gold Wing, a bike that was much better in every way than its predecessor. Likewise, BMW has kept upping the ante with its K1200LT.

Cycle Babble

Sport-tourers are motorcycles that combine the comfort and carrying capacity of a touring bike with the handling and power of a sportbike, with larger fairings and hard, lockable luggage.

All segments of the touring market didn't go into suspended animation while the Gold Wing waited patiently for a challenger to its throne. There were some exciting developments in other types of touring motorcycles, such as the *sport-touring* segment of the market. Sport-tourers combine the comfort and carrying capacity of a touring bike with the handling and excitement of a sportbike. You can think of these machines as sportbikes with larger fairings and hard, lockable luggage.

This class existed for a long time without having a proper name. In fact, almost every BMW built in the last quarter of the century falls into this group.

Although the term sport-touring *is fairly new, BMW has been building such bikes for decades.*

Kawasaki produced the first purpose-built Japanese sport-tourer with its Concours, introduced in 1986. Honda followed suit, bringing out its ST1100 in 1991. Over on the other side of the world, manufacturers such as Aprilia, Ducati, and Triumph also offer BMW competition in the sport-touring arena.

These bikes represent a compromise, giving up a bit of sporting capability to the smaller, more agile sportbikes, while sacrificing some luggage-carrying capability when compared to the ultimate behemoths. It seems a compromise many riders are willing to make. If you like to crank up the throttle in corners and cover huge expanses of geography in a single sitting, but you don't need to carry everything you own with you on a trip, these bikes may be a good compromise for you, too.

Manufacturers have also developed the touring cruiser, another subcategory of the touring bike. The touring-cruiser bikes combine the looks of cruisers with the functionality of touring bikes. With their windshields and hard luggage, they are more comfortable and convenient than cruisers, yet they retain the American look that makes cruisers so popular. Yamaha's Royal Star Venture and Victory's V92TC Touring Custom are two of the larger and more recent entries in this class. A bit down the food chain in overall bulk (but not overall capability) is Kawasaki's Vulcan Nomad. And, of course, Harley has many entries in this category because it invented the category.

The Least You Need to Know

- Dual-sport motorcycles make excellent all-around bikes, especially for beginners.
- Cruiser styling reflects the unique tastes and needs of American motorcyclists.
- Sportbikes are high-performance motorcycles designed to go fast and handle well. They usually have full-coverage bodywork and cramped riding positions, although there are some exceptions.
- Pure-dirt bikes look like dual-sports but are designed strictly for off-road use—and they are illegal to ride on the street.
- Standard-style motorcycles are characterized by comfortable riding positions and minimal bodywork.
- Touring bikes are (usually) large motorcycles with fairings; hard, lockable luggage; and other touring amenities.

Part 2

So You Want to Buy a Bike?

Now comes the most exciting part of your entire adventure: getting your first bike. It's fun just to go out and look at it, and admire its combination of form and function. You'll soon be able to visualize its details, the curves in its bodywork, and the way it smells when you park it after a ride on a warm summer day. The machine will become a part of you.

But your first bike will be as demanding as it is exciting. To keep your bike in the condition you brought it home in, you'll need to have a basic understanding of its mechanical nature. And just buying a bike in the first place can be a traumatic event. As with any form of commerce, people sell motorcycles to make money, and if you walk into a dealership unprepared, you will be their cash cow.

In this part of the book, you'll learn what kind of bike is right for you, what that bike is made of, how different bikes work, how to buy your first motorcycle without getting ripped off, and what extra gear you'll need after you buy the bike.

Chapter 4

Choosing the Right Bike

In This Chapter

- Deciding which type of motorcycle best meets your needs
- Why a smaller bike may be a good choice
- New bike or used bike? How to decide
- The hidden costs of motorcycling

You are about to enter into a relationship with a mechanical object unlike any you have had before. Owning a motorcycle is a much more intimate experience than owning a car or pickup truck, perhaps because you meld into the machine when you ride, your body encasing the mechanical heart of the bike. You become part of the machine. You ride just inches away from the engine, the source of your bike's power, and you feel and hear the internal-combustion event more directly than is possible in an enclosed vehicle.

And you control the direction in which you travel with your body, leading the bike down the road with your own movements just as you would lead a dance partner. This provides a much more immediate experience than sitting inside a glass bubble, turning a steering wheel vaguely connected to some invisible mechanism.

Given the nature of this intimate relationship, it is vital that you choose the right partner. With the dizzying array of motorcycles available, choosing that partner might seem daunting at this stage, but it's really not as confusing as it might seem. You don't have to know every detail of every bike ever made; you only need to know yourself and your own needs.

What Do You Want to Do?

Before you select a type of bike, first you need to determine what kind of riding you want to do (as discussed in Chapter 3). If you have no interest in riding on public roads and you just want a bike to ride through the swamps and forests, you should probably consider getting a strictly off-road dirtbike.

But you will probably want something you can ride on the road. Riding off-road is great fun, but by getting a bike that isn't street-legal, you cut off a lot of your future options. Unless you already have friends who are into serious off-road riding, you'll probably want a machine you can legally ride to the local hangout to visit old friends and make new ones.

Or maybe you don't give a rip about riding off-road. You might have visions of riding through corners on a high-performance sportbike, leaning over so far your knees skim the surface of the asphalt. Or perhaps you envision yourself making epic road trips aboard the biggest touring rig available. Maybe you dream of conquering the jungles on a dual-sport machine.

On the other hand, you may not even know what you want out of a bike just yet.

Whether you know exactly what you want out of the sport or you're still trying to figure that out, it's best to keep your options open. Just because you want to see the world doesn't mean you have to buy an ultimate-behemoth luxo-tourer. And just because you want to be the next speed racer doesn't mean you have to buy the bike that won at Daytona this year.

Although bikes have grown increasingly specialized over the last 15 years, they remain remarkably versatile machines.

Any bike can be a tourer if you take it on a trip. I've put 1,000-mile days on a hard-edged sportbike. I've traveled the entire United States on a big V-twin cruiser. My wife once rode a 500-cc thumper from the Canadian border to Mexico and back.

And in the right hands, any bike can be a sportbike. While riding an 18-year-old, 650-cc Japanese bike, I've shown my tail to testosterone-crazed squids (sportbike riders with more enthusiasm than talent) on the latest sporting hardware. And while riding a modern sportbike, I've been embarrassed on a twisty road by an old dude on a Harley that was older than I was.

While any bike can be used for nearly any purpose, there is a reason certain types of motorcycles are used for certain tasks more frequently than others. I still suffer from wrist problems from touring on a sportbike, and my wife bought a larger bike within weeks of returning from her trip on the thumper. And that guy who smoked me on his old Harley would probably love riding a modern sportbike, if he ever tried one.

Choosing a Versatile Motorcycle

You might think you know what you want to do before you start riding, but after you've been at it a while, you might discover an interest in an entirely different form of riding. You might get a Harley Sportster thinking you'll use it only to ride to the lake on the weekends, for example, and then develop an itch to ride to the farthest corners of North America.

That's why it's a good idea to get as versatile a motorcycle as possible for your first bike. As I said in Chapter 3, the big dual-sports are about as versatile as a bike can get. They can handle unpaved roads and worse, and they can be set up for touring.

However, you might not be interested in this type of bike. You might be turned off by the looks of the machine. Another disadvantage of the dual-sport bikes is their height: they are tall machines. While sitting up high is an advantage because it lets you see over traffic (and, more important, helps other drivers see you), it presents some challenges to those with shorter inseams. To fit on one, you need to be of at least average height, or you may find these bikes a bit of a handful in stop-and-go traffic.

Suzuki's DR650SE is an example of a dual-sport. This popular, versatile bike was twice voted "Best Dual-Sport Single" by Motorcyclist™ *magazine.*

(Photo courtesy Motorcyclist™ *magazine)*

If dual-sports aren't your thing, that doesn't mean you're out of luck. There are many versatile pure-street bikes to choose from, too.

Browse the buying guide to new bikes in Appendix A to learn more about the many types of dual-sport or pure-street bikes that might be right for you.

Getting a Good Fit

A big factor in versatility is comfort. If you are comfortable on a bike, you can ride it harder and farther. And different bodies fit on different bikes. You can't really tell by looking at it if a bike is going to fit you, either. For example, I fit nicely on Yamaha's YZF600R and could ride one from coast to coast without needing wrist surgery. But Honda's CBR600F3 puts my hands to sleep within minutes. Yet a new rider would be hard-pressed to see a noticeable difference between the two bikes if they were parked side by side, and many other riders find the Honda just as comfortable as the Yamaha.

Motorcycle *ergonomics*—the science of designing motorcycles that conform to the human body—receives a lot of attention in the motorcycling press these days. Ergonomic considerations influence all aspects of motorcycle design, from the riding position to the placement of the controls, which, in turn, contribute to the overall versatility of a motorcycle. The better a motorcycle fits you, the more comfortable you will be. The more comfortable you are, the more useful your motorcycle will be.

> **Cycle Babble**
>
> The science of **ergonomics**, or human engineering, is used to design devices (including everything from cars to chairs) that conform to the human body. Ergonomics is a prime consideration when designing motorcycles; the idea is to provide maximum efficiency while keeping operator fatigue to a minimum.

Because choosing a motorcycle is as much an emotional process as it is an intellectual one, in the end, only you will know what type of motorcycle will be right for you. But once you've selected a type of bike, getting a versatile bike that fits your body will make your entire motorcycle experience much more rewarding. I talk more about trying out and buying bikes in Chapter 7.

Starting Out Small

Probably the most common mistake new riders make when choosing their first bike is buying a bike that's too large for them to learn to ride easily.

I discuss the basics of riding in Chapter 10, but it's important to explain a little about how motorcycles work here so you'll understand this point. By nature, motorcycles are unstable vehicles: if you don't hold them up some way, they fall over. When you ride, your bike is held up by its own inertia, as well as by the gyroscopic and centrifugal forces of its spinning wheels.

But any time your motorcycle is not traveling in a perfectly straight line, its weight shifts around in a manner you may be totally unused to. When traveling, a motorcycle doesn't follow its front wheels around a corner like a car does; instead, the bike leans around corners, rotating around a central axis, much like an airplane.

Cycle Babble

Using the handlebar as a lever to lean the bike into a turn is called **countersteering** because you do it backward: if you want to turn right, you push the handlebars to the left. This makes the motorcycle lean to the right, which, in turn, makes the bike move to the right.

Because of this, you don't steer a motorcycle the way you drive a car. Instead, you *countersteer* it, using the handlebar to lever the motorcycle into a lean and initiate a turn.

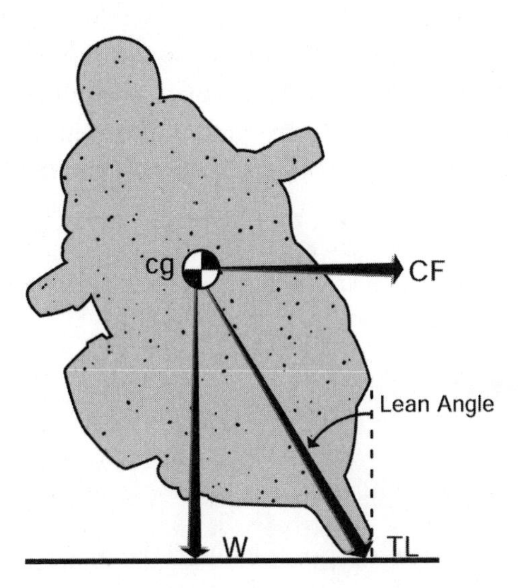

Instead of turning like a car, motorcycles lean into a turn, rotating on the machine's central axis like an airplane.

The point I'm trying to make here is that, on the road, motorcycles move around a lot in weird ways. This takes some getting used to, even on a lightweight motorcycle. On a heavier bike, this can be so disconcerting that it scares a new rider into never learning to steer the motorcycle properly.

The people who seem to run into the most trouble are those who choose a heavyweight cruiser or a big touring motorcycle for their first bike.

Perhaps it's a Freudian thing, but size seems to be some sort of a status symbol for cruiser riders. As a popular T-shirt slogan says, "Size does matter." Unfortunately, for a new rider, it matters in a negative way.

For one thing, the heavy weight makes the motorcycle tend to ride in a straight line, even when you attempt to negotiate a turn. The more bike weight you have, the more you have to wrestle the machine through every turn. In addition, excessive weight can be especially problematic in cruisers because of certain handling characteristics common to the breed. Because of the steering geometry required to give cruisers their chopperlike look, they tend not to be the best-handling bikes on the road. To many novice riders, the bikes feel as if they are going to flop over.

Trying to master a large touring bike is usually a mistake for a novice. I've seen the enthusiasm of a lot of new riders nipped in the bud after they bought an ultimate behemoth-type touring bike before they were ready. When you get in over your head on one of these machines, their heavy weight is going to hurt you. When things start to go wrong on an 800-pound motorcycle, they go wrong fast.

We all fall into the "bigger is better" trap. For years I rode a Honda ST1100, a 700-pounder and one of the finest sport-touring motorcycles in the world. I enjoyed it so much that I may never have ridden anything else, had fate not intervened. A balloon payment coming due on my condo forced me to sell the big ST1100 and get a small, cheap motorcycle. I missed the big Honda, but in the process, I rediscovered the pleasure of riding a small, nimble motorcycle. Now, if I were forced to have only one bike, I would choose a lightweight sporty motorcycle over a larger machine.

But you can go to the other extreme, too. Selecting a motorcycle that's too large can ruin your enthusiasm for the sport; if you select one that is too small, you will soon outgrow the bike.

Starting Out Slow

New sportbike riders tend not to have weight-related problems because sportbikes generally are light, maneuverable motorcycles.

Although they are not physically large machines, the problem with sportbikes has to do with power—specifically, the fact that they might have too much of it for a novice rider. Grab a handful of throttle on one of the larger machines, and you'll be traveling more than 100 mph before your brain even has a chance to register your change in speed. The slowest of these bikes can be overwhelmingly quick. Before you buy one for your first bike, you should honestly assess your self-control and your riding ability. These bikes present a challenge for even the most experienced rider.

Best Bets for New Bikers

The trick is to find the right compromise: a bike small and safe enough to learn to ride, but competent enough to keep up with you as your skills grow. There are machines in each bike category that fulfill these requirements. As I mentioned earlier, any of the dual-sports makes a great first bike if you physically fit it and like its style. And most of the standard-style motorcycles are easy to learn to ride, and you can live with them for a very long time. Most of these bikes have high sporting capabilities, too, if you find yourself drawn to sportbikes.

The middleweight cruiser class teems with good choices for a first bike if your taste runs toward custom-style motorcycles. Just about any of the 500-cc to 800-cc cruisers are bikes you will enjoy riding for a long time.

If you're adamant about getting a Harley-Davidson for your first bike, you've got choices there, too, although the Big Twins are physically large bikes and will probably be uncomfortable for most novice riders. They also cost as much as most new cars.

But Harley makes its Sportster series for people looking for a bike smaller than a Big Twin. These attractive motorcycles represent good values for the money. And because Harley addressed the Sportster's biggest problem—vibration—for 2004, the Sportster has become an excellent choice for the beginning rider.

Harley's ultimate behemoth, the CVO Screamin' Eagle Electra Glide ($28,595), shown on the left, dwarfs Harley's entry-level bike, the 883 Sportster ($6,495).

If you hanker to see the world on your bike, you're in luck, even if you're a beginner. Any bike that fits you and has enough power to keep up with traffic can be outfitted for touring. You can tour on a dual-sport, standard, cruiser, or sporty bike; you don't need an ultimate behemoth. Don't get me wrong: the big touring bikes are fantastic machines. I've owned one myself and used it more than any other bike. These bikes are just too heavy for a novice rider.

New or Used?

When you've selected a type of motorcycle, you need to decide whether you want to buy a new bike or a used one.

Price is probably the prime determining factor in this decision. If money is no object, you can just waltz into a dealership and buy any bike that strikes your fancy. You can buy two or three of them if you're that well off, so you don't even have to make any choices.

But most of us have to make prudent decisions when it comes to expenditures, especially when it comes to spending money on recreational activities such as motorcycling. If you're on a budget, buying a used bike can be a wise decision.

We will go into the details of buying a used bike in Chapter 7. In general, though, modern motorcycles are pretty tough to destroy, and unless the previous owner really went out of his or her way to trash the thing, most used bikes are in fairly good condition. This is especially true of motorcycles that appeal to more mature riders, such as touring bikes, cruisers, and standards. It is less true of sportbikes, which tend to lead harder lives than other types of motorcycles. Dual-sports can go either way. They are usually in fair condition, unless the owner has attempted to do serious off-road riding on them.

Motorcycology

We won't discuss buying used off-road motorcycles because these are primarily race bikes, or bikes that have been ridden by expert riders under extremely stressful conditions. If you choose to purchase a used off-road motorcycle, you should be prepared to entirely rebuild it.

One disadvantage of buying a used bike is that you are never quite certain what you are getting. Another disadvantage of buying used is that you don't usually get a warranty. I show you how to minimize your risks in Chapter 7.

But given the reliable nature of modern bikes, these disadvantages are fairly insignificant. The advantage of buying used is that used bikes are less expensive than new ones. This is especially true of Japanese motorcycles, which historically have had fairly poor resale value. For example, Kawasaki's 2004 Ninja 500R retails for $4,799. At that price, the little Ninja represents one of the best values in motorcycling. But you can find a used fixer-upper for as little as $1,000. Nice, clean, used models can be found for as little as $1,500 to $2,000. These bikes may be 10 years old or more, but they are the same basic motorcycle as the new model.

Harley-Davidsons prove the exception. People have had to wait months to buy new Harleys, so the used market has gone insane. I've seen a 1998 Sportster 1200 Custom, a bike that listed for $8,700, advertised in a newspaper for $13,000.

A premium of $4,300 is quite a price to pay for being impatient. I strongly recommend waiting to buy a new one, given the current market climate. Fortunately for buyers (and unfortunately for those looking to turn a quick buck), that climate seems to have changed. Already you can find new Harleys sitting for sale on showroom floors, a situation unheard of a couple of years ago. When supply and demand equalize, only a fool would pay more for a used bike than a new bike.

While buying a used bike may make the most sense from a pure dollars-and-cents point of view, buying a new bike has its advantages, too. When you buy a new bike, you get a warranty. While the odds of a modern bike breaking down are slim, it does happen, and when it does, that warranty is nice to have.

Another benefit of buying a new bike is that it can be easier to finance. Often the dealer will be able to finance the machine, saving you the hassle of procuring your own loan. And many manufacturers offer attractive low-interest financing packages.

Buying a new bike frees you from some of the worries of buying a used bike. Knowing the machine's complete history has certain benefits. When you are a bike's only owner, you can break it in properly yourself, and you know the bike has been properly maintained.

Plus, there's the intangible benefit of riding a brand-new motorcycle. There's nothing quite like the feeling of riding away from a dealership on your brand-new bike.

The Costs of Cycling

The most obvious (and largest) cost of motorcycling is the cost of the bike itself. New streetbikes range from a low of around $3,000 for a Kawasaki Ninja 250R to a high of $32,000 for a Ducati 999R. Most new bikes fall into the range of $7,000 to $15,000.

Used-bike prices can vary even more than new-bike prices. I tell you where to find price references for specific bikes in Chapter 7, but expect to spend at least $2,500 to $5,000 for a good used motorcycle (unless you're a skilled bargain hunter).

No matter what type of bike you buy, or whether you buy new or used, you will find some unexpected costs. Some of these costs, such as buying insurance, will become apparent soon after you write the check for the bike. Others, such as the cost of basic maintenance, will rear their ugly heads only after you've racked up a few miles.

These costs aren't obvious to a new rider, and a little knowledge ahead of time can influence your choice of a bike. As you will learn, that choice will, in turn, influence those hidden costs.

When shopping for a new motorcycle, you can save a lot of money by remaining flexible about which make and model to buy. Say you've decided to purchase a midsize cruiser, such as Kawasaki's Vulcan 800 Classic. While searching for such a bike, you find a decade-old Honda 800 Shadow in mint condition at one third the price of the Kawasaki. While the Kawasaki is a fine motorcycle, the Shadow is capable of providing every bit as much enjoyment, and with its shaft drive and hydraulically adjusted valves, the Honda will save you hundreds of dollars per year in maintenance costs over the Kawasaki. You can pocket the money saved and use it to finance a cross-country motorcycle trip.

You can also save a lot of money by watching for carryover models. While shopping for the best deal on a Honda 750 Shadow, you might run across a brand-new last year's model Kawasaki 800 Vulcan for $1,500 less. In this case, maintenance costs will be roughly equal because both bikes have manually adjusted valves and chain drives; if you keep an open mind, that will be an extra $1,500 in your pocket.

Buying a used bike is where the process most diverges from buying a car. Because motorcycle prices can fluctuate widely from region to region, depending on how large a market an area has, accurate price guides are difficult to compile.

Further complicating the creation of useful price guides is the wide variation in the condition of each motorcycle. One seller's Yamaha 1100 Special can be in mint condition at 60,000 miles, while the next guy's can be a hunk of junk at 10,000 miles.

When deciding how much a bike is worth, a guidebook's value assessment is only part of the equation. In addition to things such as condition and completeness, you have to look at routine wear and tear. Keeping a motorcycle in tip-top running condition is an expensive proposition. A bike with a fresh tuneup is definitely worth more than a bike that needs a tuneup.

Another item that increases a bike's value is fresh tires. You should be able to tell by looking whether the tires have low miles: Check the depth of the tread at the edges of the tire compared to the depth of the tread at the center. A good pair of quality tires can run you well over $300, with mounting and balancing, so factor that into your price determination.

On the other hand, new tires of low quality actually detract from the value of a bike, at least in my personal equation. If a bike has a pair of bargain-brand tires, I have to decide whether to ride on tires that I consider undesirable or to toss out a nearly new set of tires and spend $300 on another pair. If a bike is wearing a pair of budget-brand tires, I automatically deduct $250 from my offer.

> **Steer Clear**
>
> Before upping your offer because the seller assures you that a bike has had a recent tuneup, make sure that he or she can provide documented proof that the tuneup has been performed.

It's a good idea to speak with as many other owners of a certain model as you can before making a purchase (here again, belonging to a club can be beneficial). Also check any service bulletins that may have been issued to your dealer on a certain model before buying that model.

These rough guidelines may help, but in the end, it's just going to be you and the seller. The entire process may boil down to how badly you want to buy the bike or how much the owner wants to sell it. One thing I can guarantee: if you buy the motorcycle that's right for you, one or two years from now, as you're riding down the road enjoying your machine, you will not be thinking, "Damn, I paid too much for this thing."

Making the Deal

Now comes the most crucial (and most nervewracking) part of the entire process: negotiating the deal. You've decided what the motorcycle is worth to you, and the seller knows what the bike is worth to him or her. Now the two of you have to see if those figures jibe.

For me, negotiating the price of a motorcycle isn't the same as negotiating the price of anything else. People have more of an emotional attachment to motorcycles than they do to other goods: you're buying someone's passion. Whereas I have no moral qualms telling someone they're insane if they think a car or a radio is worth a ridiculous sum of money, I'll politely decline purchasing a motorcycle if the owner has an unrealistic opinion of its value. Its emotional value to that person may be such that the bike actually is worth the price to the owner (but not to me).

In such situations, you'll have to use your own judgment of the seller. If he or she seems reasonable, bring out the source you're using to arrive at your price and explain that their price is a bit steep. If the seller seems like a lunatic, extricate yourself from the situation as quickly as possible.

On the other hand, if the price is in the ballpark, I'll haggle until I get it in my acceptable window. If I can't, I'll usually give up (unless I really want the bike). There are often a lot of motorcycles out there, and it's generally a buyer's market.

In the end, this is a decision only you can make. I've provided you with the basics, but when you're face to face with the seller, trying to make a decision that will affect your life for years to come, you have to be the final judge.

The Least You Need to Know

- The quality of a dealership and of its service department is almost as important as the quality of the motorcycle itself.
- Clubs are a great source of motorcycles and information about motorcycles.
- Before taking a motorcycle out for a test ride, inspect it as if your life depends on it—because it does.
- Be flexible when choosing a motorcycle.

Chapter 8

Insider Tips on Buying a Bike

In This Chapter

- Keeping your maintenance costs down by selecting a low-maintenance bike
- Getting the best price from a dealership
- Financing a bike at the lowest interest rate
- Saving money on insurance

In Chapter 7, I told you how to buy your first bike. Now let me give you a few hints on other costs and responsibilities associated with buying a motorcycle, such as maintaining, financing, and insuring that bike. I'll also give you advice on trading bikes and some more tips on getting the best prices.

The purchase price of a motorcycle is just the tip of the iceberg when it comes to expenses you'll incur when owning a bike. Maintenance will be a huge expense, but I'm going to give you some hints on how to minimize that expense.

A smart shopper can also minimize the costs of financing and insuring a bike. I'm going to show you some ways to save money when you finance and insure a bike. I'm also going to offer some tips on trading in a bike, if you ever decide to do so.

Minimizing Maintenance Costs

Your choice of a bike can determine how much maintenance you'll need to do. Sometimes engineers design motorcycles with certain high-maintenance features to increase the performance of a bike. More often than not, though, features that make a motorcycle easier (and cheaper) to maintain are excluded just to save production costs.

If you're after extremely high performance, you'll have to accept the fact that you'll have to spend more money on maintenance. But if you're willing to accept a slightly lower level of performance, you can look for certain features and practice certain riding habits that will help you keep maintenance costs down.

Three elements, in particular, will affect your maintenance costs: the shaft drive, the centerstand, and the valves. (See Chapters 16 and 17 for a description of these parts.)

Getting Shafted

Select a bike with a shaft drive. As you'll see in Chapters 16 and 17, chain maintenance is the most frequent procedure you'll need to perform on your bike. It's also the dirtiest.

Sporty bikes will usually have a chain because chains tend to disrupt handling less than shafts. If you want such a bike, you'll usually have to accept a chain as part of the package. But there has been a trend in recent years to use chains on types of bikes that, by nature, aren't the best in handling, such as midsize cruisers. This is purely a cost-cutting measure on the part of the manufacturers.

If you want to buy a midsize Japanese cruiser, my advice is to get an older, used one because these usually have shaft drives.

Another option is to select a bike with a belt-drive system. These can be a good compromise between the handling benefits of a chain and the maintenance benefits of a shaft. Belt-drive systems, such as the one used by Harley-Davidson, require less maintenance than chains, but only slightly more than shafts. The main drawback of Harley's belt-drive system is that fixing one can be an expensive proposition.

Getting Centered: The Benefits of a Centerstand

Make certain that your bike comes equipped with a centerstand. All Japanese bikes used to come with centerstands—it was one of the things that set them apart from Harley-Davidsons, which have never been equipped with modern centerstands.

In the 1980s, Japanese manufacturers began excluding centerstands from ultra-high-performance sportbikes because the designs of the exhaust systems used on those bikes prohibited the mounting of centerstands and also because centerstands hindered cornering clearance.

But in the past few years, manufacturers have also begun excluding them from bikes that already have limited cornering clearance, such as cruisers. This is another cost-cutting measure. Combine the lack of a centerstand with a chain drive, and I guarantee that you will create new expletives while maintaining your bike. Understand, though, that the reality of modern motorcycling is that many owners purchase aftermarket service stands. (Service stands generally support one end of the bike or the other, and are separate from the motorcycle. Centerstands bolt to the motorcycle's frame.) These days, it's simply the price of being a motorcyclist.

Hydraulically Adjusted Valves

One of the costliest aspects of maintaining a motorcycle is adjusting the amount the valves move up and down.

This is a crucial (and often neglected) part of motorcycle maintenance.

It is also an expensive part of motorcycle maintenance. On most modern motorcycles, valve adjustment is too complex a job for an inexperienced mechanic to tackle alone. Most riders take their bikes into shops to have the procedure performed.

If the motorcycle has any bodywork that the mechanic has to remove to gain access to the valves, or if the motorcycle is constructed in a way that requires the mechanic to go to heroic lengths to gain access to the valves, labor costs will be even higher.

Fortunately, modern metallurgy and manufacturing techniques mean that valve adjustments on new motorcycles don't have to be done nearly as often as in the past. Keep that in mind when you're trying to choose between an older bike and a brand-new one.

There is another way to avoid this expensive bit of maintenance. Back in the early 1980s, Honda introduced several motorcycle models that had overhead-cam engines with hydraulically adjusted valves. Suzuki and Kawasaki followed suit, introducing cruisers with similar systems. All new Harleys come with hydraulically adjusted valves. Such systems completely eliminate the costs of valve adjustments.

Getting the Best Deal

To get the best deal on a bike, you're best off dealing directly with a sales manager. As I said in Chapter 7, call all the dealerships within the distance you are willing to drive (both to buy the bike and to get it serviced), and have the sales manager quote you an *out-the-door price.* This will be the amount you'll actually pay and will include all hidden costs, such as taxes, licenses, and other fees.

> **Cycle Babble**
>
> The **out-the-door price** is the amount you'll actually pay for a bike, factoring in all hidden costs such as taxes, licenses, and other fees.

If the manager beats around the bush and won't give you a straight out-the-door price, he or she could be planning to stick you with some hidden costs. This may give you some insight into how the dealer will handle any warranty work or other issues that might come up later, so you might want to shop elsewhere if the dealer is evasive.

You might already know that you'll find the best buys on bikes in the off season—in the fall and winter. What you might not know is that you'll find the very best buys on the last Saturday of a month because, at that time, dealers are anxious to meet their monthly sales quotas.

To Your Credit: Financing

Most people don't have the cash on hand to buy a new motorcycle, so many people are forced to finance bikes. The interest paid in finance charges can represent a significant amount of the overall cost of owning a motorcycle, so before you even go looking for a bike, you should arrange the lowest-priced financing you can find.

First, call at least three banks to get the following information:

- The interest rates for unsecured personal loans with payments spread out over both a 36-month period and a 48-month period.
- The same information about a loan if it is secured by the title to your bike.
- The monthly payment for a $10,000 loan in each instance.

You use the amount of $10,000 so that you can calculate your payments based on the amount you borrow. For example, if a bank quotes you a monthly payment of $320 for an unsecured, 36-month loan of $10,000, you can divide $320 by 10, and you'll know that you're being charged $32 a month for every $1,000 you borrow. If you borrow $4,000 to buy a Kawasaki 500 Ninja, just multiply 32 by 4 to learn what your monthly payments will be. Here are a few more tips on how to make it easier to finance your new bike at a dealership—and more:

- Have personal information ready and in order. The dealer or loan officer will want to see a payroll check stub, will want to know how long you've been at the job, and will pull your credit report. You should also get a credit report on your own to make sure everything is accurate.
- Even if you have less than stellar credit, you might be able to get financing. What a dealer/loan officer wants to see is that you've got a good, solid job to handle your outstanding debt.
- Make the biggest downpayment you can afford. It will significantly reduce your monthly loan payments. A good starting point is 25 percent.
- Know that there are alternatives to getting a loan from the dealership. For instance, check out financing the bike through motorcycle-manufacturer lending institutions. Or check the independents, such as Household Retail Services, Inc., used by many dealers. And don't forget resources on the web. Check out www.bestloandeals.com, www.cyclebytel.com, www.motorcyclelender.com, and www.123motorcycleloans.com on the Internet.

Getting Insured

Most states require you to at least have liability insurance before you can operate a vehicle on public roads. If you finance your bike and use its title as security, you need to have full coverage. Full coverage isn't a bad idea anyway if your bike is worth a significant amount of money, but be prepared: full-coverage insurance on a bike is expensive, especially if you live in a major metropolitan area. However, you can do some things to minimize your expenses.

As I said in Chapter 4, most companies base insurance rates on several factors, such as the type of bike, the size of its engine, and the amount of expensive body work on the bike. They also take your driving record into account.

There's nothing you can do about your driving history (you can't change the past), but you can minimize your insurance costs by choosing a bike that is under 600 cc and has minimal bodywork. The list of new bikes under 600 cc without plastic fairings is short:

Aprilia RS50

Honda Rebel

Honda Nighthawk

Honda VLX Shadow

Kawasaki Eliminator 125

Kawasaki KLR250

Kawasaki Vulcan 500 LTD

MZ RT125/RT125 SM

Suzuki DR200SE

Suzuki GS500F

Yamaha Virago 250

Yamaha XT225

The list of used bikes that meet this criteria isn't much longer. In addition to used models of the bikes in the preceding list, it includes a few more choices:

Honda CB650SC/CB700SC Nighthawk

Honda FT500/VT500 Ascot

Honda VF500C V30 Magna

Honda VT500/VT600/VT700 Shadow

Honda XL350R/XL500R/XL600R

Kawasaki EN450 454 LTD/EN500 Vulcan 500

Kawasaki KLR600

Kawasaki KZ550/KZ550 LTD/KZ550 Spectre

Kawasaki ZL600 Eliminator

Kawasaki ZR550 Zephyr

KTM 400/XCe

Suzuki DR350SE

Suzuki GS550E/L

Suzuki GSF400 Bandit

Yamaha XJ550 Seca/Maxim (although some Secas came with a small bikini fairing)

Yamaha XT550/XT600

Yamaha YX600 Radian

All these bikes will work as a first bike. Some will work better than others, and some will be better buys than others (see Appendixes A and B for lists of which are the best first bikes and which are the best buys). All will be relatively inexpensive to insure, especially the older, less expensive models.

Another trick for getting lower rates on your full-coverage insurance is to get a policy with a high deductible. Purchasing a policy with a $500 deductible instead of a $250 deductible means that you'll pay the first $500 to repair the bike if something happens to it. This might seem like a lot of money to shell out in case of an accident, but it won't take you long to save that much on your premiums.

Besides, if you do file a claim, almost every company will raise your rates an exorbitant amount (probably by as much as you'll spend just to fix the bike yourself if you have a higher deductible). If you do make a claim, most of the time, you will pay for it one way or another. Usually, it costs less to fix it yourself in the long run.

Trading Bikes

If your first bike isn't what you had hoped, or if you're ready to move up to a different bike, you may face the decision of whether to trade it in at the dealership to get money toward your new bike.

Usually, you will get more money selling your bike straight out. In a couple of cases, I've made more by trading a bike, but the vast majority of times I've traded, I've lost money. In both cases where I came out ahead, I had an unusual motorcycle—one the dealer already had a buyer lined up for. If I had been able to find such a buyer on my own, I would have made more money than I did when I traded.

The only advantage of trading is convenience. When trading bikes, convenience is usually expensive. You will almost always get more money selling your old bike yourself, and you will always get a better price if you buy your new bike without a trade.

The Least You Need to Know

- You'll save a lot of money over time by choosing a low-maintenance motorcycle.
- Make certain you know the out-the-door price before buying a bike.
- Interest can be a significant part of the overall cost of buying a bike, so shop around.
- In the long run, you can save a lot of money on insurance by having a policy with a fairly high deductible.

Chapter 9

Getting the Gear

In This Chapter

- The facts and myths of helmet use
- Which type of helmet provides the most protection
- Essential protective gear
- Gear that will help you beat the elements
- Where to find the best deals on accessories

We who define ourselves as motorcyclists tend to forget that, at their very core, motorcycles are toys. While we might use them for practical transportation, we primarily use them for fun. And part of the fun of owning a toy is buying accessories for it. Would Barbie be so popular if you couldn't change her outfits?

Fortunately, motorcyclists can choose from a variety of accessories and gear that even Barbie would envy. And not all of that gear is just for fashion or fun; a large part of it serves practical purposes. While some items I'll discuss in this chapter are optional, others are absolutely essential.

Helmets: Home Is Where Your Head Is

Topping your list of essential items should be your helmet.

The issue of helmet use causes more debate than any other issue in motorcycling, which is insane: it's like arguing for or against smallpox vaccinations during the nineteenth century.

Make no mistake about it: not wearing a helmet is stupid. According to a long-term study conducted by Professor Harry Hurt for the University of Southern California's Head Protection Research Laboratory, you're five times more likely to suffer a serious head injury if you have an accident while not wearing a helmet than you are if you crash while wearing one. Every study ever conducted backs up Hurt's findings.

Given the overwhelming evidence supporting the effectiveness of helmets, you'd think everyone would wear one, but you'd be wrong. Stand on any street corner in a state without helmet laws, and you'll see as many bare heads as you will see helmeted heads. People go to extreme lengths to justify their choice to not wear a helmet, but none of their justifications holds up in the face of all the available research. The arguments that helmets break necks, block vision, impair hearing, and cause overheating have been proven myths by every study ever conducted.

I believe most people who don't wear helmets make their decision based on peer pressure. Otherwise reasonable, intelligent adults seem more afraid of facing the ridicule of their comrades than they are of living out the rest of their lives as produce. I actually had a man at the annual motorcycle rally in Sturgis tell me he always wore a helmet but wasn't wearing one during the rally because his friends weren't wearing theirs. I was a rebel, I told him, and I wore mine anyway.

I was once in his position. I rode for more than a decade without a helmet, mainly because, when I was young, I hung out with hardcore Harley bikers, and they would have thought I was some kind of wimp had I worn a helmet.

When I was 25, I took a job working as an orderly in a rehabilitation hospital in the head-and-spine-injury unit. One patient I worked with was a victim of a motorcycle crash. He didn't break a single bone in his accident, and had he been wearing a helmet, he would have walked away with nothing but his pride injured. But he wasn't wearing one, and he hit his head on a rock.

While his body was perfectly healthy, the patient couldn't remember where he was from one minute to the next. One of my jobs was to lead him to the cafeteria every day because he forgot its location from one meal to the next.

That spring, my wife and I both bought motorcycle helmets, and I haven't ridden without one since.

Besides protecting your head, a good-fitting helmet actually makes riding more comfortable. Helmets reduce road noise, keep the wind blast out of your face, and keep bugs and other debris out of your eyes.

How Helmets Are Made

Helmets help keep the contents of your head on the inside rather than the outside by using four basic components in their construction:

- **The outer shell.** The outside of a helmet, usually constructed of fiberglass or injection-molded plastic, disperses energy from an impact across a broad area of the helmet before that energy reaches your head.
- **The impact-absorbing lining.** This area inside the outer shell, usually made of a dense layer of expanded polystyrene, absorbs most of the shock caused by an impact.
- **The comfort padding.** This innermost layer of soft foam and cloth conforms to your head and is primarily responsible for how comfortable the helmet is.
- **The retention system.** This consists of the strap—connected to the bottom of the helmet—that goes under your chin and holds the helmet on.

Helmets come in a variety of styles, from small, bowl-shape half-helmets that protect your brain stem and not much else, to sleek, fully enclosed helmets that protect everything above your neck. In between are the three-quarter, or open-face helmets, which cover most of your head but leave your face unprotected. These give better protection than half-helmets, but if your face contacts the pavement at speed, an open-face helmet will provide you with a one-way ticket on the ugly train. Neither half-helmets nor open-face helmets offer the comfort full-face helmets provide by shielding the wearer from the elements. Whichever type of helmet you choose, the important thing is to choose a helmet. It is the single most crucial piece of motorcycle gear.

Choosing the Right Helmet

Helmets come in a variety of styles and prices. You can get a full-face helmet for less than $100, while high-end helmets can run more than $700.

Why do some helmets cost more than others? There are a variety of reasons. Paint schemes add to the price of a helmet; expect to pay more for a helmet with fancy graphics than for a solid-color helmet. (If the paint scheme replicates the helmet of a top racer, expect to pay more yet.) Some expensive helmets are more comfortable than cheaper helmets, while others are not.

A top-line helmet such as this Shoei RF-1000 Voltage helmet can cost as much as two cheap helmets, but it's worth it. There's a reason why cheap helmets are cheap.

(Photo courtesy of the manufacturer)

Some helmets cost more because they use more expensive material in their outer shells. This may contribute to comfort by making the helmet lighter, but it doesn't necessarily make the helmet any safer.

Safety First

All helmets have to meet minimum safety standards set by the Department of Transportation (DOT). Two other organizations, the American National Standards Institute (ANSI) and the Snell Memorial Foundation, also certify helmets. A Snell certification is something I look for on a helmet. Snell won't certify a half- or open-face helmet, as the DOT will, and it also has more exacting standards for the retention system than the DOT.

CAUTION

Steer Clear

If you choose a half-helmet, be certain you are getting one approved by the DOT. Unscrupulous dealers have placed DOT stickers (stickers applied to the helmet listing the helmet as DOT approved) on unsafe novelty helmets. Genuine DOT-approved helmets also have a label permanently attached to the inside of the helmet displaying DOT information, such as the date of manufacture. Make sure you're getting the real thing.

Getting a Good Fit

Once you get used to wearing a helmet, you won't feel comfortable riding without one. Of course, that assumes that you've picked a helmet that fits you well. A helmet that is too loose might flop around while you're riding, obstructing your vision, and a helmet that is too tight will live up to the worst predictions of the antihelmet crowd.

If all heads were the same shape, choosing a helmet would be simple: you'd just match your helmet size to your hat size. Unfortunately, helmets have to conform to your entire head rather than just the crown of your head.

A helmet should feel fairly snug on your head to prevent it from sliding around and possibly obscuring your vision or falling off in an accident. It may feel too tight when you first put it on. When in place, a properly fitting helmet shouldn't slide around on your head. At the same time, you need to watch for *pressure points*—places where the helmet pushes uncomfortably against your head.

When you try on a helmet, wear it around the store for a bit, and when you take it off, note any soreness or red spots. Wearing a helmet that exerts pressure on your head can turn into a brutal form of torture after an extended period; improperly fitted helmets have permanently turned many riders against helmet use. If the helmet you are trying on touches pressure points, try on a larger size or a different brand or model.

CAUTION

Steer Clear

Because of the difficulty involved in selecting a properly fitting helmet, I strongly advise you to purchase your first one from a store where you can try on different models and sizes. While you can often save money by purchasing accessories through mail-order companies, you won't be saving any money if you can't wear the helmet you order from a magazine ad because it doesn't fit.

CAUTION

Steer Clear

Denim actually provides better abrasion resistance than fashion-weight leather, which is used in the construction of most leather garments available from sources that don't specialize in motorcycle gear. Make certain that your riding gear is constructed of competition-weight leather (leather that is at least 1.3 mm thick): leave the fashion-weight stuff to the supermodels and biker wannabes.

In Style: What to Wear

Although we can do a lot to make motorcycle riding safer, the fact remains that motorcycles tend to fall over more often than cars. Think about your soft skin hitting the hard pavement, and you start to see why we wear special clothing when we ride.

The following list describes the bare-minimum amount of protective gear you need to wear when riding:

- Over-the-ankle leather boots
- Leather, full-fingered gloves
- Long pants
- A riding jacket

This list defines the absolute minimal amount of clothing you can wear to ride safely, especially concerning the last two items (pants and jacket). You may have seen people riding in shorts, tennis shoes, and nothing else. My advice is to not become attached to these people because, should they survive even the most minor spill, they will not emerge from the experience as people you'd want to look at on a regular basis.

Denim actually provides a fair amount of abrasion resistance and should be considered the lowest acceptable standard for protective pants and jackets, but many riders prefer the safety (and style) of a purpose-designed riding suit. These suits, usually constructed of leather or special synthetic materials, such as Kevlar and Cordura nylon, offer superior abrasion resistance and often have built-in armor to protect vital areas of a rider's body.

Looking Good in Leather

Competition-weight leather (leather that is at least 1.3 mm thick) provides the best crash protection of any material, period. That's why it's the material of choice for racing suits. I can guarantee you (from personal experience) that buying a new jacket is much less painful than getting road rash, which is what riders call the abrasions from a crash.

Not all that long ago, a motorcyclist had one choice when it came to protective gear: the traditional leather biker jacket, like Marlon Brando wore in *The Wild One*. This lack of choice had its advantages: Back then, you knew who rode a bike and who didn't.

The variety of styles and colors now available for leather riding gear probably has a lot to do with the popularity of leather in the fashion world. No longer are motorcyclists forced to choose between Marlon Brando's biker jacket and nothing at all. Today's jackets and complete riding suits are available in as many styles and colors as are motorcycles themselves. And traditional black leather riding gear is now available in shapes and styles to complement every body type.

Once a motorcyclist looking for a protective jacket had just one choice: the black leather biker jacket.

(Photo © 1998 Darwin Holmstrom)

Synthetic Riding Suits: Ties Optional

While leather is still the optimum material for crash protection, an increasing number of riders choose synthetic riding suits. The advantages of leather are most apparent at extremely high speeds (which is why racers choose leather), but at speeds under triple-digit velocities, synthetic suits provide all the protection you are likely to need.

> **Motorcycology**
>
> Aerostich Riderwear led the revolution in synthetic riding gear, and its riding suits, jackets, and pants still set the industry standard. But there is another reason to purchase Aerostich riding gear: it's cool. Wearing an Aerostich Roadcrafter suit or Darien jacket and pants into any motorcycle hangout will automatically mark you as one of motorcycling's elite troops.

These suits have certain advantages over leather. Most of them are machine-washable, unlike leather, which must be sent to a cleaner. And many of them are waterproof or water-resistant, eliminating the need for special rain gear. Plus, these synthetic suits can easily be worn over regular clothing, a tremendous advantage for people who use their motorcycles to commute to work. Many synthetic suits are constructed with removable liners, allowing the rider to use them over a broad range of weather conditions. In hot weather, riders can wear light clothing beneath their suits, and as the temperatures drop, riders can put in the liners and wear extra layers of clothing. Aerostich even offers an electric liner for its Darien jacket.

Aerostich's Darien Gore-Tex-lined jacket and pants, which feature body armor in crucial places, combine safety and outstanding protection from the elements.

(Photo © 1998 Darwin Holmstrom)

Gloves: How Much Blood Can You Lose Through the Palm of Your Hand?

Many riders—even those mentioned earlier, who wear nothing but a pair of shorts and some sandals—wear a pair of gloves when they are riding, if for no other reason than for comfort.

Always wear a sturdy pair of leather gloves, preferably a pair with gauntlets that extend over your wrists. A good pair of gloves designed specifically for motorcycle use will have extra leather on the palms, knuckles, and fingers. This provides additional protection against abrasion in case of an accident.

Riders who like to consider themselves tough often wear fingerless gloves. While these will provide some palm protection in the event of a crash, they really offer very little hand protection. Plus, while you are riding, the wind stretches out the finger openings, and bugs can get blown in. Getting stung by a bee on the palm of your hand can make your ride home a painful and dangerous experience. Full-fingered leather gloves prevent this.

In fact, bees are one major reason to wear protective gear. They are a major part of the riding experience; sooner or later, you will get stung. Wearing gloves is one of the most effective ways you can avoid bee stings. I especially like gloves with large gauntlets that go well past the sleeve opening on my jacket; this keeps the little buggers from flying up my jacket sleeve and stinging my arm.

Motorcycle Moments

One of the bloodiest accidents I've ever seen involved a rider who went down at more than 70 mph without gloves. He had a helmet on and wasn't seriously injured, except that he completely peeled off the skin from the palms of his hands. He lost more than a pint of blood through just the wounds on his hands.

A good pair of riding gloves will provide both comfort and protection.

(Photo © 1998 Darwin Holmstrom)

Fancy Footwear

Even choosing footwear for riding requires some thoughtful consideration. You need to wear a pair of over-the-ankle leather boots to protect your ankles from being burned by the exhaust pipes and from stones and other debris. You also need to take other factors into account when selecting a pair of boots.

On a motorcycle, your feet are an important part of your motorcycle's chassis: they are what hold up the motorcycle when you are at rest. In effect, when you aren't moving, the soles of your shoes are like an extra set of tires. Because of this, you'll want to wear a pair of boots with grippy soles. While fashionable cowboy boots provide adequate ankle protection, their leather soles are far too slippery for them to be safe riding shoes. If you wear cowboy boots, make certain they are work-style cowboy boots with grippy rubber soles. That holds true for any style of boot you choose.

I prefer a pull-on boot over a lace-up boot, and not just because they take less time to put on. I worry about laces coming loose and getting caught in moving parts.

Motorcyclists seem to develop unnatural attachments to their boots, perhaps because they are such an integral part of riding. I have a couple of pairs of riding boots that I've elevated to the status of pets.

My favorite boots are a pair of Harley-Davidson lineman-style boots I've had since college. These are the big, up-to-the-knee black leather boots that scare people when you walk into the room wearing them. I've ridden through thousands of miles of rain and snow in them. I've even crashed in them, and they still have the original pair of soles.

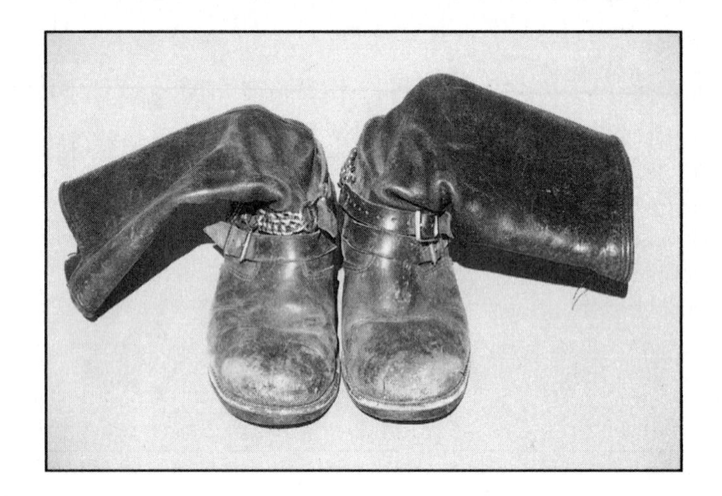

A good pair of boots, such as the author's Harley-Davidson lineman's boots, will outlast several motorcycles.

(Photo © 1998 Darwin Holmstrom)

Extreme Riding Gear

Nothing surpasses the pleasure of seeing the world on a motorcycle because, on a bike, you are right there, in the thick of it. That means you get to smell the freshly cut hay alongside the road you're riding down. The morning sun recharges you, just as it recharges the flora.

The downside of all this nature worship is that you will experience the world in its entirety, and you must take the bad with the good. That means being prepared for any kind of weather.

Rain Gear

Ride long enough, and your rain suit will become as much of a part of your everyday riding gear as your helmet: you won't leave home without it. A good rain suit can turn a miserable, wet ride into a tolerable or even fun one.

Motorcycology

When selecting a rain suit, choose as brightly colored a suit as possible. Visibility is especially important when it comes to gear you will wear in low-visibility situations, such as rain. Don't buy a black rain suit. Face it, you're not going to look cool while riding a motorcycle in the rain, regardless of how tough your rain suit looks. Since being cool is out of the question, you might as well be safe.

Rain suits are either one- or two-piece suits, made of polyvinyl chloride (PVC) or coated nylon. I prefer the one-piece suits because rain can seep in between the pants and the jacket on some two-piece suits.

PVC provides better rain protection than most coated nylon suits, but because it is so sticky to the touch, it can be difficult to get on and off. To get around this, the best PVC suits have a nylon mesh lining that slides against your leather riding gear. Look for a suit that has such lining in both the upper and lower portions.

Motorcycology

Think of rain gear as insurance against rain. If you need it, you'll be glad you have it; if you don't need it, you'll be glad anyway because you had nice weather for your ride.

In my experience, the best rain gear is a waterproof riding suit, such as the Aerostich Darien jacket and pants, which are made of Gore-Tex Cordura material. With these, you don't have to bother putting a rain suit on when foul weather approaches and taking it off when it passes. Even the best rain suits are a hassle to put on by the side of the road on a windy day, and when they get wet, they can be real buggers to get off over leather.

As backward as it may seem, I've encountered a lot bikers who refuse to wear rain gear. This strikes me as so odd. I know from long years of experience that few things in this world are as miserable as spending an entire day in drenched leather.

You can get a bare-bones two-piece rain suit for well under $50. Expect to spend more than $100 for a top-quality one-piece suit.

Ride long enough, and your rain suit will become part of your everyday riding gear: You won't leave home without it.

(Photo © 1998 Darwin Holmstrom)

Freezing to Death: Beating the Cold

Motorcyclists tend to get cold more often than they get hot. Even on a relatively mild day—say, 65°F—the windchill on a motorcycle traveling at 65 mph can approach freezing. Hypothermia (a condition in which your body temperature drops to dangerously low levels) is a very real danger on a bike. As I said earlier, in cold weather, a synthetic motorcycle suit can be a real lifesaver, but even those who can't afford such a suit can throw together the proper gear for riding on a cool day.

Motorcycology

The only drawback of thermal underwear is that it tends to be bulky under your clothes. If this is a problem, another option is to wear silk long underwear. While this doesn't provide the warmth of thermal underwear, it still keeps you warm, without the added bulk.

Thermal underwear is a given if you plan to ride when it's cool. On a bike without fairing, I wear thermal underwear (tops and bottoms) whenever the temperature dips below 70°F.

On really cold days, I wear jeans and a turtleneck sweater over my thermal underwear. I like to wear a sweatshirt over that, along with either chaps or riding pants. When the temperatures get too cold, the summer leather riding suits usually go into hibernation.

Even if you can't afford a Darien jacket with an electric liner, you can still benefit from electrically heated clothing on a budget. Aerostich and several other companies make electrically heated vests that you can wear under your jacket. These vests can keep you toasty on even the coldest ride. On super-cold days, I've worn an electric vest under my rain gear, even though it wasn't raining. The vest warmed up the entire inside of the suit and kept me as warm as if I'd been driving a car.

Motorcycology

I've found that a one-piece pair of thermal underwear (a union suit) is preferable to the traditional two-piece set. When you dress in bulky layers, your clothes tend to ride up, creating a gap of bare skin between the top and bottom pieces of a two-piece suit. You can avoid this with a union suit.

Keeping your hands warm can go a long way toward keeping your whole body warm. Several companies offer electrically heated handgrip kits, and BMW offers them as an option on its bikes. You can also purchase something called Hippo Hands, sheaths that attach to your handlebars and surround your controls. These devices may look odd, but they provide exceptional protection against the elements.

For the ultimate in cold-weather gear, Aerostich makes this electric liner that zips into its Darien jacket.

(Photo © 1998 Darwin Holmstrom)

Baked, Boiled, or Fried: Beating the Heat

All motorcyclists have to deal with the heat. Riding all day under the hot sun takes a lot out of your body. You can become dangerously dehydrated and even suffer heat stroke. At the very least, you may become tired, and your judgment and riding skills will suffer.

One of my most dangerous riding experiences occurred because of dehydration. I got a mild case of food poisoning in Las Vegas, but I didn't realize it until I was headed across the Arizona desert. At the worst possible moment I could imagine, I realized I couldn't keep down water. I spent a difficult (and dangerous) day making my way from gas station to gas station, until I finally had the sense to call it quits and get a motel room.

Since that episode, I've learned a lot about riding in heat. The most important thing to remember is to keep hydrated. Always drink plenty of fluids, and on really hot days, drink fluids especially designed to rehydrate your cells, such as sports drinks. Remember that caffeine is a diuretic and will deplete your body's store of water rather than replenish it. If you feel thirsty, you have already gone too long without a drink. If you ride much in hot climates, you should really invest in a CamelBak or some other brand of water reservoir. Fill these with ice, and in addition to providing you with refreshing water to drink, they will keep you cool during the day.

Another method for keeping cool is to soak your shirt under your riding gear. This works especially well with a heavily ventilated jacket such as an Aerostich Darien. You can control the rate of evaporation of the water on your shirt by opening and closing vents in the jacket.

The right gear is crucial for hot-weather riding. Most leather makers now offer perforated leather riding gear, which lets air flow through the garment. A few companies even offer mesh jackets with protective armor, sort of like the gear worn by off-road riders. These help you keep cool but still provide reasonable abrasion protection. Joe Rocket's Santa Fe jacket is a very popular jacket of this type.

Again, synthetic riding suits make excellent hot-weather riding gear. You can remove the lining from most of these and just use the outer shell, which retains all the armor and protective qualities. The suits themselves have many zippered vents, allowing you to control airflow. Aerostich recommends wearing long pants and a long-sleeve shirt under its suits because, theoretically, its Cordura can melt under extremely high temperatures (but in all the years of manufacturing, examining, and repairing suits that have been through crashes, they have yet to find one case of this happening). While I can't condone this practice, your risks would probably be minimal if you chose to wear just shorts and a T-shirt under your Aerostich suit on an extremely hot day. You would still have far more abrasion protection than someone riding in jeans and a light jacket.

Lightweight, ventilated jackets such as this Coretech from Tour Master provide outstanding ventilation and keep you relatively cool on hot days. What's more, Tour Master's top-line jacket here also features triple-density armor in strategic places and an available zip-in/zip-out liner.

Accessories: All the Extras

A good part of the fun of owning a motorcycle is getting all the accessories that go along with it. Motorcyclists may try to convince you otherwise, but they lie. They love modifying their bikes and collecting gadgets.

A huge array of accessories is available for every type of bike and every type of biker, from cruiser windshields to travel trailers, to global positioning units (computers that use satellites to tell you where you are) and bike-to-bike communicators. Some are mere novelties, things mainly used to amuse your friends when you stop for a cup of coffee. Other accessories come closer to necessities.

Motorcycology

If you choose to mount a windshield to your bike, select one that you can see over without the top of the windshield cutting across your line of vision. The airflow over a well-designed windshield will go over your face, directing wind, bugs, and debris to the top of your helmet or over it. Most Plexiglas windshields aren't optically clear enough to provide an undistorted view of the road if you look directly through them. This is especially problematic at night.

On the more frivolous side are the purely cosmetic items, things that serve no purpose except to alter a bike's looks.

CAUTION

Steer Clear

Even a simple addition such as a sissybar—the backrest put behind the passenger's portion of the saddle—can make a bike behave in a frightening manner at high speeds.

Most accessories available today are usually harmless. That wasn't always true, especially during the chopper craze of the 1960s and 1970s. Some of the popular accessories of the day, such as high "sissybar" backrests and high handlebars, could induce high-speed wobbles in some bike's handling. Some accessories, such as extended forks and aftermarket frames with steep rakes, actually made a motorcycle downright dangerous to ride.

Today's accessories can still have unintended side effects. A while back, I bought a Yamaha Venture, an ultimate behemoth type of touring bike, on which the previous owner had installed a pair of chrome covers over the vents in the side panel. While he probably found these covers attractive, they trapped heat in the engine compartment and made the bike run hot, so I removed them.

The owner had also installed a strange set of 1950s-era taillights around the license plate frame. At first, I didn't care for the way these Elvis lights, as I call them, looked, but after awhile, they grew on me, so I kept them. Besides, anything that makes you more visible to traffic is a functional accessory.

Windshields

On the closer-to-necessity side are windshields. While a bike with a sporty, forward-leaning riding position can get by without a windshield because the rider is naturally braced against the wind, on more laid-back bikes (such as cruisers), an effective windshield can make the difference between a comfortable ride and a trip to the chiropractor.

A quality windshield, such as this Street Shield from National Cycle, can make any motorcycle a more comfortable place to spend time.

(Photo © 1998 Darwin Holmstrom)

Saddlebags

Saddlebags are probably the most useful accessory you can add to your bike, turning it from a pretty plaything into a practical form of transportation. Hard bags, which are more or less suitcases mounted to the bike, are the most useful because they offer better weather protection, plus most of them can be locked. Unfortunately, few motorcycles offer them as options (although the number is growing). You can purchase them for many bikes from aftermarket manufacturers, such as GIVI. These tend to be expensive, but if you can afford a set, it is money well spent.

You'll probably end up buying a pair of soft saddlebags that you mount over your seat. These are usually made of vinyl, leather, or nylon.

Saddlebags change a motorcycle from a toy into a practical form of transportation. Chase Harper's ET 4000 Saddlebags provide just about all the carrying capacity you'll need.

(Photo © 1998 Darwin Holmstrom)

Tankbags

Tankbags also add much to a motorcycle's usefulness. These are similar to soft saddlebags, usually constructed of nylon, but they mount on top of the fuel tank. These can be mounted by adjustable straps or by using magnetic mounts that consist of strong magnets in the base of the bags that stick to the tank. Of course, this requires that your tank be constructed of metal; such a system won't work on plastic tanks or tank covers.

Tankbags are great for traveling, not only because they offer extra storage, but because most of them also have a clear map pocket on top. If you've ever tried to unfold a map and read it at the side of a road on a windy day, you'll appreciate this feature.

CAUTION

Steer Clear

Be careful of what you pack in a tankbag. I once crashed, and my motorcycle did a cartwheel, ejecting me from the saddle. In my tankbag I had a metal toolkit. When I went off the bike, I landed with the tankbag under my chest. I was uninjured, except for several broken ribs from the tankbag containing the toolkit. Moral of the story? Never carry anything in your tankbag you wouldn't want to use for a pillow.

The major drawback of using a tankbag is that the straps can scratch the paint on your gas tank.

The variety of accessories available could fill its own book, and since they reflect an owner's individual taste, only you can decide which ones are right for your bike.

Once you've become accustomed to the convenience of a tankbag, such as this 1150 expandable tankbag from Chase Harper, you'll use the bag every time you ride.

(Photo © 1998 Darwin Holmstrom)

Magazines

Some of the most useful accessories are things that you neither wear nor mount on your motorcycles. Magazines—or, more precisely, the valuable information contained in magazines—can help you become a much better motorcyclist. That information might even save your life some day. This is as true of online magazines as it is of print magazines.

Not that I'm biased or anything, but the magazines in Primedia's Motorcycle Group, magazines such as *Motorcyclist*, *Motorcycle Cruiser*, *Sport Rider*, and *Dirt Rider*, contain some of the best information found anywhere.

Where to Buy Accessories

Where you buy those accessories is up to you, too. You can buy your gear from a local dealer, or you can buy from one of several mail-order firms that sell just about every accessory available, usually at discount prices. Both methods have drawbacks, and both have benefits.

When you buy from a local dealer, you see what you're getting: you can try on a helmet or a garment, or see if a windshield fits your bike without obstructing your view. And if you do buy something that won't fit you or your bike (although the chances of that happening are slim because the staff can help you select the correct item in the first place), you can always bring it back. Another advantage of buying local is that you often can get the item right away and don't have to wait for it to be shipped.

Motorcycology

Often the price difference between buying local and ordering from a discount company is not all that great, especially after figuring in shipping and handling charges. Chances are, your local dealer can come reasonably close to those prices, if given the chance.

On the other hand, the mail-order places usually have a much wider variety of items than any local shop could afford to carry. Plus, they usually sell those items for less than the shops. The drawbacks are that you don't get to check the fit of the items before purchasing them, and returning them can also be a hassle.

One other drawback of buying from a mail-order company is that you won't be supporting your local shops. A lot of smaller shops operate on a slim profit margin, and it wouldn't take much to put many of them out of business. When you buy from some company in a distant location, you could help put your local dealer out of business. This might not seem like it would concern you in any practical way, but it does. If an emergency arises and you need to repair your bike right now, that local dealer is awfully nice to have.

For a comprehensive list of companies that provide motorcycle accessories, see Appendix C.

The Least You Need to Know

- Although some states allow you to choose whether you wear a helmet, if you have a functioning brain, there is no real choice.
- Wear competition-weight leather to protect your body from the elements and in case of a crash.

- Not wearing gloves can turn a minor mishap into a visit to the emergency room.
- Rain suits can take the misery out of rain.
- Although mail-order companies may offer a wide range of motorcycle accessories, your local dealer can help you choose the right accessories and avoid the need to return items.

Part 3

On the Road

Starting up your bike and hitting the road: this is what motorcycling is all about. All the rest of the motorcycling experience pales when compared to actually riding.

Riding is fun, but it's also serious business, with grave consequences if you make a mistake. Because of the serious nature of riding, you need to be prepared.

This part of the book covers a variety of survival strategies for the street, as well as the basics of how to ride. I also discuss hazards that you might encounter and what to do in case of an emergency. So get your helmet and riding gear, and make sure your bike is ready to roll, because we're going riding.

Chapter 10

Preparing to Hit the Road

In This Chapter

- How to get in the right frame of mind for riding
- Understanding the licensing procedure
- How the Motorcycle Safety Foundation can help you learn to ride
- What switches and levers do
- Mastering the preride inspection

You're just about ready to hit the road, but first you need to learn how to ride. You need to learn what the controls on a bike do and how you make them do that. You'll need to learn how to prepare your motorcycle for the road, and you'll also need to prepare yourself.

Before you can even ride a bike, you have to get an instructional (learner's) permit. After you learn to ride, you'll want to get your motorcycle endorsement. Not only will this keep you out of trouble with the law, but it will also statistically lower your chances of getting killed on your bike.

If you haven't ridden before, you'll need to start from scratch. The things you learned when you learned to drive a car don't apply to motorcycles.

Every day you ride, you will encounter unexpected challenges, such as all kinds of crazed car drivers. In any encounter between a car and a motorcycle, the car has the advantage.

You'll have enough uncontrollable events to worry about while you're riding. You don't need to worry about things you can control, such as the condition of your motorcycle. That's why you'll need to inspect certain components on your bike each time you ride.

And you'll need to examine your own head before each ride. There's no room on a bike for a distracted or angry rider. If you are not totally in the moment, totally aware of where you are and what you are doing, you can endanger yourself.

In this chapter, I'll explain what you need to do to get your permit and motorcycle endorsement. I'll also show you how to use the controls on your bike, how to prepare your bike for each ride, and how to mentally prepare yourself for each ride.

Getting in Your Right Mind: Mental Motorcycling

Riding a bike requires your undivided attention. If you preoccupy yourself thinking about the meeting you're late for while you commute to work on your bike, you might never make that meeting at all.

Before you head out onto the public roads, you have to make sure your mind is right. As Strother Martin (the overseer in the film *Cool Hand Luke*) might have said, motorcyclists whose minds ain't right get to spend the rest of eternity in the box.

CAUTION

Steer Clear

Nothing gets your mind less right for riding than messing it up with alcohol or other drugs. Just one beer can upset your balance in ways you can't perceive, and that can have fatal consequences. According to the Motorcycle Safety Foundation, 50 percent of all people killed on motorcycles had alcohol in their blood—and of that 50 percent, two thirds had had only one or two drinks before their accidents.

You need to clear your mind of distractions before you get on your bike. Do whatever it takes to get your mind right (including going to the bathroom—you'd be surprised at how your concentration can suffer when you've got a full bladder).

Another great distraction is anger at other drivers. Anger on the road is dangerous; it will cloud your judgment, and you need that to make the split-second decisions required to survive in traffic. You need to remain calm and collected in every situation, regardless of whether you are right or wrong. While you may have the right of way, the person in the car has your life in his or her hands. Don't start vehicular arguments with someone who can hurt you simply by turning a steering wheel. Instead, calmly remove yourself from such situations. Get as far away from the offending vehicle as possible.

Getting Licensed

Every state in the Union requires riders to obtain a special endorsement on their driver's license before operating a motorcycle. While this may seem like just another hoop to jump through, these states are doing you a favor. According to the Motorcycle Safety Foundation, unlicensed riders account for the majority of accident victims; by getting a license, you vastly increase your odds of not becoming a statistic. Licensing programs help get a safer, more knowledgeable population of motorcyclists out on the street.

Motorcycle tests, both written and riding, have improved a great deal since I first got my license back in the early 1980s. I'd have to say my first experience with the licensing procedure was useless. Whoever compiled the test obviously had no motorcycle experience, and the questions had no relevance to the knowledge needed to survive on a motorcycle.

I had a pleasant surprise when I retook the written test in the early 1990s; it actually asked useful questions. You had to know things about real-world motorcycling to pass.

Each state has a different written test with different questions. The most useful tests are those devised in conjunction with the Motorcycle Safety Foundation. To obtain a study guide for your state's test, call your local Department of Motor Vehicles.

Getting Your Learner's Permit

The first step in getting licensed is to get your permit, which you receive upon successfully completing the written part of your test. The purpose of the permit is to allow you to get out and practice in the real world before taking your test. You should get your permit even before you actually learn to ride so that you can legally practice your riding.

In most states, getting your permit will allow you to ride during daylight hours without a passenger. Most states have extra requirements for permitted riders, such as not allowing them to ride after dark or allowing them to ride on limited-access highways only. You will be required to wear a helmet if you have just a permit—but that shouldn't matter to you because, after reading Chapter 9, you want to wear your helmet all the time anyway.

Getting Your Endorsement

You'll get your endorsement, the notation on your driver's license officially designating you as a motorcyclist, after you complete the riding portion of your test. For this, you'll be required to demonstrate your riding skills on either a closed course or public streets.

When I took my test, I just rode around a city block, did a U-turn in the street without putting my foot down, and basically didn't kill myself. A tester watched from the sidewalk, and when I returned, he gave me my license, along with a speech informing me of the reasons why I should become an organ donor. This portion of the test has improved somewhat since then, but it still teaches you very little about the skills you'll need to survive on the mean streets. To gain those, your best bet is to take a Motorcycle Safety Foundation RiderCourse.

The Motorcycle Safety Foundation

A nationwide not-for-profit organization established in March 1973, the Motorcycle Safety Foundation (MSF) works to make motorcycling a safer activity and has developed programs recognized around the world for their excellence and effectiveness. The MSF does the following:

- It works to make high-quality rider-training programs, designed for both new and experienced riders, available to as wide a population as possible.
- It works with state and national governments and organizations to promote motorcycle safety and to help adopt effective motorcycle-operator licensing practices.
- It collects data and information on motorcycle safety and works to get that information out to the public.

Motorcycology

Another advantage of completing an MSF RiderCourse is that many insurance companies give you a break on your premiums if you successfully complete the course. It is the single best thing you can do to ensure that you have a long and healthy career as a motorcyclist.

There is nothing you can do to better prepare yourself for the challenges of motorcycling than to take an MSF RiderCourse. That applies to experienced riders as well as novices. The MSF has worked to make such courses available across the entire United States. Even if you have to drive a few miles to reach the RiderCourse nearest you, you can find no better use of your time if you're serious about motorcycling. To find the RiderCourse nearest you, call the Motorcycle Safety Foundation at 1-800-446-9227 or check out www.msf-usa.org on the web.

In addition to possibly saving your butt somewhere down the line, taking an MSF RiderCourse has immediate practical value. More than 20 states will grant you your motorcycle endorsement upon successfully completing a RiderCourse, saving you the trouble of going to a busy Department of Motor Vehicles office and taking a test. Even if the state still makes you take the test, many states give you extra credit for completing an approved RiderCourse.

And for off-road enthusiasts, the MSF offers its DirtBike School. It's a one-day course that emphasizes the mental and physical skills required for dirtbike riding, and, of course, safety is paramount. Class sizes are kept small to ensure plenty of individual attention from the MSF-certified coaches, and students can be assured of getting the proper fundamentals to have big fun off-road. For more information, check out www.dirtbikeschool.com on the web; you also can enroll with a single phone call to 1-877-288-7093.

Control Freaks: How to Ride a Motorcycle

On a motorcycle, you control the machine with your body, leaning into curves rather than steering the bike. This is why motorcycling provides you with a freedom no other form of transportation can. But controlling a bike requires more than just throwing your weight around. To be able to ride a bike, you need to orchestrate a complex series of actions between both your hands and your feet, all performed simultaneously, in perfect synchronicity.

Primary Controls

You use six major controls to operate just about every motorcycle made since World War II (with the exception of a couple of oddball bikes that use automatic transmissions). The location of these controls has been standardized on all motorcycles manufactured after the mid-1970s (although the location of the shifter and rear brake may be reversed on certain European and American motorcycles manufactured before that time). The following figures illustrate the standard places where you'll find controls on all but a few rare, collectible motorcycles.

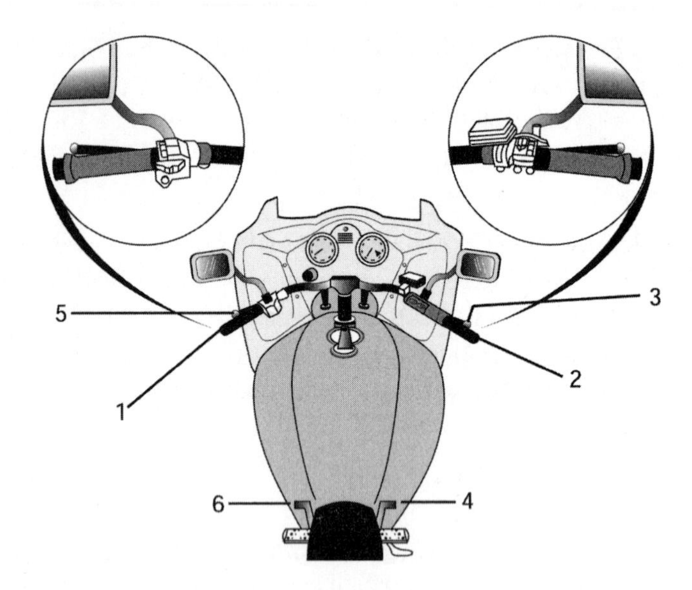

The six primary controls you'll use to ride your bike.

1. The **handlebars** are the levers attached to the top of the fork that you use to control the bike's direction. (Note that I didn't say *steer* the bike: remember, at anything higher than parking-lot speeds, you *countersteer* the bike, using the handlebars to lever the bike over, not steer it.)

2. The **throttle** is a twist grip located on the right end of the handlebar. This controls your speed. You twist the grip toward you to increase the amount of fuel getting into the engine, thus increasing your speed. All properly functioning modern throttles have springs that automatically return them to the closed position.

3. The **front brake lever** is the lever mounted to the right side of the handlebar, in front of the throttle, that controls the front brake.

4. The **rear brake lever** is the lever near the right footpeg that controls the rear brake and (on some models with linked braking systems) the front brake.

5. The **clutch lever** is located on the left end of the handlebar (the mirror image of the front brake lever). It controls the clutch and is used to help shift gears.

6. The **shift lever** is located near the left footpeg. It moves the shifting forks in the transmission, which, in turn, shift the transmission's gears.

By using these controls with your hands and feet, you can make the motorcycle stop and go, and you can control the bike's direction. While you are riding, you constantly use these controls—often using all of them at the same time.

Secondary Controls

In addition to the six primary controls, you'll need to use a variety of other controls to ride a bike effectively. The most important of these are illustrated in the following figure.

1. The **ignition switch** is similar to the ignition switch in cars, except that it usually locks the fork as a theft deterrent, it operates a parking light, and it is separate from the starter. You don't turn the key to start a bike like you do a car.

2. The **electric-starter button** is on the right end of the handlebar near the throttle. Nearly every motorcycle made today comes with an electric starter, which you operate by pressing this button.

3. The **kick-start lever** is an oddity on most bikes made today, except for some smaller dual-sports and strictly off-road bikes, but you may encounter it on certain used bikes. It's usually located near the right footpeg (although it's located on the left side on certain European bikes). To work this device, you need to kick the lever in a downward motion with your foot.

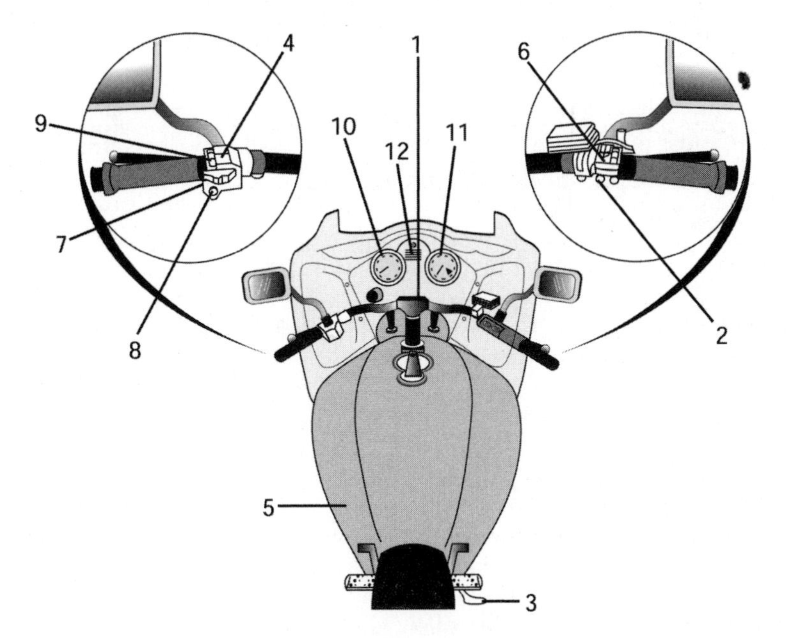

The secondary controls you'll use to ride your bike.

4. The **choke or enrichment control** is a lever or a knob that is located in various positions but is usually found on the handlebars; you use it to help start your bike. This used to be a fairly straightforward system, but it has become more complex with the advent of fuel-injection systems and onboard computer technology.

5. The **fuel petcock** is a valve that controls the flow of fuel from the gas tank to the induction system; it usually has positions for On, Off, Reserve, and Prime. Prime is used only after the engine has not been run for an extended period of time; it fills the float bowls with fuel before starting the engine.

6. The **engine cut-off switch** (or kill switch) turns off the engine. If you can't start your bike, the first thing you should check is whether the kill switch is in the Off position.

7. All street-legal motorcycles manufactured in the past 25 years are equipped with **turn signals.**

Motorcycology

Fuel petcocks are much less important on modern bikes than on older bikes; many modern bikes with fuel pumps don't even use traditional petcocks. Even on those that do have one, you'll seldom need to bother with it. On older bikes, you'll need to turn this switch off each time you park the bike and remember to turn it on when you restart it. The one big advantage of petcocks is their Reserve feature, which saves a small amount of fuel in the bottom of the tank, in case you run out.

Unlike cars, many bikes don't have a self-canceling feature built into their turn-signal switches. On most modern bikes, you operate the turn signals by pushing the switch toward the direction in which you want to turn, and then you push it straight in to cancel the turn signal.

8. Your **horn** can save your life, so don't be timid about using it. You operate most horns by pushing a button located next to the turn-signal switch.

9. The **headlight dimmer switch** switches the headlight between high- and low-beam modes. On most modern bikes, you can't turn off the lights, so this switch just changes beams.

10. The **speedometer** indicates your speed.

11. The **tachometer** indicates the number of revolutions your engine is turning each minute.

12. The **indicator lights** (sometimes known as idiot lights) are primarily the same as the indicator lights on your car, with the exception of a neutral indicator light (usually green) that indicates when the transmission is in neutral.

Motorcycology

You'll use your idiot lights more on a bike than you do on a car, especially the neutral light and the turn-signal indicator. Because most bikes don't have self-canceling turn signals, it's easy to forget that they're on.

Although these are all peripheral system controls used to augment riding rather than directly to ride the bike, you will need to use most, if not all, of them every time you ride.

The Preride Inspection

Motorcycles require more upkeep than cars. This has always been the case, and it is still a fact of motorcycling life, even with the technological advances you learned about in earlier chapters. The consequences of a systems failure on a bike are much more severe than they are if something goes wrong with your car. Take a blown tire, for example. When a tire blows on your car, you can have difficulty controlling it. When the same thing happens on a bike, the danger level increases exponentially.

The best way to avoid a catastrophic failure is to inspect your motorcycle on a regular basis. Some items need to be checked more often than others; some should be checked each time you go out for a ride.

The Motorcycle Safety Foundation uses the *T-CLOCK method* to help remember what to check during the preride inspection:

T	Tires and wheels
C	Controls
L	Lights and electrics
O	Oils and fluids
C	Chassis and chain
K	Kickstand

This method is useful, but I'm going to present a simpler one because I've found that by making the preride inspection too complicated, you encourage riders to ignore the whole thing completely.

I try to check all the items on the T-CLOCK list fairly regularly, but to be honest, I don't check them all every time I ride. A lot depends on the bike I'm riding; for example, if I know that a bike doesn't use oil, I might check the oil only once a week. If the bike is an oil burner, I might check it in the morning and then check it a couple more times as the day progresses.

I've found that the cables and other controls on modern bikes seem to need less attention than those on older bikes; I might go a couple of weeks without attending to my cables and controls, depending on the conditions I've been riding under. As for chains, I prefer shaft-driven bikes, so I can eliminate that messy procedure entirely.

I do check for loose bolts in the chassis and make certain the spring is attached to the kickstand each time I ride. The two things I consider absolutely essential to check before each ride are the tires and lights.

Checking the Tires

I check the air pressure in my tires each morning before I start my bike. I keep an air-pressure gauge in my jacket pocket, and I check the tires when they are cold (when the air inside them warms up, which it does very quickly while you ride, the pressure reads higher). Not only is riding with the proper air pressure in your tires safer, but it also makes your tires last longer. Check your owner's manual to find the proper air-pressure level for your motorcycle.

Whenever I check my air pressure, I also look over the tires themselves to check their wear and to look for any abnormalities, such as bulges, damage to the carcass, and cracking in the sidewalls. I also make sure I haven't picked up a nail or a chunk of glass. I will not ride on a tire I have any questions about. Neither should you.

Keep a tire gauge in your jacket or on your bike so you can check the air pressure each morning.

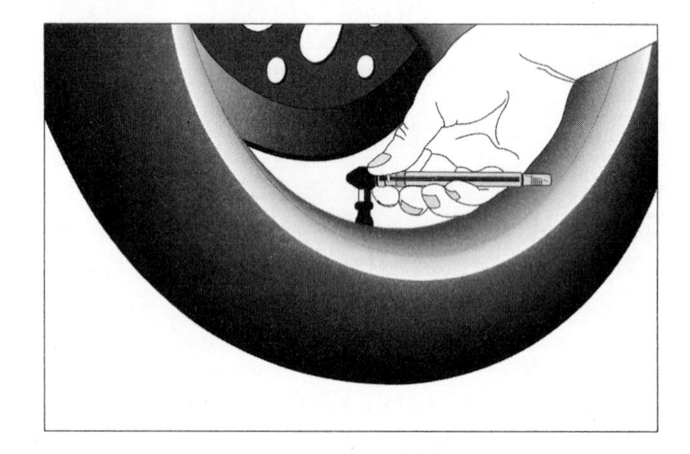

The best way to avoid a blowout is to keep a close eye on your tires and to make certain they are free of debris, such nails or other objects that could puncture the tire. Change your tires as soon as they wear down to an unacceptable level.

At the same time I check the tires, I make certain that the bolts holding the axles in place are tight. Probably the one thing worse than having a flat tire would be having a wheel assembly fall off completely.

Motorcycle Moments

A friend of mine once lost the front tire on his Harley chopper while we were riding to a rally together because his axle bolts vibrated loose. He went end over end and landed in a ditch about 50 feet from his bike. Although he wasn't wearing a helmet, he seemed to be unhurt, except for a few cuts and bruises. We loaded his bike into a friend's truck and continued to the rally. My friend appeared to be none the worse for wear and tear, but later we learned he'd suffered a severe concussion, and to this day he doesn't remember a thing about that rally.

Looking at Lights

Your lighting system is fairly simple to overlook, but it can get you into a lot of trouble.

If your brake lights aren't working, you can end up with a Chevrolet enema before you even get out of town. Motorcycles have extraordinary stopping power, and car drivers, by and large, don't give themselves enough room to stop when they're following you. Brake lights are not much protection to keep tailgaters from embedding themselves into your nether regions, but they are all you have (at least until someone designs an antitailgating device that uses a 70-mm cannon mounted on your saddlebag).

Motorcycology

Motorcycle headlights usually have two elements: one for high beam and one for low beam. Only one element burns out at a time in a properly functioning system, so you should still have a low-beam element if your high-beam burns out, and vice versa. However, be warned that the remaining element will burn out soon after the first, leaving you in the dark. It's a good idea to always pack a spare headlight bulb and taillamp bulb in your gear.

Motorcycle headlights and taillights seem to fail more frequently than their automotive counterparts, probably because of increased vibration. Because most motorcycles have only one headlight, if it burns out, you will be up the creek when the sun goes down. It's a good idea to check both the high beam and low beam of your headlight when you check your taillight and brake light.

This might seem like a lot of preparation before you can ride, and it is. But the consequences of being unprepared on a bike are just too great.

Learn the controls of your motorcycle. Memorize them and test yourself on them. In an emergency situation, your life can depend on your split-second reactions. You can't afford to lose any time in reacting because you had to think about where a control was: that microsecond can cost you your life.

And internalize the habit of giving your bike a preride inspection. You might feel tempted to skip it when you're late for work or are trying to get to a movie on time, but the possible consequences of some sort of failure of your motorcycle could be so severe that you might never see a movie or be able to work again. Take a few minutes to check over your machine before you take your life in your hands. Those minutes may add years to your life.

The Least You Need to Know

- Unlicensed riders account for the majority of all motorcycle fatalities.
- There is no better way to learn to ride than to take a RiderCourse from the Motorcycle Safety Foundation.
- The controls on a bike are completely different from the controls on a car.
- You'll need to use both your hands and both your feet, often all at the same time, to ride a motorcycle.
- Because the consequences of equipment failure on a bike are so much greater than on a car, you need to take a few minutes before each ride to inspect certain key components.

Chapter 11

Learning to Ride

In This Chapter

- How to control your bike
- The basic skills you need to start and stop a motorcycle
- Applying the brakes or throttle
- How to turn and change lanes

You're finally ready to hit the road. Everything you've learned so far has been to help prepare you for this moment. For some of you, what comes next will seem natural, and much of what I discuss may seem obvious. Others will find mastering your motorcycle a bit more challenging.

Those of you who have less difficulty need to assimilate this information as much as those who struggle—perhaps even more so. While your instincts will help you understand the dynamics involved in piloting a motorcycle, they won't provide you with all the skills you need to survive the brutal streets you are about to enter. Your natural abilities may even make you a bit lazy, and you'll quickly develop bad habits if left to your own devices.

I've found that people who have to put more thought into learning to ride a bike eventually become safer motorcyclists than those who ride instinctively. Having to think about all the things they need to do seems to make them mentally more involved in riding, thus helping them develop safe habits from the beginning.

In this chapter, I'm going to provide you with the basic skills you need to ride a motorcycle. In Chapter 12, I'll go into more advanced techniques. You should read both chapters before venturing out on the public roads.

Steering Clear

Some people seem to intuitively understand how to operate a motorcycle, while others need to consciously learn to do so. Neither group makes inherently better or worse motorcyclists. The latter group simply has to put a bit more mental energy into learning to ride.

I belong to the first group. When I was about 8 years old, my neighbor got a minibike and let my brother and me ride it. I had no problem and instinctively *countersteered.* My brother didn't do so well. His brain told him to turn the handlebars to the right if he wanted to go right, which on the surface, makes sense. In reality, a motorcycle doesn't work that way. He turned the bars to the right, the minibike veered left, he ended up in some hedges, and my neighbor's mother refused to let us ride the minibike again.

Cycle Babble

Countersteering refers to turning the handlebars on a motorcycle in the opposite direction than the direction in which you want to turn. Countersteering is the only way to get a motorcycle to change directions at speeds of more than 10 mph.

Unlike a car, a motorcycle can't turn if it doesn't lean. You steer a bike by making it lean rather than turning the wheel. You do this by countersteering, or turning the handlebars in the opposite direction in which you want to turn. While your brain may try to convince you otherwise and force you to rely on the instincts used to drive a car, your brain is wrong. The laws of physics will prevail over your brain every single time.

When you turn the handlebar toward the right, the wheel moves toward the right—so far, common sense and physics are in complete agreement. The rest of the motorcycle obeys other laws of physics, though. The bike wants to keep moving in a straight line. But because you have essentially steered the wheel out from under the bike, the motorcycle rolls on its center of gravity, forcing the motorcycle to lean to the left.

When the motorcycle leans far enough over (the lean angle necessary to initiate a turn varies with speed—the faster you are going, the more you'll have to lean), the angle between the tire's contact patch (the area of the tire touching the pavement) actually points in the opposite direction from which you initially turned the handlebars. This is true at any speeds over about 10 mph.

The point is, you must countersteer a motorcycle, or turn it in the opposite direction in which you want to go, to control its direction. If you don't, you will end up like my brother on that minibike, except that you probably won't be lucky enough to have a big shrub to land in.

Now that I've hammered that point into your head, it's time to crank up your bike's engine and go riding.

Parking-Lot Practice

Before you begin learning to ride, you need to find a safe place to practice, such as an empty parking lot, where there are no other vehicles. Practice basic starting, turning, and stopping procedures until you are comfortable with your ability to start, turn, and stop before venturing out into traffic. Just mastering the basics of riding a motorcycle will prove challenging enough; you don't need to compound these challenges by adding the risks posed by other drivers. Better yet, take a Motorcycle Safety Foundation RiderCourse, in which you'll learn these skills in a controlled environment under the guidance of a trained instructor (see Chapter 10 for details).

Starting the Beast

Even just getting on a bike requires a little knowledge. To begin, you always mount a motorcycle from the left side because the kickstand is located on that side, so it will be leaning in that direction (provided it is not on the *centerstand,* a stand that supports the motorcycle in an upright position). Hold both handgrips on the handlebar to prevent the bike from moving, and swing your leg over the seat. When you're standing securely over the bike, straighten it with the handlebars. After you've comfortably balanced the bike, rest your weight on the seat.

Cycle Babble

A **centerstand** is a supporting stand located just in front of a motorcycle's rear wheel that secures the bike in an upright position.

Never forget to raise the kickstand when you get on a bike because the protruding stand can jam into the pavement while you are riding and cause you to lose control of the bike and crash. To do this, use your left heel to kick the kickstand into the up position after you have balanced the bike.

Motorcycology

As silly as this may sound, don't forget to keep your feet planted on the ground whenever your motorcycle is stopped. Many people have actually fallen over while parked because they put their feet on the pegs before they were moving or, more commonly, forgot to put their feet down when they stopped.

If the bike is resting on its centerstand, cover the front brake lever with your right hand (rest it in position so you can stop the bike once it starts to roll), and gently rock the bike forward, causing it to roll off the stand. When it is down off the centerstand, the centerstand will spring into the up position—as soon as this happens, stop the bike from rolling by applying the front brake. Once you're down, it's a good idea to check to make certain that the kickstand is in the up position—sometimes riders initially park the bike using the kickstand and then place it on the centerstand, forgetting to raise the kickstand.

The starting procedure varies with each motorcycle. For example, if you have an older motorcycle (anything manufactured before the late 1970s), you'll probably have to turn on the fuel petcock before starting the bike (see Chapter 10). Otherwise, the bike won't start. Or, if it does, it will begin to sputter and then die, as float bowls empty. This seems to happen at precisely the wrong moment. Most modern bikes have vacuum-operated petcocks that open as soon as the starter button is pushed and close when the engine is shut down.

Start Your Ignition

The next step is to turn on the ignition switch and make sure that the kill switch is not in the Off position. Even the most experienced motorcyclist sometimes bumps the kill switch into the Off position and then wears his or her battery down trying to start the beast. You can save yourself a lot of grief by getting into the habit of automatically turning the switch to the On position each time you turn on the ignition switch.

The ignition switch is usually located on the dash, up near the instrument panel, but a recent trend is to locate the switch in some odd position under the seat or fuel tank, (where the switches were located on motorcycles manufactured before about 1970). This retro touch, which emulates the switch location on some Harley-Davidson models, appears on many of the newer Japanese cruisers.

Next, make certain your transmission is in neutral. Accidentally hitting the starter button while the bike is in gear can be a good way to fall over in your driveway, which is one of the worst ways to start out your ride. This is why the neutral light is so important on a motorcycle, but you can't always trust the light. On some bikes, the neutral light may light up when the gearshift lever is in a certain position, even if it hasn't completely disengaged the gears in the transmission.

Rock the bike back and forth to make certain you are in neutral—if you are in gear, you won't be able to move the bike more than a small distance before the rear wheel refuses to turn. If this happens, gently move the shift lever up or down until you can roll the motorcycle freely. If you have a bike that consistently gives you a false neutral reading, you may have transmission or clutch problems.

After you've switched on the ignition, you'll more than likely need to set your choke, especially if the engine is cold. How much choke you have to use varies from bike to bike. This is almost a mystical procedure, and you'll need to use every one of your senses to learn the exact combination of choke and throttle needed. You'll need to listen to the engine turning over, feel it catch and begin to fire, smell the exhaust to see if you are giving it too much throttle and flooding the carburetors, watch the tachometer once the engine starts, and adjust the choke accordingly. A properly running motorcycle with perfectly adjusted controls usually needs very little throttle to start when cold, although it may need a bit more when warm. Unfortunately, we seldom achieve absolute perfection in tuning our engines, causing the procedure to vary widely.

Now pull in the clutch lever. Even though you've shifted to neutral, the light is shining brightly, and you've checked to make certain the transmission is in neutral, you can never be too careful on a motorcycle.

Here the procedure for starting a bike with an electric starter differs from the procedure for starting one with a kick starter. On electrically starting bikes, you start the engine with the press of a button. With the clutch lever pulled in, push the starter button; the bike should fire up. It will make a brief grinding sound as the starter spins the flywheel in the engine. Then when the engine fires (when the fuel charges in the cylinders begin to burn), you will hear the internal-combustion process taking place. When you hear this, release the starter button immediately.

Motorcycology

Different manufacturers use a variety of safety devices to ensure that you don't start a bike while it is in gear, such as starters that operate only when the clutch lever is pulled in or when the transmission is in neutral. Unfortunately, there is no standard, agreed-upon procedure.

If the engine doesn't fire immediately, don't hold the button down for an extended period of time because this will drain the battery, burn out the starter, and cause other damage. Usually, if the engine doesn't fire immediately, the problem will be something as simple as your forgetting to turn on the fuel petcock or accidentally bumping the kill switch to the Off position.

Kick-Starting Your Bike

Kick-starting is pretty much the same, except that instead of just pushing a button, you'll need to use the kick-starting lever.

First, fold out the lever, or the peg at the top of the lever. If the lever is located on the right side of the bike (as it will be on all but a few European bikes), lean the bike slightly to the left to give your hands more leverage against the force of your kick. This supports the bike during the starting procedure.

Quickly and forcefully kick the lever downward. The inertia of the engine will want to make the lever slam back up again on many bikes, slapping it against your shin or ankle with tremendous force if your foot slips off the peg; make certain that you have a firm footing on the peg before kicking. Repeat this procedure until the bike starts. You'll soon understand the appeal of electric starters.

If all this sounds like a lot of bother, just be glad you're riding a modern bike. This procedure is simple compared to starting an old Triumph Thunderbird or Harley XLCH Sportster (probably the most difficult-to-start bike in history).

Taking Off: The Friction Zone

Taking off on a motorcycle is a lot like taking off in a car with a manual transmission, except that the controls are reversed (you operate the throttle, clutch, and front brake with your hands and operate the shifter with your foot), and you have to balance a bike and take off at the same time.

You let the clutch lever out to transmit power from the engine to the rear wheel on a bike, just as you do in a car. The Motorcycle Safety Foundation describes the area in the clutch lever's travel where power first begins to transmit to the rear tire as the friction zone, a description I find useful. To find the friction zone, first pull the clutch lever in toward the handgrip, and then shift the gear lever down into first gear.

Now, with both feet on the ground, slowly ease out the clutch lever until you hear the engine begin to slow down. As the engine slows, the bike begins to move forward—you're in the friction zone.

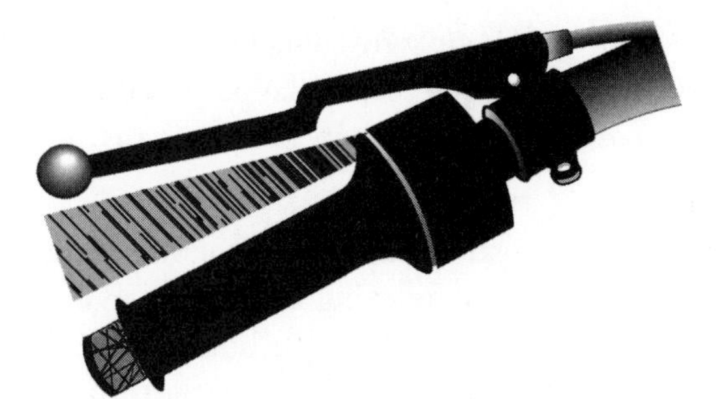

Although the friction zone varies slightly from bike to bike, depending on such factors as clutch wear and adjustment, it falls near the middle of a clutch lever's travel on a properly functioning bike.

To continue through the friction zone, you have to apply the throttle to give the engine enough fuel, or the bike will stall. But if you give it too much fuel, you'll spin out of control and crash, which, as I said, is a horrible way to begin any ride. And if you let the clutch out too fast, you'll either stall or spin out of control. It's a delicate operation, one that will become second nature to you soon enough but that requires some practice for now. When you start the bike for the first time, practice getting the clutch into the friction zone a few times before riding, easing out the clutch lever until you find the friction zone and then pulling it back in.

Motorcycology

All motorcycles now sold in the United States use a standard shifting pattern, described as one-down, four-up (or five- or three-up, depending on the number of gears). This means that you push the lever down to engage first gear and up to engage the remaining gears, with neutral found between first and second gears. This may vary on older American and European motorcycles.

When you feel that you are ready to ride, ease out the clutch, giving the engine just enough gas not to stall. If you feel the engine about to stall, pull the clutch lever back in. And if you're accelerating too fast, ease up on the throttle. If you feel any loss of control, pull the clutch lever back in and gently apply the brakes.

Stopping What You've Started

I've noticed one common mistake people tend to make when they teach others how to ride: they show their students how to start without showing them how to stop. You'll see these people running around parking lots, chasing their students, shrieking, "Pull in the clutch! Pull in the clutch!" It's easy to forget that stopping is as important as starting, and for the beginner, it can be nearly as difficult a skill to master.

To come to a complete stop, you'll need to use both your hands and both your feet at the same time. In one motion, you pull in the clutch lever with your left hand and squeeze the front brake lever with your right, while shifting down to first gear with your left foot and pressing down on the rear brake pedal with your right. Remember, when stopping, it's almost as important to keep the clutch disengaged as it is to use the brakes.

Motorcycology

As silly as it is, the myth that you'll flip and go over the handlebars if you use the front brake persists among certain groups of motorcyclists (usually the same folks who don't wear helmets). The front brake provides 70 percent or more of your stopping power and should be considered your primary brake. Some bikes even have linked-brake systems to assist front brake application.

Cycle Babble

There are two basic types of motorcycle crashes: **low-siding,** when you slide down, falling toward the inside of the corner, and **high-siding,** which happens when you start to slide in one direction and then flip over in the opposite direction.

Using the brakes on a bike is much more challenging than using the brakes on a car. For starters, you'll have to use both your right hand and your right foot to brake, rather than just using your right foot as in a car. Plus, riding a two-wheeled vehicle introduces all kinds of weird chassis dynamics into the situation. I'll discuss these dynamics at greater length in Chapter 12.

Your front brake is the most important of the two brakes. An average motorcycle relies on the front brake for 70 to 80 percent of its stopping power.

You don't want to squeeze the brakes too hard, or you'll lock up your tires and skid, especially the rear tire, which locks up more easily than the front tire. According to the California Highway Patrol, a rider locking up his or her rear brake is a factor in the majority of crashes. If your rear tire starts to skid, there's a good chance you'll either *low-side* (fall toward the inside of a corner) or *high-side* (start to slide in one direction and then flip over in the other direction). When you high-side, you cause it by releasing the brake while skidding, thereby allowing the rear tire to regain traction and jerking the motorcycle in the opposite direction.

Braking Practice

Locking up your brakes can be a very dangerous situation for an inexperienced rider. To help avoid it, practice stopping quickly in the parking lot, being careful not to lock up the brakes. Only when you are comfortable with your ability to feel what the tires are doing through the brake lever and brake pedal should you venture out on public roads.

Even after you master braking, you need to practice emergency stops. Go to an abandoned parking lot and practice stopping as hard as you can. First, practice stopping using just the front brake. At the slightest hint of the front tire locking up, release the front brake. If you lock up the front tire, you more than likely will fall down. Once you know the limits of your front brake and can instinctively apply it forcefully and quickly, begin adding a small amount of rear brake at the same time as you apply the front brake. Remember that the front brake does most of the work, and the rear brake locks the tire up much easier than the front, so you won't apply nearly as much pressure to the rear brake as you do to the front.

Parking the Bike

Once your bike is stopped, extend the kickstand to the down position and then gently lean the bike to the left until it rests securely on the stand. If your bike has one, it's a good idea to park the bike on its centerstand if the ground is fairly level. A centerstand provides a more secure perch than the kickstand.

If you've ever watched someone struggle to put a bike on its centerstand, you've probably watched him or her do it wrong. There's usually a trick to putting most bikes on their centerstands without throwing out your back:

1. First, stand beside the bike, facing it from the left side, and grasp both handlebar grips.
2. When you have a firm grip on the bike, take your right foot and lower the centerstand until you feel both its feet resting securely on the ground.
3. Then balance the bike by the handlebars so that it rests perfectly upright.
4. Next, move one hand down and grasp the motorcycle frame under the rider's portion of the saddle (this gives you more leverage). Many motorcycles, such as Honda's ST1100, have retractable handles to grasp when raising the bike onto its centerstand. Make certain that you have a good bite on the *centerstand tang*, the part sticking out that you place just in front of the heel of your boot, before raising the bike, because you'll be using your foot and leg to lift the bike.

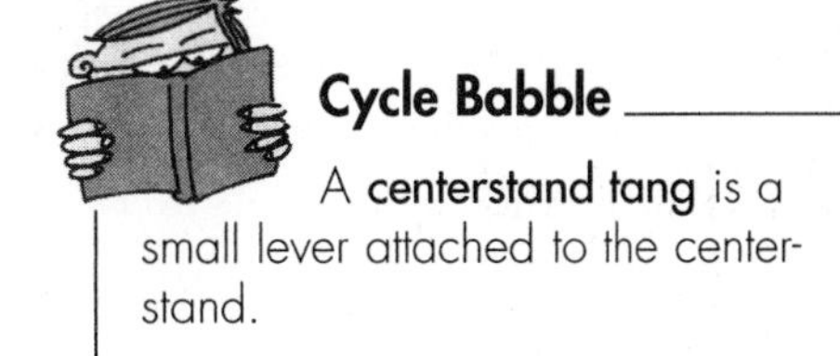

Cycle Babble

A **centerstand tang** is a small lever attached to the centerstand.

5. Lock the centerstand tang against your heel so that your boot does not slide. Once everything is secure, push down and backward on the tang with your leg while rolling the bike backward with your arms. A well-balanced bike should roll right back up on its centerstand.

Some bikes require more strength than others to lift on their centerstands, but if you do it right, you should be able to raise any bike up on the centerstand by yourself.

Make certain that your boot is firmly planted on the centerstand tang before you lift the bike up on its centerstand.

(Photo © 1998 Darwin Holmstrom)

Shifting Gears

As with any manual transmission, you'll need to shift your motorcycle's gears as engine speeds increase and decrease. Shifting up allows you to ride faster, and shifting down allows you to ride slower.

You shift up when your rpm increase to a certain point: upshift too late, and you'll rev your engine excessively; upshift too early, and you'll lug your engine (lugging refers to the chugging sound an engine makes when it is in danger of stalling). The idea is to keep the engine in its powerband (the rpm range in which the engine generates most of its power).

You want to keep the engine in its powerband for safety reasons as well as mechanical and performance reasons. Technically, when an engine is in its powerband, it is operating at its peak efficiency, which is good for the mechanical components in the engine and allows the motorcycle to accelerate quickly. If the engine is not in its powerband because it is running at too many rpm, it causes excessive wear on its mechanical parts; if it is not in the powerband because the revs are too low, it can cause detonation in the cylinders (tiny, uncontrolled explosions that can damage components), buildup of unburned hydrocarbons, and lack of power.

It's the lack of power that poses a safety problem. In the real world, you will encounter situations in which you'll need to accelerate quickly to avoid an accident. If you don't have the engine in its powerband, you'll need to waste precious split seconds downshifting, and a split second can mean the difference between a near miss and a tragic accident.

To shift up, roll off the throttle at the same time that you squeeze in the clutch lever. When the throttle is fully closed and the clutch is disengaged, move the shift lever up with your toe in a firm, smooth movement until the lever stops. If you hesitate during the shift, you might not get it into the next gear. This is called finding a *false neutral* and can be potentially dangerous. When you have engaged the next gear (you can hear this happen and feel it with your foot), ease the clutch lever back out and slowly roll the throttle back up to speed.

Cycle Babble

The transmission's inability to engage gears is called finding a **false neutral** because, although the transmission is not in neutral, it behaves as though it is.

You downshift as you decrease your speed. You need to do this with the same finesse as you upshift because, by downshifting when the engine is revving too high, you can lock up your rear tire just as if you had applied too much brake, causing you to lose control and crash.

To downshift, roll off the throttle and squeeze the clutch. Firmly press down on the shift lever, and then apply a small amount of throttle as you ease out the clutch lever. When coming to a complete stop, you may shift all the way down to neutral without releasing the clutch, but again, you'll want to do this gradually. Many motorcycle transmissions can be damaged by shifting to a lower gear at too high a speed, even if the clutch lever is pulled in. This is especially problematic on older bikes or bikes with worn clutches.

Motorcycology

You can slow your progress by carefully downshifting, a process that causes *engine braking*. To do this, you shift down one gear at a time, releasing the clutch after each downshift. But be careful not to do this too aggressively, or you can lock up the rear wheel and lose control. This is an especially useful technique when navigating mountain roads, helping you keep your brakes cooler so they remain near their peak efficiency.

If you're serious about performing your own maintenance, your best bet is to buy an actual shop manual for your bike. These manuals, designed as guides for authorized dealer mechanics, are specific to your bike and generally tell you the best way to perform each procedure. These manuals are expensive, but they will save you money in the long run.

If you buy a used bike that is no longer in production, you might not be able to find a shop manual. In such cases, your best bet is to buy one of the aftermarket manuals from publishers such as Clymer, Haynes, or Helm Inc. If you can't find a manual for your exact model, you should be able to find one for another bike using the same family of engine. This isn't an ideal solution, but it's better than nothing.

Keeping the Shiny Side Up: Supporting the Bike

Before doing any work on your bike, make certain it's securely positioned. If your bike has a centerstand, use it for procedures that don't require you to remove any heavy parts from the bike, such as changing oil and tightening the chain.

If you need to remove heavy parts, such as wheels and tires, you'll need to find another method of supporting the bike because when you remove the parts, you'll change the weight distribution of the bike, upsetting the balance on the centerstand. You'll also need to use an alternative method of supporting the bike if it's not equipped with a centerstand.

I use a variety of materials to support my bikes, depending on the bike. I've created stable stands by using cinderblocks with two-by-fours as buffers to keep from damaging the parts under my bike. The key is to make certain that your blocking is stable.

Some companies sell special motorcycle lifts. While these are expensive, a good lift is your safest, most secure method of supporting your bike while you work on it. Some companies sell rear-end stands that prop a bike up by the swingarm, which are fairly affordable.

CAUTION

Steer Clear

If your bike has a fairing that extends around the bottom of the engine, remove this before placing your bike on any kind of support. The plastic cowling isn't strong enough to support the bike and will break under the machine's weight.

Oil: Your Bike's Blood

Oil serves three purposes in your bike's engine:

- Oil reduces friction and wear, making all internal parts move more smoothly and efficiently.
- Oil dissipates heat. It carries heat away from the moving parts of an engine as it flows over them. On some bikes, oil is sprayed on the hottest parts of an engine, such as the underside of the piston domes, to enhance heat dissipation.
- Oil cleans the inside of your engine. The inside of your engine is filled with metal parts that rub together at tremendous speeds, causing microscopic particles of metal to shear off. Your oil removes these particles and traps them in your oil filter.

Two-stroke engines use oil differently than four-stroke engines (see Chapter 6). In a two-stroke, the oil enters the engine with the air/fuel charge and is burned up and eliminated with the exhaust, causing the characteristic blue smoke coming from exhaust pipe. This is why the EPA isn't very fond of two-strokes.

Cycle Babble

In a **wet-sump system,** oil is stored in the engine's crankcase. In a **dry-sump system,** oil is stored in an external tank.

Four-strokes circulate their oil, using either a *dry-sump system,* in which the oil is stored in an external container, or a *wet-sump system,* in which the oil is contained in the engine's crankcase. Most bikes use wet-sump systems.

Checking the Oil Level

On a two-stroke, you'll need to check the oil level every day because two-strokes are designed to burn oil. On a modern, properly running four-stroke, though, you need to check the oil level only two or three times a week. If you have a bike that uses lots of oil, check more often.

On two-strokes and dry-sump four-strokes, you'll check the oil level in the external tank, usually located either beneath the seat or within the frame itself (although on some late-model Harleys, the tank is down by the transmission). On a wet-sump four-stroke, you'll check the oil level at the bottom of the engine. In all cases, you'll either check by inserting a dipstick (a flat blade connected to the filler cap) into the oil tank, or you'll simply look into a sight glass (a window into the tank). The sight-glass method is much easier and less messy.

Motorcycology

When you are checking oil, your bike should be in an upright position (unless otherwise stated in the owner's manual). On bikes without centerstands, this means you need two people: one to support the bike and the other to check the oil.

Another thing to keep in mind is that most bikes require you to simply rest the cap in the hole to get an accurate reading on the dipstick, rather than requiring that you screw the cap down. Your owner's manual will tell you which method to use.

If the oil level gets down near the add mark, fill the tank back up to the full mark, but be careful. It usually takes much less oil than you might imagine to fill the tank to the full mark, and overfilling your tank can cause as many problems as running it too low. Pour in a small amount and then recheck the level. Keep doing this until you reach the full mark.

Changin' Oil

The single most important thing you can do to ensure a long engine life for your motorcycle is to perform regular oil changes. As you ride your bike, two things happen to your oil:

- The molecules in the oil break apart, causing the oil to lose its lubricating properties.
- The oil gets contaminated with the microscopic particles that wear away from the parts inside your engine, causing the oil to become more abrasive.

Motorcycology

Recent friction-modifying additives used in some automotive oils may seriously damage your bike, so you should use motorcycle-specific oil. I use an automotive synthetic oil (Mobil 1), which so far has not incorporated the offending additives. It's much less expensive than motorcycle-specific oil and performs well. However, if Mobil begins putting friction-modifying additives in Mobil 1, I'll switch to a motorcycle-specific oil.

Steer Clear

Drain the oil when the engine is hot because then the oil will be less viscous and will drain completely. This creates a challenge because the oil will be scalding hot, as will the engine and other components. Be especially careful to avoid the exhaust pipes, which can cause serious burns.

Here's how to change your oil:

1. Drain the oil. Locate the drain plug, which is somewhere on the bottom of the engine on wet-sump systems (the location varies with dry sumps), and place your pan-shape container under the plug. When you remove the plug (usually a hex-head bolt), the oil will come out with some force, so take that into account when placing the pan.
2. Remove the filter. Change the filter every time you change the oil. There are two types of filters—the canister type, which has a replaceable filter element located in a canister attached to the engine, and the spin-on type, which spins on and off like an automotive oil filter.

When removing a canister-type filter, be extremely careful not to strip the fastener(s) holding the canister on, and thoroughly clean the area around the canister before removal. There will be a spring and some metal washers inside the canister to hold the filter in place. Note their location for when you install the new filter; after you remove the old filter, wipe out the inside of the canister with a clean rag. Be careful not to lose the spring or the washers.

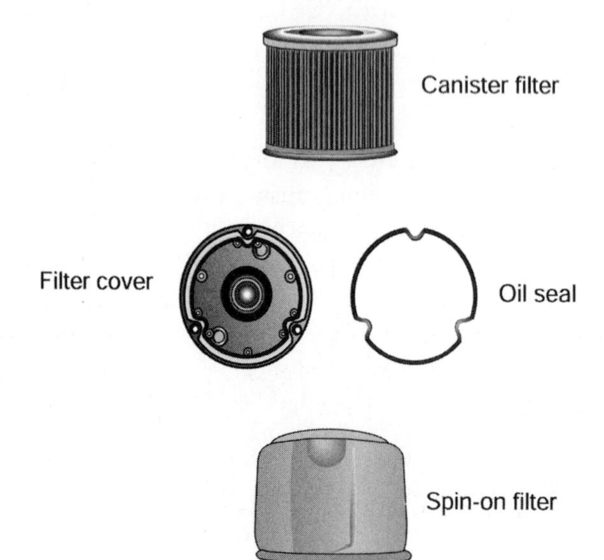

A spin-on oil filter is much more convenient to change than a canister-type filter.

3. Clean and replace the drain plug when the engine is done draining. Some drain plugs have a magnetic tip to collect metal shavings from inside the engine. Thoroughly clean the tip before replacing the plug. Most drain plugs have an aluminum crush washer to enhance the plug's seal. Make certain that you don't lose this washer when removing the plug. Also make certain that the surface of the engine is clean before you replace the plug/washer combo.

4. Replace the filter. With a spin-on filter, lightly smear a drop or two of clean oil around the rubber seal attached to the new filter before mounting it, to create an oil-tight seal between the filter and engine. Do not overtighten.

   A canister-type filter will come with a rubber O-ring seal for the canister. Make certain to use a new O-ring with each change. When you have the seal in place, lightly smear it with a drop or two of clean oil, making sure you don't get any foreign material on the O-ring, before replacing the canister. Mount the new filter inside the canister, making certain to assemble the spring and washers correctly. And when tightening the fastener(s), be extra careful not to strip the threads. Because of the spring holding the filter in place within the canister, it is easy to get the canister slightly askew when mounting it, which could lead to thread misalignment. If you encounter the slightest resistance when replacing the fastener(s), make certain that everything is aligned before proceeding.

5. Fill with fresh, clean oil, using the recommendations in your owner's manual for the type of oil and the amount. Next, restart your engine to pump oil into the filter. Be extra careful when doing this, and don't rev the throttle any more than is necessary because your engine will not be properly lubricated upon startup. Let the engine idle for about a minute; then shut it off and recheck the oil level. It will have gone down because of the oil pumped into the filter, so refill to the full mark on the dipstick.

After you have changed the oil, keep a close watch on the oil level, and visually check for leaks around the drain plug and filter. The most likely source for an oil leak is around the filter in a canister-type unit. If you get even a small particle of foreign material between the rubber seal and the engine, you might notice leakage from the canister. This will only get worse. If this happens, you need to get a new rubber seal and do the whole thing over again.

Air Filters: Clearing the Sinuses

Air filters prevent dust and dirt from getting sucked into your engine, but over time they become plugged up with all that dust and dirt. When this happens, your bike doesn't get enough air to properly mix with the fuel charge entering your engine, leading to poor performance and increased gas consumption. Air filters are made of paper or foam. Foam filters must be soaked in a special oil. They're located in a bike's airbox, a chamber connected to the carburetors. When a filter becomes clogged, you have to replace it (if it is a paper type) or clean it (if it is made of foam).

First, you need to remove the filter. On modern bikes, the airbox is usually located under the gas tank or under the seat. See your owner's manual for the removal procedure because it varies with each model of bike.

Next, replace a paper filter, or clean and re-oil a foam filter according to your owner's manual's instructions. Afterward, replace the filter.

Motorcycology

Replacing a stock paper air filter with a quality aftermarket filter can noticeably improve your bike's performance if it has a fuel-injection system that can compensate for the increased airflow. If your bike has carbs, though, a freer-flowing aftermarket filter can cause some problems. To meet EPA emissions requirements, many bikes have carburetors that mix more air with the fuel charge than is optimal for combustion. This reduces emissions, but it also decreases performance and causes the engine to run hotter than before. By using an aftermarket filter, you increase the airflow even more, which can raise engine temperatures to dangerous levels, especially on an air-cooled bike. Because of this, it might be a good idea to have a qualified mechanic rejet (insert new parts that increase the flow of gasoline) your carburetors if you install an aftermarket air filter.

Batteries: An Electrifying Experience

Batteries are one area in which motorcycle technology has more than kept pace with automotive technology. Motorcycle batteries need far less attention. Indeed, many bikes these days come with sealed batteries that need no—as in none, zero—maintenance.

Now, locating the battery might very well be a problem. Batteries used to be located under a bike's seat, but now you can find them anywhere, from up by the headlight to back by the swingarm. Consult your manual.

Once you've found the battery, check the electrolyte level by looking at the side of the battery. The battery case is made of translucent plastic, allowing you to see the level of the fluid inside. If the level is slightly low, add distilled water.

Several things can cause extremely low electrolyte levels. Your battery may have cracked or in some way come apart and is leaking, in which case you'll need to replace it immediately. Or you may have tipped the bike over or leaned it far enough for the electrolyte to drip out the overflow tube at the top of the battery. Or your charging system may be malfunctioning, overcharging your battery and evaporating the fluid. If you suspect charging-system problems and you're not a skilled mechanic, it's probably time to take the bike in for professional help.

Keeping Cool

Today most bikes use some sort of supplemental cooling system. Some bikes spray cooling oil from the engine's sump on internal hot spots. Other bikes use a liquid-cooling system similar to that found in most cars. The liquid-cooling system is the most common on today's streetbikes and requires some maintenance on your part.

At least once a week, you should check your coolant level. Usually, you do this by checking your overflow tank, a white plastic tank located in a position remote from the radiator. When you do this, you should also give your radiator hoses a visual inspection, looking for cracks and leaks. If you need to fill the system with coolant, use a mixture of motorcycle-specific antifreeze and distilled water, as recommended in your owner's manual. Every couple of years, you should replace the coolant.

CAUTION

Steer Clear

Be extra careful about what kind of antifreeze you use in your motorcycle. Automotive antifreeze contains silica, an abrasive designed to keep the cooling system polished inside. This abrasive can damage a motorcycle's water pump, leading to engine failure and expensive repairs.

Chain Maintenance

If you have a chain-driven motorcycle, maintaining your chain will become your most frequently performed chore. You'll probably need to adjust the tension of the chain, clean it, and lubricate it roughly twice a month (more often if you put a lot of miles on your bike).

Checking the Tension

To check the tension, grasp the chain on the underside of the swingarm, about halfway between the front and rear chain sprockets, and move the chain up and down. Check several spots on the chain by rolling the bike ahead and rechecking the tension. If the chain moves up and down more than about an inch, it needs to be tightened. If the amount the chain moves varies from spot to spot, the chain may have a tight spot. If the tight spot is severe enough, you may need to replace the chain. I'll tell you how to do that in Chapter 17.

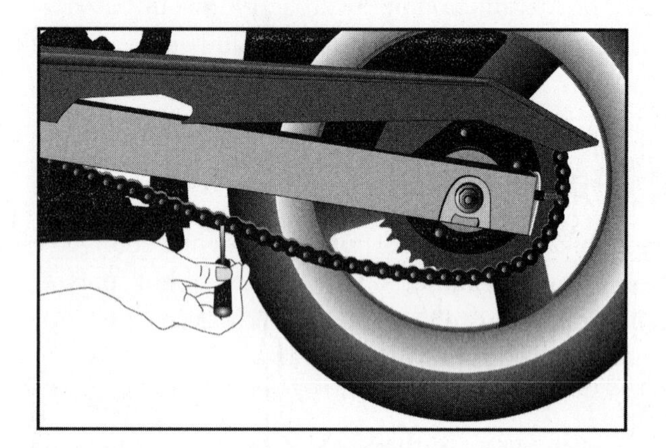

Check the tension along the chain's lower run, about halfway between the front and rear sprockets.

Adjusting the Chain

To adjust the chain, place the bike on the centerstand, or rest it on its side stand if you have no centerstand, and recheck the chain's tension. On the centerstand, your chain's tension may vary from when you first checked it because the distance between the sprockets may differ slightly. On the centerstand, the swingarm hangs lower than when the bike is resting on the wheels, arcing the rear sprocket closer to the front and making the chain feel looser. Take this difference into account when adjusting the chain. If you adjust the chain to its proper tension on the centerstand, it may become too tight when off the centerstand, and a too-tight chain can break and shoot off your bike like a missile.

Loosen the axle nut(s). You will have to remove a security pin on most bikes when undoing the axle nut(s). Once the nut(s) are loose, you can adjust the chain. You do this by adjusting bolts on the end of the swingarm on either side of the wheel. Usually, there will be hex-head nuts on each bolt—an inner nut to move the axle, and an outer nut to lock the other in place when finished. Loosen the outer nut and then carefully adjust the inner nut, moving the nut on one side of the wheel a small amount and then moving the other nut an equal amount.

When you have tightened your chain by the desired amount, tighten down the outside nuts. Retighten the axle, and insert a new security pin. When you adjust axle bolts, make certain that you adjust the bolts on either side of the wheel evenly, or you will cause your back wheel to become misaligned with your front wheel.

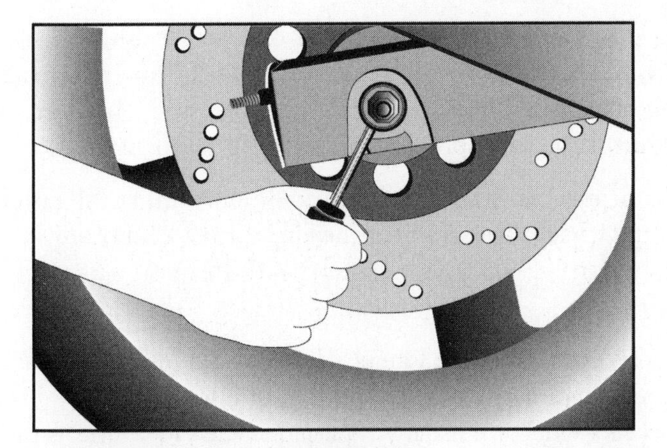

Loosen but don't remove the axle bolt.

Make certain to adjust the bolts on each side of the wheel the exact same amount. Don't overtighten the chain.

The procedure for adjusting your chain varies from bike to bike, but most bikes use some form of this method. Some bikes have a bolt on the back of the swingarm, with the locking nut between the bolt and the swingarm. A few bikes, especially modern sportbikes with single-sided swingarms, use an eccentric cam on the axles to adjust chain tension. See your owner's manual for the procedure for adjusting these types of chains.

Cleaning and Lubricating Your Chain

To get the most use out of a chain, you'll need to keep it clean and lubricated. Most bikes now use longer-lasting O-ring chains (chains with internal lubricant kept in place by rubber seals), but these still need surface lubrication. The problem with O-ring chains is that many substances degrade rubber O-rings, including common lubricants and cleaning solvents. Use only cleaners and lubricants approved for use on O-ring chains.

To clean a chain, place an O-ring-approved cleaner on a soft brush, and use that to clean the grime off the chain. When you get all the crud off, wipe the chain dry before applying fresh lubricant. This is a messy, dirty, frustrating job, but it greatly increases chain life, and chains and sprockets are extremely expensive.

To lubricate your chain, aim the spray from the can of lubricant at the inside of the chain while rotating the wheel to evenly coat the chain. Like all motorcycle maintenance, this is infinitely easier if you have a centerstand. Clean off excess lubricant from the wheels and tires.

Motorcycle drive chains now last much longer than they did just a few years ago, but they also cost a lot more than they used to. And they still wear out. Add in the cost of replacing drive sprockets (which are usually replaced at the same time as the chain), and you're looking at spending $200 to $300.

You can minimize wear on your chain by not beating on your bike. The harder you accelerate, the more you stretch your chain.

Shaft Maintenance

Although shaft drive systems require much less maintenance than chain drives, you will need to change the oil in the rear gearcase assembly on the back wheel once or twice a year. This is a simple process. Drain the old oil by removing the drain plug at the bottom of the housing, replace the plug, and refill the housing back to the recommended level by removing a plug at the top of the housing and pouring the gear oil in there. Gear oil is extremely heavy oil (usually 80W) that you can buy at nearly all motorcycle dealerships. To check the oil level, remove the filler plug and visually check the level.

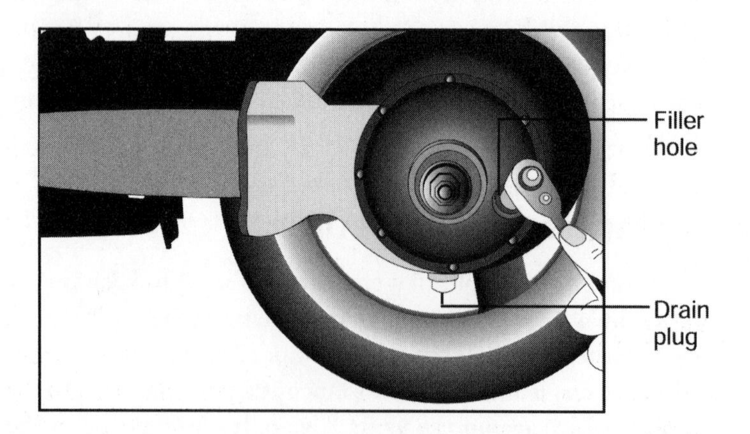

Filling oil in the gearcase a couple of times a year is far easier than cleaning, lubing, and adjusting your chain.

Cleaning Up

Some of us clean our bikes obsessively, while others prefer to let the grime accumulate. Sooner or later, though, even the grubbiest motorcycle needs a bath. Even if you like your bike grubby, it's a good idea to clean your bike once in a while, if for no other reason than that cleaning allows you to inspect the bike thoroughly, checking for fluid leaks, loose bolts, and other problems.

Don't use pressure washers on your bike because many delicate parts are more exposed on a motorcycle than on a car. A pressure washer can force dirt and grime between seals, causing bearing failures and other problems. Instead, get a large bucket of warm, soapy water; a sponge; a soft brush; a chamois, and a bunch of soft towels and rags, and wash your bike by hand. It's not that hard if you follow the proper procedure:

1. Degrease the bike. Apply degreaser to the grimiest parts of the bike, such as the engine, wheels, and swingarm, with a soft brush. A hard brush may scratch painted surfaces.
2. Wash the bike with soap and water. Wash the bike from top to bottom with the sponge, making certain that you wash off all the degreaser. Use a small brush (such as a toothbrush) to get in those hard-to-reach places. Wipe the bike dry with the chamois cloth.

CAUTION

Steer Clear

When washing your bike, use a special low-salt detergent. Normal household detergents have a high alkali content and can cause erosion.

3. Polish the bike. Use chrome polish on chromed metal surfaces (but not chromed plastic surfaces because the polish may melt the plastic). Every so often, use a light polish to buff out the paint, but don't use this every time you wash because it takes off a thin layer of paint with every use.
4. When you are done, apply a hard wax to the painted bodywork and buff it out until it shines. This is especially important after polishing the paint because the polish softens the paint and the wax protects it. Apply a light coat of lubricant, like WD-40, to unpainted metal surfaces to prevent erosion.

On Ice: Storing Your Bike

Winter storage is the worst part of owning a bike. It's not difficult, but it means you won't be able to ride until spring. First, clean the bike so that it doesn't corrode over the winter. Make certain that the bike is dry before storing it. Change the engine oil and replace the oil filter just as you normally would.

Drain the carburetor float bowls by turning off the fuel petcock and running the bike until the engine dies. You can also drain the float bowls by opening their drain screws, which are located at the bottom of each carb's float bowl, but be careful not to let gas drip onto hot surfaces. Fill the fuel tank to the very top; this prevents corrosion from forming on the inner surfaces of the gas tank. Finally, add a fuel-stabilizing additive to the tank. Alternatively, you could completely empty the fuel tank and then spray the inside of the fuel tank with a rust inhibitor.

Unscrew the spark plugs and pour in a single tablespoon of clean engine oil. Using either the electric starter or the kick starter, spin the engine over a few times to spread the oil around. Inflate the tires to their recommended pressures, and, if possible, place the motorcycle on blocks so the tires are off the ground. Finally, remove the battery and store it in a warm place, and your bike is ready for winter.

In the spring, you'll need to replace the battery, refill the float bowls by turning the fuel petcock to the Prime position, and again change the oil. If you've done everything right, your bike should start right up.

The Least You Need to Know

- Buy quality tools—it's less expensive in the long run than buying cheap tools.
- Before working on your bike, make certain it's properly supported so that it doesn't fall on you.
- Don't use automotive antifreeze in a motorcycle.
- Overtightening your chain can cause as many problems as not tightening it at all.
- Clean your bike regularly and store it carefully.

Chapter 17

Rx: Repair

In This Chapter

- Should you take your bike in or fix it yourself?
- Saving money by removing your own wheels
- Fixing potentially dangerous brake problems
- Replacing your chain and sprockets

In this chapter, I'm going to tell you about more in-depth repair procedures than I went over in Chapter 16. I'm going to explain how to perform the most common repairs you will encounter, such as changing tires, replacing brake pads, bleeding brake lines, and replacing chains and sprockets. On most bikes, the procedures generally follow those I outline here. There will be minor differences, which is why you'll also need a repair manual. For more specific repairs, you're going to have to rely solely on your repair manual.

If you can master working on your own bike, you will attain new levels of freedom and autonomy. And you'll save a pile of money. But mastering these procedures will take much time and effort on your part. You'll need to invest in the proper tools. You'll need patience.

Take It In or Do It Yourself?

Should you take your bike in to have someone else work on it, or should you do the work yourself?

A lot of that decision depends on whether you can find a shop you trust. (As I mentioned in Chapter 7, you should have done your research on this before you bought your bike.) A good, trustworthy shop will have trained mechanics with the right tools for every situation. But a bad shop can bung up your bike worse than you could yourself—and then charge you a lot of money for it.

> **Motorcycology**
>
> Remember that properly supporting your bike is even more important when performing the repairs in this chapter than it was when performing the maintenance procedures in Chapter 16.

If you learn to do the work yourself, you'll never be at the mercy of some shop's schedule for getting your bike fixed. And you'll develop skills that could prove valuable in an emergency. But you'll also have to buy a lot of expensive equipment.

There are benefits to both methods of repair. Ultimately, you'll be the only person who can decide which method is best for you.

Where the Rubber Meets the Road: Tires

Tires are one of the items you need to inspect each time you ride. Look over your tires each morning, checking for cracks, cuts, irregular swelling, and objects such as rocks or nails embedded in the tread. Check tire wear—a tire that looks okay one morning can be noticeably worn the next, especially if you've been riding hard or the air temperature has been high (tires wear faster when the pavement is hot).

Worn tires impair your bike's handling, especially in the rain, and are more likely to suffer catastrophic failure than newer tires. Your tires should have wear bars that appear as the tires age, but chances are, your tires' performance and safety will have begun to deteriorate long before the wear bars appear.

Get in the habit of checking the air pressure in your tires before each ride. A sudden loss of air indicates a potentially serious problem. Minor fluctuations in air pressure are normal and are often caused by changes in the air temperature. If your air pressure is a little low, inflate the tire until it reaches the pressure recommended in your owner's manual. If it is drastically low, examine the tread for a hidden nail or some other object that may have punctured the tire.

If a tire is punctured, repair is possible. You can patch a tube or put a plug in a tubeless tire, but I don't recommend either maneuver, except as a way to get your bike to a repair shop. The consequences of a blowout are too great. Replacing a tire or an inner tube is much cheaper than undergoing months of painful rehab therapy.

Removing the Rear Wheel

If you need a tire replaced, you should let a repair shop with the proper equipment do the job. That equipment is too specialized and too expensive for most amateur mechanics to have in their own shops, and the consequences of incorrectly mounting a tire are too great. But when you need to change a tire, you can save a lot of money by removing the wheels yourself and bringing the wheel assembly into a shop.

The method for removing motorcycle wheels differs with each bike, depending on the method of securing the axle, the drive system, and the brake system. Some bikes require the disassembly of suspension components or bodywork. The method described here is for a chain-driven motorcycle with disc brakes. Consult your repair manual for specific details.

1. First, remove the axle. To do this, remove the split keys securing the axle nut(s) in place, and then undo the nut(s). Some axles may have additional pinch bolts securing them in place that aren't obvious upon first inspection of the assembly. Make certain that you have loosened or removed all bolts holding the axle in place, and then gently tap the axle through the swingarm with a soft-faced mallet.

Motorcycology

When removing the axle, make certain that you are passing the axle through the swingarm in the correct direction. Many axles have a big end on one side and a securing bolt on the other. If the axle won't move in the direction you are tapping, or if it stops moving abruptly, make certain that you're not trying to push it through the swingarm in the wrong direction.

Be gentle when tapping the axle through the swingarm. If it takes more than a light tap, chances are, something has not been properly loosened.

2. Once you have the axle past one side of the swingarm, it should move freely through the wheel. A couple of things may hinder its progress. If the chain is too tight, it may pull the wheel forward, causing the axle to bind. If this is the case, loosen the axle adjustment bolts, being careful to adjust the bolts on both sides an equal amount. If the wheel falls down a bit after you move the axle through one side of the swingarm, it will also cause the axle to bind. You may have to support the wheel with your knee while removing the axle to prevent this.

   Some bikes will require you to unhook the rear shocks from the swingarm, allowing it to drop low enough for the axle to clear the exhaust pipes. In extreme cases, you may have to remove the exhaust pipes entirely.

3. Next, remove the wheel. Remove the spacers between the wheel and the swingarm, making notes of their location. To help remember their locations for reassembly, I lay them out on a rag, along with the axle, in the exact order they go on the bike. Push the wheel forward and unhook the chain when there is enough slack. Move the chain away from the wheel. You may need to remove the chain guard to allow you to move the chain free of the wheel.

CAUTION

Steer Clear

Never ride hard just after you have mounted new tires. New tires are slippery for the first few dozen miles, so ride with extra caution while breaking them in. At first, they may have less traction than the ones you just replaced.

You may have to remove some items to get the tire to clear the swingarm.

On shaft-drive bikes, wheel removal is usually easier than on chain-driven bikes. The main difference is that you pull the wheel away from the pinion housing to unhook it from the drive system rather than pushing it forward and removing the chain.

You may have to undo the brake caliper to make room to remove the wheel. If you have to do so, hold the caliper while you remove the wheel, and then make certain that it is securely supported until reassembly. Don't let the caliper hang by its hose.

4. When you have had the tire changed and the wheel balanced, reassemble by reversing the process. Don't forget to install a new split key to lock the axle bolt in place. Make certain that everything is properly assembled before riding, and stop to check all the bolts frequently the first few times you go riding.

Removing the Front Wheel

Removing the front wheel is similar to removing the rear wheel, except that it's a bit easier because you don't have a drive system to deal with or a swingarm to work around. You may have to remove a speedometer cable, though.

Because you won't have to work around a swingarm or drive system, the front wheel is easier to remove than the rear wheel on most bikes.

To remove the wheel, first unhook the speedometer cable, if necessary. Then remove the axle. On many bikes, the easiest way to do this is to undo the end caps at the bottom of the fork, allowing the axle along with the entire wheel-tire assembly to drop out the bottom. If it works that way, simply roll the tire ahead, remove the axle bolts, and pull the axle out. Other bikes require you to remove the axle bolt(s) and push the axle through the wheel to remove the assembly, much as I discussed doing with the rear wheel. Either way, note the location of any spacers between the wheel and the fork.

You may have to remove the brake calipers to remove the front wheel. If so, make certain that you don't let them hang by their hoses.

To reassemble, just reverse the procedure.

Tires can prove to be major wallet drainers. Motorcycle tires cost much more than their automotive counterparts, running as high as $300 apiece for premium sport radials. And they won't last nearly as long as a car tire. A person who logs a lot of miles can easily expect to run through at least one set of tires per year.

A Screeching Halt: Brakes

In all my years of riding, I've seen only two people get killed in motorcycle accidents, both on a racetrack. One of them was killed when his front brake lever came off. This illustrates just how important your brakes are. If even the least complicated part of the system fails, it could cost you your life.

There are two kinds of brakes: *disc brakes* and *drum brakes*. Most modern bikes use disc brakes in front. Many also use disc brakes in back, but some still use drum rear brakes. Disc brakes slow your motorcycle by squeezing pistons inside a caliper, which is attached to your frame or fork and doesn't rotate, against a disc attached to your wheel, slowing both the disc and the wheel it is attached to. Drum brakes work by expanding the brake shoes—stationary, horseshoe-shape devices inside your wheel hub—against the inner surface of the hub, which is part of the rotating wheel.

> **Cycle Babble**
>
> Many bikes use a combination of **disc brakes** on the front and **drum brakes** on the rear. You will find this combination especially common on cruisers. Disc brakes use stationary calipers that squeeze pads against discs that rotate with the wheel, while drum brakes use horseshoe-shape brake shoes that expand against the inner surface of the wheel hub.

With disc brakes, you will need to periodically change the brake pads—metal-backed fiber pads located at the ends of the pistons in the calipers. These pads are the surfaces that actually contact the brake disc, and they wear down over time.

With drum brakes, you will need to replace the shoes as they wear down.

Checking Brake Pads

The procedure for checking pad wear varies according to the design of the caliper. Some allow you to simply look between the caliper and the disc, but many designs have a cover on top of the caliper that can be pried off with a screwdriver. This gives you a clear view of the pads. Some designs require you to remove the caliper entirely to inspect the pads.

If the brake-pad material is wearing thin, it is time to replace the pads. Sometimes the material will change in texture over time, especially if the pads have been subjected to extreme heat or some contaminant. If you notice a decrease in your brakes' performance, you should replace the pads, even if they appear to have enough material on them.

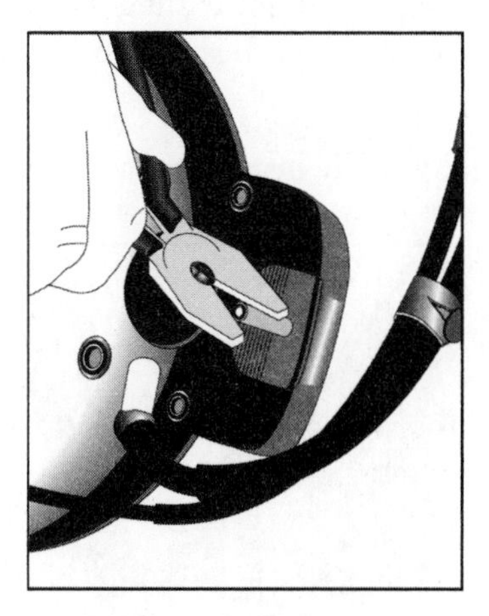

On many calipers, you can visually inspect the pads by popping off a cover on the top of the caliper with a screwdriver.

Replacing Brake Pads

Again, the procedure for replacing brake pads varies from caliper to caliper, so the instructions presented here are *just a general guide.*

On some designs, the correct procedure doesn't require you to remove the calipers. Others require you to do so. This is usually accomplished by removing the two bolts holding the caliper to its carrier or to a fork leg. However you do it, make sure you keep all the parts scrupulously, surgically clean, including the brake pads themselves, the master cylinder caps, and the caps' rubber diaphragms. Most manufacturers sell their own brand of aerosol cleaners and lubricant, usually including something for cleaning ignition contact points or brake parts. Use it as freely as you would water.

> CAUTION
>
> **Steer Clear**
>
> When the caliper is removed from the disc, or when you remove the pads from the caliper, do not squeeze the brake lever. Also be careful not to contaminate the caliper or pads with brake fluid, oil, or dirt because this can cause your brakes to malfunction.

The pads are held in place by pins that pass through the caliper body. The pins are retained by some sort of clip or by a split key. First remove the clip or key, being careful not to lose any pieces; they don't come with the new pads. When you are unfamiliar with the procedure, it helps to take notes on the order in which you remove parts.

Remove the pads with a pair of pliers, and insert the new pads. Because your new pads will be thicker than the old, worn pads, you may have to ease the piston back into the caliper. This should require little force. If you need to use something to push the piston back in the caliper, use something soft, such as a wooden stick, instead of a metal object, such as a screwdriver, because the metal can damage seals and the surface of the piston.

While the pads are out, visually inspect the pistons' dust seals for any tears.

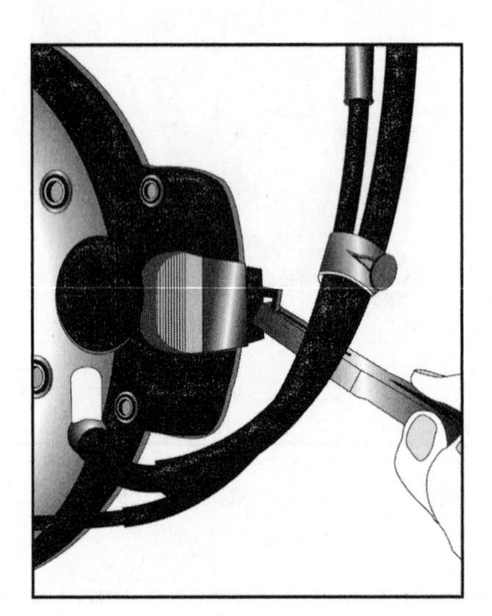

Because the old pads were worn, you may have to move pistons back in their calipers when replacing brake pads.

After you have inserted the pads, simply reverse this procedure, referring to your notes for the correct order of assembly. If your brake uses clips to retain the pad pins, you can reuse those. If you have a split key retaining the pins, use new split keys instead of reusing the old ones.

Motorcycology

A certain amount of grooving in the disc surface is natural, but if it becomes too grooved, braking performance can diminish and pad wear can accelerate. The only repair for a grooved disc on a bike is replacement, an expensive proposition.

When you check your brake pads, you should also check your discs (these are the metal rotors the caliper presses the pads against). If you replace your pads before they become too worn, your discs should last a long time. But if your pads wear down too far, they can damage the discs. You can check your disc by looking at it and feeling its surface for irregularities.

Checking Shoes

The only way to check the brake shoes is to remove the wheel from the bike, which I explained earlier in this chapter. After you remove the wheel, pull the backing plate from the brake drum. This should be so loose that it will fall off on its own if you tip the wheel upside down—but don't do that because the fall could damage the brakes.

It's difficult to judge the wear of the brake shoes by visual inspection because you really don't know what they are supposed to look like. Rely on your manual to provide you with information on acceptable shoe-wear limits.

> CAUTION
>
> **Steer Clear**
>
> The springs holding the brake shoes in place are strong, so be careful not to pinch your fingers when removing and replacing shoes.

Replacing Shoes

The brake shoes are held in place by strong springs as well as clips on some designs. Remove the clip, and squeeze the brakes together to release the tension on the springs. Remove the springs and lift the shoes out. Install the new brake shoes by reversing the procedure. Just as with replacing disc-brake pads, keep everything frighteningly clean.

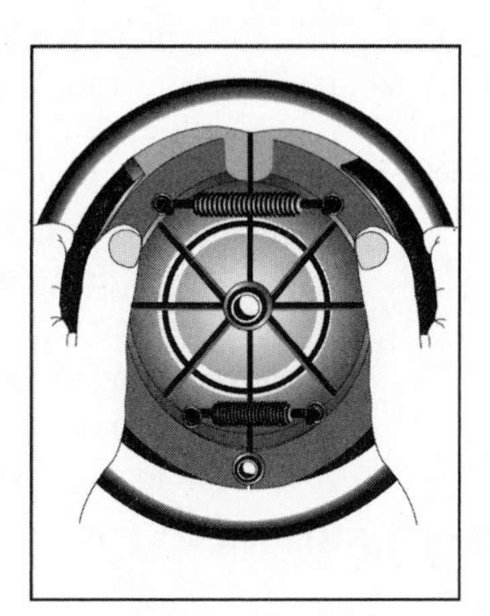

Two strong springs hold the brake shoes in place.

Brake-Lever Adjustment

Many bikes come with adjustable brake and clutch levers, items that improve both comfort and safety because they allow you to react more quickly in an emergency. Most handlebar levers adjust by rotating a numbered dial located at the lever pivot.

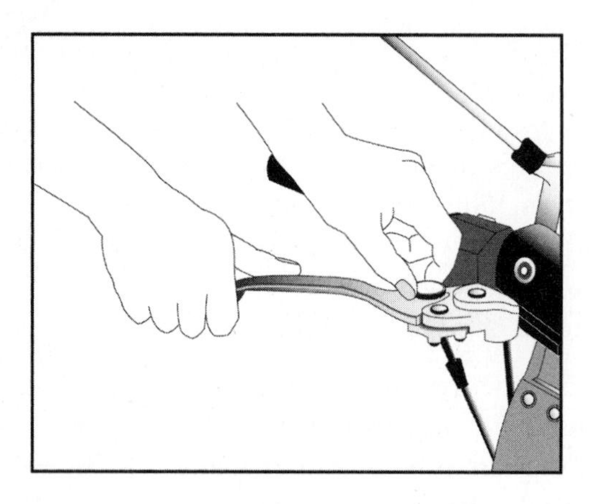

Adjusting your brake levers can decrease your reaction time in an emergency, saving your life.

The pedal angle on your foot brake often is also adjustable, and finding the proper angle can make a huge difference in your reaction time and your riding comfort. On drum rear brakes, the angle is usually adjusted by a movable stop, a bolt located near the rear of the pedal. This bolt usually has a lock nut similar to that used on the rear-axle adjusting bolt. On disc rear brakes, the adjusting bolt will be part of the lever connecting the brake pedal to the master cylinder, and it works in much the same way as a drum-brake lever adjuster.

Motorcycology

The distance between the rear wheel and the engine varies slightly as the bike moves up and down on its suspension. The rear-wheel assembly is sprung—that is, it moves with the suspension. This is why you need to leave some free play in components connected to both the rear wheel and the frame or engine, like the rear drum-brake lever and the drive chain.

On drum brakes, you will have an adjustment for free play located on the lever that actuates the brake shoes. You will need to tighten the nut on the end of the connecting rod as the brake shoes wear. Be careful not to overtighten the free play, or suspension motion might accidentally activate the brake. You need to keep enough free play to allow the bike to move up and down on its suspension without activating the brake.

A Bloody Mess: Bleeding the Brake Lines

Disc brakes operate by moving hydraulic fluid from the master cylinder—the reservoir to which the brake lever is connected—and the calipers. The fluid, which comes in several varieties that can't be intermixed (the variety your bike needs is stamped on its master-cylinder reservoir cover), is one of the nastiest substances you will ever encounter. It melts plastic, disintegrates paint, and does nasty things to the human body.

It also absorbs water, meaning that if you have a leak in your system, you have to fix it immediately because water makes the fluid mushy and decreases your braking power. Even if you don't have a leak, atmospheric moisture will condense in your brake system over time, so you'll need to replace the fluid every couple of years anyway.

After you replace the fluid, you'll need to bleed the air out of the braking system. (Sometimes you'll need to do this even when you don't change the fluid, just to get air out of the system.) This is a messy job that can do damage to both you and your bike, so take your time when performing this procedure. To bleed the brakes, follow these steps:

1. Remove the reservoir cap at the top of your master cylinder by unscrewing the screws holding it in. This cap has a rubber diaphragm underneath it. Remove this to expose the fluid. You may want to wrap a cloth around the bottom of the master cylinder to capture leaked fluid before it reaches any painted metal or plastic parts. Keep the reservoir cap and its rubber diaphragm fetishistically clean.

CAUTION

Steer Clear

Never use brake fluid from a container that has been opened—it may contain fluid absorbed from the atmosphere. Always use a fresh container. And make certain that you're using the correct type for your brake system. The cover of your master cylinder will be marked DOT 3, DOT 4, DOT 5, or DOT 5.1, referring to the type of fluid needed. Use *only* that type of fluid.

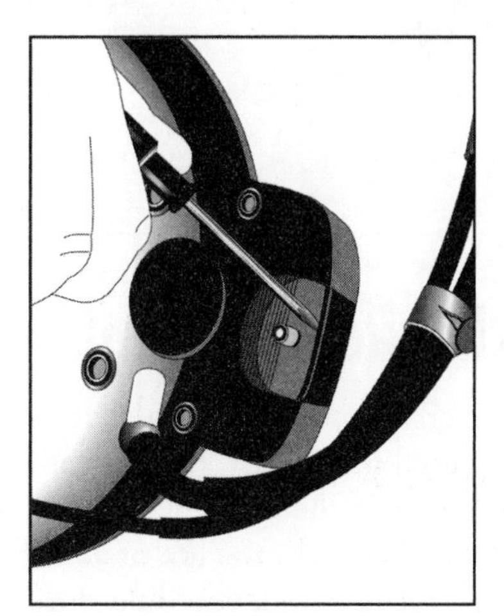

Each motorcycle uses a slightly different procedure for removing and reinstalling brake pads. It's a good idea to have a shop manual for your specific model of motorcycle before attempting to replace brake pads. And it's a bad idea to poke around inside the caliper with a metal tool such as the screwdriver shown in this illustration. Use a wooden stick to pry apart the pads after installation, to avoid damaging the pad material.

2. Fill the reservoir with fluid. Use only fluid from a sealed container (old cans of fluid absorb water from the atmosphere), and use only the fluid your braking system was designed for. Be careful not to spill because the fluid will wreak havoc on the bike's finish. Then replace the diaphragm.

3. Bleed the brakes. There will be an odd-looking nipple on your caliper. Put one end of a clear plastic tube over the nipple, and put the other end of the tube in a jar with some hydraulic fluid inside. Loosen the nipple approximately one turn, and squeeze the brake lever gently, causing fluid to flow through the tube. Tighten the nipple and release the lever. If you see bubbles in the tube, repeat the process until they disappear. Refill the reservoir and refit the rubber diaphragm before squeezing the brake lever. Repeat this procedure for each caliper.

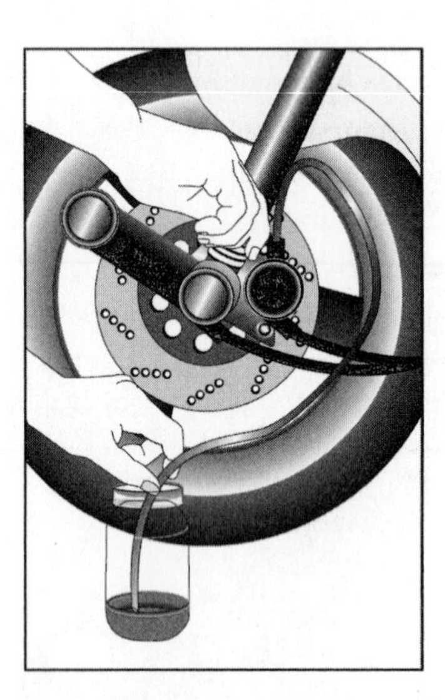

You'll need to have a length of clear plastic tubing on hand to bleed your brakes without making a mess.

Chain and Sprocket Replacement

As mentioned in Chapter 16, modern O-ring chains last much longer than the conventional roller chains used in the past, but they also cost much more to replace. Proper maintenance—keeping the chain clean, well lubricated, and properly adjusted—can significantly increase the life of your chain, but sooner or later, you'll need to replace it. And when you do, you'll need to replace the sprockets to which the chain is connected.

Chains have a repair link, also known as a master link—a link that can be disassembled for chain repair—or they are of the continuous-loop variety. Replacing a continuous-loop chain requires special tools and is best left to a professional. The procedure here applies to chains with split repair links:

1. Clean the chain and sprocket area. This is the dirtiest, grimiest area on your bike. Cleaning the area will make your job much easier.
2. Remove anything that blocks access to your sprockets. You will have to remove the rear wheel and the casing covering the front sprocket. You may also have to remove your chain guard and other items.
3. Disassemble the chain's repair link. Using your pliers, squeeze the spring clip off of its pins. Then you can remove the side plate and push the link out the other side. You can now remove the chain.
4. Remove the sprockets. The bolts holding the sprockets on will be tight and difficult to remove. It might be easier to loosen the bolts on the rear sprocket when the wheel is still mounted on the bike. To do this, have someone hold the rear brake and help stabilize the bike, and break the bolts loose before removing the wheel. Once the bolts holding the sprockets on are removed, you should be able to lift off the sprockets.

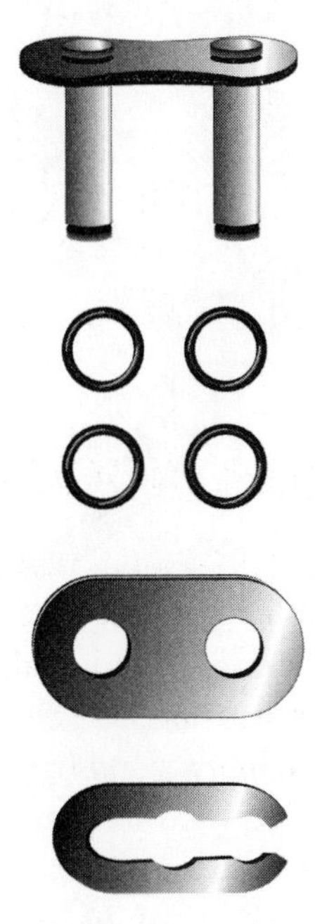

The instructions for assembling your chain's split repair link will be provided with the chain.

It might be easier to break loose the bolts on the rear sprocket before removing the rear wheel.

5. Replace the sprockets and coat the bolt threads with a locking compound, such as blue Loctite. Then tighten the bolts to the torque specs in your owner's manual or shop manual. Finally, reinstall the rear wheel assembly.
6. Put on the new chain. The new chain will be slightly shorter than the old one, so you'll need to adjust your rear axle accordingly, remembering to turn the bolts on either side of the wheel evenly to maintain wheel alignment. Place a newspaper under the chain so that it doesn't get dirty if you drop it, and then feed the chain over the rear sprocket, along the top of the swingarm, and then over the front sprocket. This will allow you to connect the chain on the bottom of the swingarm, where you'll have more room to work.

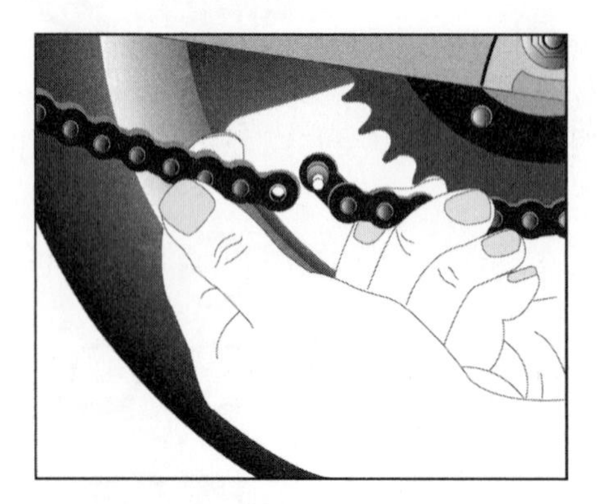

You'll need to loosen the chain adjusters to connect the chain because the new chain will be shorter than the old one. Make certain to move both adjusting bolts the same distance, to retain wheel alignment.

7. Assemble the split/master link with the rubber O-rings. (The chain's manufacturer will include instructions for doing this with the chain.) Then insert the split link through the two ends of the chain, connecting the chain. Place an O-ring over each exposed pin, put the side plate over the pins, and push the retaining clip over the pins, making certain that the closed end of the clip faces toward the chain's direction of travel. This means that the closed end will be facing the rear sprocket if you're working on the part of the chain that lies under the swingarm.

8. Adjust the chain to the proper tension, as described in Chapter 16, and then make certain that all bolts are tight. The chain might require readjusting quite a bit when it is new, so check the tension more often than normal.

Steer Clear

Make certain that you replace the split/master link retaining clip's round/closed end facing the direction the chain travels. In that position, the split-link retaining clip has its open end facing away from the chain's direction of travel. If the split end is facing the direction in which the chain moves, road debris could wedge between the clip, causing it to come loose and leading to the loss of your chain.

As you perform these procedures, you will get a better idea of your mechanical abilities. You may find that you have a knack for doing your own repair. If so, cautiously branch out, performing more of your own repairs.

Even if you can afford to have someone else do all this work, if you learn to perform your own maintenance and repair, you'll derive more satisfaction from the motorcycle ownership experience.

The Least You Need to Know

- Check your tire pressure before every ride.
- New tires are slippery and need some time to be broken in properly before they provide all their potential traction.
- Always use the brake fluid your brake system was designed to use, and use only brake fluid from a sealed container.
- When replacing the split link in a drive chain, make certain that the round/closed end of the retainer clip points in the direction in which the chain moves.

Chapter 18

Creative Customizing and Collecting

In This Chapter

- Why customize your bike?
- Types of custom motorcycles
- Setting goals for customizing your bike
- What to look for when collecting motorcycles

In 1885, Gottlieb Daimler cobbled together the Einspur, the first gasoline-powered, purpose-built motorcycle. The vehicle was just a testbed for his engine, and as soon as he had a motor strong enough to power a four-wheeled vehicle, he abandoned his Einspur. History is a bit unclear about what happened to the vehicle after that. My guess is that it fell into the hands of the first motorcycle enthusiast, who promptly customized the thing.

Motorcyclists have been customizing their machines since the beginning of the sport. Whether we ride a run-of-the-mill Universal Japanese Motorcycle (UJM) or a priceless collectible bike, we can't resist personalizing our machines.

Motorcyclists also like to collect motorcycles. People collect bikes for different reasons. Some collect bikes as investments, although the value of such investments has not been proven. Most of us collect bikes just because we like them. (Motorcycles seem to follow you home sometimes.)

In this chapter, I'm going to help you decide whether you should customize your bike and how to get started. I'm also going to explain the basics of collecting bikes. I'll offer advice on which bikes may be good investments, but mostly I'm going to try to help you find motorcycles that make you happy. Ask any serious collector, and he or she will tell you that's what it's all about.

Why Customize?

Originally, people modified their motorcycles to improve them in some way. In the early years of the sport, for example, many motorcyclists added a windshield, some saddlebags, or perhaps a sidecar to their bikes.

After World War II, customization in the United States focused on improving performance. Young American men and women had been exposed to lightweight, high-performance European motorcycles during the war. When they came home, the old U.S. bikes just didn't cut it. Most motorcycle riders had to figure out alternative methods to get higher performance out of their bikes.

How'd they do it? They simply lightened their bikes. They unbolted every nonessential part they could unbolt or torch. This became the pattern for customization in this country, and to this day, the *bobbers*, as the original chopped customs were called, set the pattern for U.S.-style custom bikes.

> **Cycle Babble**
>
> The custom bikes American riders built after World War II were called **bobbers** because owners cut off, or "bobbed," much of the bodywork.

As the performance levels of stock motorcycles climbed, it became less necessary to customize a bike to attain more speed. But people now customize for other reasons, too.

Some people customize for style. Modifications such as lowering a bike's suspension, altering its steering geometry, and adding *ape-hanger* (tall) handlebars—the modifications that have come to define the term *custom* for many people—actually detract from a bike's performance, but scores of people do these things to their bikes anyway. (Many of the radically customized motorcycles you see in bike shows are actually unrideable.)

But there's an alternate movement in the realm of motorcycle customization. Many people still modify their bikes to increase their usefulness. People add aftermarket suspension components to improve a bike's handling. They mount windshields, more comfortable seats, and hard luggage to make a motorcycle a better long-distance tourer. They add aftermarket air filters and rejet their carburetors, not only to make their bikes faster, but also to make them more efficient. In a way, customization has come full circle.

Cycle Babble

The term **ape hangers** was coined at the height of the custom-bike movement to describe tall handlebars that forced the rider to reach skyward to grasp the controls, making the rider adopt an ape-like posture. Harley-Davidson recently copyrighted this term, but it has been around since at least the 1960s.

Comparing Customs

Ask a typical American to describe a custom bike, and he or she will most likely describe the radical chopper-type bike. Such bikes account for the largest segment of customization in the United States, but elsewhere in the world, other types of customs have been more prevalent. In the past few years, some of the other styles of customs have been gaining in popularity in the United States, especially the streetfighters (also known as hooligan or naked bikes) that have long been popular in Europe.

Choppers

Choppers define American motorcycle style. The original bobbers were American hot rods, stripped-down Harleys, and Indians built for speed. As other, faster motorcycles became available, custom Harleys evolved from the bobbers of the 1940s into the choppers of the 1960s. By then, chopper style had become carved in stone: extended forks; high handlebars; a low, fat tire on the back; a tall, skinny tire up front; and a tall backrest or sissybar.

In the 1970s and 1980s, choppers evolved into low riders, becoming longer and lower. Now low-rider customs are more common than traditional choppers, although the original choppers' style has made a strong comeback in the past few years.

Steer Clear

I don't recommend building a chopper-type custom. Such bikes tend to be so foul-handling that they are unsafe. Riding a motorcycle is challenging enough on a bike you can steer. If you want to own such a machine, I recommend buying one from an established customizer who knows what he or she is doing when building the bike.

The original bobbers were either Harleys or Indians. When the British began exporting large numbers of bikes to the United States in the 1950s, these, too, became popular bikes to chop. Initially, customizers also chopped Japanese bikes, but by the early 1980s, Harleys once again ruled the custom-bike market in the United States. But due to the difficulty of obtaining new Harleys, along with their soaring prices, Japanese bikes have become a force of their own in the custom scene. You can now buy aftermarket customizing parts for a variety of Japanese cruisers.

Although typical choppers with extended forks looked pretty groovy, the bikes handled so poorly that they were unsafe to ride.

(Photo © 1998 Darwin Holmstrom)

Harley-Davidsons have long been the motorcycles of choice for customizing projects, but in recent years, Japanese bikes, such as this Honda Shadow, have become more popular among customizers.

(Photo © 1998 Darwin Holmstrom)

Café Racers

While Americans were busy chopping their Harleys, the Europeans took a different approach to customization. For many postwar Europeans, motorcycles were the only form of transportation to which they had access. In Europe, motorcycles were (and still are) used more frequently as practical transportation than in the United States.

Thus, customization tended to be more heavily focused on practical improvements. That, combined with the more liberal attitude toward riding fast in many European countries, meant that Europeans were more interested in building faster, better-handling customs than they were in adding higher ape-hanger handlebars and taller sissybars.

In the 1950s and early 1960s, a discernible European style of custom began to emerge. These bikes were inspired by European racing motorcycles. Owners moved their footpegs toward the rear and lowered their handlebars, often using handlebars that bolted directly onto the fork legs. This placed the rider in a crouched, forward-leaning position. Some owners adapted small fairings to their bikes to mimic the fairings used by racers.

These bikes became known as *café racers*, supposedly because their owners hung out in cafés and raced each other from café to café. Such bikes have always had a cult following in the United States, a following that continues to grow over time. There are probably more café racers in the United States right now than at any time in history. In some cities, such as Minneapolis and San Francisco, the popularity of café racers rivals that of custom Harleys.

Cycle Babble

Café racers are motorcycles modified to resemble racing motorcycles from the 1950s and '60s.

When taken to the extreme, café racers can be as uncomfortable to ride as choppers. But when modified correctly, café racers handle much better than choppers. Another benefit of building a café racer instead of building a chopper is that it's much cheaper. To build a respectable chopper, you'll need to start with either a Harley-Davidson or one of the big Japanese cruisers—an expensive proposition either way.

You can do a very nice café custom job on just about any older Japanese motorcycle—bikes you can pick up for less money than you'd spend on tax and a license for a big new cruiser.

Café racers, such as this Rickman-frame Honda 750 from the mid-1970s, have long been popular in Europe and are gaining popularity in the United States as well.

(Photo © 1998 Darwin Holmstrom)

Streetfighters

While Yankees progressed from choppers to low riders, in Europe, café bikes evolved into *streetfighters:* stripped-down, hopped-up road warriors of the type the original postwar customizers in this country might have devised if they had had access to modern technology.

Streetfighters are all about function, and the first ones had no bodywork, no fancy paint, and no chrome.

As sportbikes became increasingly complex, they also became increasingly expensive to buy and more expensive to repair after minor crashes. Insurance companies began writing off perfectly functional sportbikes rather than replacing expensive bodywork.

Cycle Babble

Streetfighters, or hooligan bikes, or naked bikes, as they are sometimes called in the United States, are bare-bones sportbikes stripped of all extraneous body work.

European motorcyclists started rescuing those damaged bikes, but instead of replacing expensive bodywork, they just trash-canned all the plastic. Like American customizers in the 1940s, they chopped off all the extraneous parts, replacing only what was needed, such as the headlight. In fact, they often bolted on a couple of headlights. When the whole thing was ready, they applied a coat of flat-black paint (to protect the surfaces of the exposed metal, not for any cosmetic reasons) and then went out and rode the wheels off these streetfighters.

These bikes proved to be so popular that the manufacturers got in the act. A variety of companies began marketing sporting bikes without any bodywork, but no one got the streetfighter look down as well as Triumph. The latest Speed Triple T509 embodies the streetfighter look.

Triumph nailed the streetfighter look with its latest Speed Triple T509.

(Photo courtesy Motorcyclist™ *magazine)*

So You Want to Customize Your Bike ...

If you are interested in customizing your bike, you need to ask yourself a few questions:

1. What do I want from my bike? Do I want to improve some functional aspect, such as comfort or handling? Do I want to improve my bike's performance? Do I just want to change my bike's appearance? What you want from your bike will guide you when deciding what changes to make.
2. What compromises am I willing to make to get what I want? A motorcycle represents a series of compromises made by the designers and engineers who created it. They made those compromises for a reason. Altering one aspect of your bike can cause unintended consequences in some other aspect. Honestly assess what you are willing to sacrifice before making any changes.
3. How much am I willing to spend? There are many small, inexpensive alterations you can make to your bike that will improve its comfort, handling, appearance, and performance. But making major alterations usually costs a lot, and there's no guarantee you'll achieve your desired results. Before embarking on a major modification of your motorcycle, make certain that you know what you want, that your intended modification will achieve that goal, and that the results will be worth what they'll cost you.

Steer Clear

Don't make drastic modifications to your bike until you are certain of your goals. Making a radical alteration that turns out to make the bike less appealing can be an expensive misstep.

Only after you've answered these questions should you make any major modifications to your bike.

By nature, customizing is a personal process. Only you know what you want and need from your bike. Part of your task as a new motorcyclist will be to learn as much as possible about your bike. As you become more familiar with your machine, you'll have a better idea of how to modify it to suit you.

I recommend starting out small. Identify an aspect of your bike you'd like to improve, such as comfort. Perhaps you can add a windshield or a better seat. Make incremental changes when possible. That will help you avoid making serious mistakes that will be difficult (and expensive) to correct.

Discussing various methods for modifying your bike will fill a book in itself. Fortunately, there are many fine books available on the subject. You can order most of these from Whitehorse Press or Motorbooks International (see Appendix C).

Classic, Collectible, or Just Old? Collecting Motorcycles

Ride long enough, and you'll notice something about motorcycles: no one can own just one. Becoming a motorcycle collector is an insidious process. It starts when you buy a better bike but can't quite bring yourself to sell your trusty old one. Then you'll decide to explore a different aspect of riding, such as off-road riding or touring, so you'll buy a bike suited for that purpose. But you still won't be able to part with the other two. Then you'll run across a pristine example of a classic bike you've always wanted, and you'll just happen to have enough money to buy it, so ….

By this time, you're too far gone to turn back. Like it or not, you're a collector. But it could be worse. Peter Egan, who writes for *Cycle World* magazine, once wrote that everyone needs at least four motorcycles: one for touring, one for sport riding, one for riding off-road, and one classic bike to keep it all in perspective. So go ahead and indulge yourself. Motorcycles have gotten much more expensive in the past 15 years, but they are still cheap compared to cars. And they take up less space. You can park up to six bikes in the space of one car, with some careful packing.

Collector's Choice

In the late 1980s and early 1990s, some investors decided British motorcycles were going to rapidly appreciate in value, and overnight, the price of Triumphs, Nortons, and BSAs skyrocketed. Many of the people buying these bikes were not motorcyclists: they were investors out to get rich.

Some people did get rich off of the entire debacle, but for the most part, it wasn't the investors—it was the people who sold the motorcycles at inflated prices. The Brit-bike boom lasted a few years, and then prices declined. British bikes still cost more than they used to, even when their prices are adjusted for inflation and appreciation, but they're back down to somewhat reasonable levels.

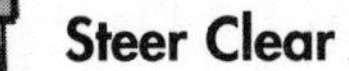

Steer Clear

Don't collect motorcycles because you think you'll make money. You won't. Even if you pick a winner, you'll be lucky to recoup the money you spend on upkeep and maintenance. If you want to get rich, try the stock market. If you want to collect motorcycles, collect bikes you like.

The lesson to be learned from all this is that you shouldn't buy a bike solely as a financial investment. It's a risky proposition, at best. Even if you get lucky and buy a bike that does increase in value, it probably won't increase enough to cover the expenses you incur while you own it.

If you're interested in a particular type or brand of bike, you can look for a particular model or year that may someday be worth more than other models or years, but that is a secondary consideration. When deciding what to collect, your first concern should be collecting bikes you like.

What Do You Like?

Before you start collecting bikes, ask yourself what you like. Do you like classic Japanese bikes? Do you like the brutal efficiency of BMWs? How about the fluid style of Italian sportbikes? Or the simple elegance of British bikes? Perhaps you like classic American motorcycles. Whatever your style, your individual preferences are of key importance when you begin collecting bikes.

What's Your Mechanical Skill Level?

How much time and energy are you willing to devote to the upkeep of your bikes? An American or British bike will require a lot more work to keep running than a Japanese bike or a BMW. Italian bikes will fall somewhere in between. Know your abilities before you start buying bikes with maintenance requirements that you are unprepared to deal with.

What's Your Budget?

You also need to ask yourself how much you're willing to spend. With the exception of Japanese bikes, any of the motorcycles mentioned in this chapter will take a serious bite out of your bank account. You can still pick up a decent British bike or a BMW for under $4,000, but if your taste runs toward Italian or American bikes, you'd better have considerably more cash available.

You can still find nice, older Japanese bikes for fairly low prices, though. The prices of a few early models, such as Honda's Benly Super Sport 125, have shot through the roof. But you can still pick up a very nice mid-1970s CB750 for under $1,500, and you can find clean examples of other Japanese bikes for less than that. Few of these bikes will ever have any serious investment value, but they're fun to ride and easy to maintain, and they make great projects for café chops.

With the passage of time, Japanese motorcycles have joined the ranks of true classics. Those that have, such as this Honda Benly Super Sport 125, will run you well into the five-figure price range.

(Photo © 1998 Darwin Holmstrom)

What Constitutes a Classic?

Classifying a bike as a classic is an almost mystical process. To be a true classic, a bike needs to have just the right combination of rarity, competence, and charisma to tickle collectors right in their reptilian stems.

Some bikes are firmly established as classics. No one questions the status of bikes such as Moto Guzzi's V7 Sport, Ducati's Round Case 750SS, Mike Hailwood Replicas, Harley's Knuckleheads and Panheads, Indian's Chiefs and Fours, any Brough or Vincent, BMW's R60s, Ariel's Square Fours, Norton's Commandos, or BSA's Gold Stars. But to get one of these bikes, be prepared to shell out some serious cash. And be prepared to wait because there are only a handful of some of these bikes on U.S. soil, and most of those are owned by collectors who have little interest in selling them.

If you decide to fork over the big bucks to buy a classic, make certain that you're getting the real thing. For example, earlier Triumph Bonnevilles are much sought after by collectors, while collectors tend to show little interest in the later models with dry-sump oil reservoirs in their frames. And if you invest your life savings in a Round Case Ducati SS, make certain that you're getting the real thing, because other Ducati models can be converted into convincing SS replicas.

One way to tell a true Round Case Ducati 750SS from a fake is to check the frame. Most SS models didn't have provisions for mounting a centerstand, and on most fakes, the mounting lugs will have been grounded off. But some very early race bikes did have some mounting lugs, and these are the most collectible of all Ducatis. Compounding this confusion is the historically shoddy record-keeping of the Ducati factory. Given the complexity involved, your best bet is to hire a recognized expert to authenticate the bike. Such a service won't come cheap, but if you have enough money to purchase this particular bike, you can certainly afford to authenticate your investment.

If you decide you can't live without a true classic, such as this Vincent Rapide (left) or Ariel Square Four, you'd better have access to some serious cash.

(Photo © 1998 Darwin Holmstrom)

How can you tell whether a bike is for real? Read all you can about a particular bike before buying one. If a bike's really a classic, there will be a plethora of books about it. Appendix C lists the names and addresses of a couple of publishers who specialize in motorcycle books. Call and get their catalogs, and you'll find books on every classic bike made.

Steer Clear

When shopping for a classic bike, make certain you're getting the real thing. Buying a fake can be one of the most expensive mistakes you'll ever make.

If you're interested in collecting classic bikes, get in touch with your local antique motorcycle club. Members of such organizations can provide you with more knowledge about classic motorcycles than any other source. And these people love motorcycles. You'll find no shortage of advice, and you may even be able to find someone who can help you locate the exact bike you're looking for.

Future Classics?

Given the scarcity and cost of true classics, collecting might seem out of most people's reach. And it can be a real gamble. Your odds of losing money are much greater than your odds of making money. That's why I recommend buying only bikes you like and bikes you will use.

That doesn't mean you can't have a lot of fun and possibly even make some money someday. There are useful bikes that qualify as great buys right now that might become classics sometime in the future.

Say, for example, that after you've become a proficient rider, you decide to buy a hardcore sportbike. You can buy any of the Japanese sportbikes.

Or, for about the same price as a 600-cc Japanese sportbike, you can buy a used Ducati 900SS. The 600-cc might be a bit faster than the Ducati, but the Ducati is faster than you'll ever be able to ride on public roads. And it's easier to ride fast than most 600-cc. In other words, it's more sportbike than you'll ever be able to use in the real world. It will require more maintenance, and you'll need to know a mechanic skilled in adjusting its valve gear, but down the road, it may be worth the bother.

Hang on to the Ducati for 10 or 20 years, and then compare its value to the value of a 20-year-old run-of-the-mill Japanese 600. While the 600 will be worth far less, the Ducati will be worth what you paid for it, provided that you've taken good care of it. And if that particular model of Ducati appreciates, as some people speculate it might, you could come out ahead. If you factor in your maintenance costs and inflation, you still would have done better to invest in the stock market, but a Ducati is much more fun to ride than a few thousand shares of Martha Stewart's stock.

By nature of their rarity or oddity, other bikes may someday become collectibles—bikes such as Yamaha's GTS, a sport-tourer with an automotive-style front suspension instead of traditional forks, and Honda's six-cylinder CBX. But if you buy one of these, do so because you want the bike. That way, you'll have more fun, and you won't be disappointed if you don't make a fortune.

If you're trying to decide between getting this Ducati 900SS FE or buying a top-shelf Japanese sportbike, you may want to ask yourself which will likely be worth more money 10 years from now.

(Photo courtesy Motorcyclist™ *magazine)*

The Least You Need to Know

- Some modifications can make a motorcycle dangerous to ride.
- Get to know your bike and what you want from it before modifying it.
- If you want to get rich, invest in the stock market, not in classic motorcycles.
- When shopping for a classic, make certain you're getting the real thing.

Part 5

The Motorcycling Community

So far, I've concentrated on you and your motorcycle. From a safety perspective, that's the most important part of riding because when you're out on the road, you're all you have to depend on.

But there's much more to motorcycling than just solitary riding. You have now become part of an extended family: the motorcycle community. In this part, I tell you about different aspects of that community and what it has to offer you.

Chapter 19

Join the Club: Motorcycle Clubs

In This Chapter

- What motorcycle clubs can offer you
- The different types of motorcycle clubs
- The importance of the American Motorcyclist Association
- Finding a motorcycle club that's right for you

Motorcycles and motorcycling have fascinated me for as long as I can remember. When I was six years old, I was already figuring out a way to get a motorcycle for myself. Not long after I finally got my first bike, I discovered an aspect of motorcycling I hadn't even considered before: the motorcycling community. I started to hang out with other kids who had motorcycles, and we began riding together.

The main benefit of joining a motorcycle club is camaraderie. Motorcyclists often feel out of place around nonmotorcyclists, like the odd gearhead in the crowd. Motorcycle clubs provide social outlets for motorcyclists, a place we can get together with our own kind and talk about riding and bikes without having to worry about boring each other. A club is a nexus where the motorcycling community comes together.

Whatever your interests, you'll find a motorcycle club with members who share those interests. In this chapter, I'll discuss different types of clubs. I'll also tell you what these organizations have to offer you.

How Motorcycle Clubs Were Born

A lot of the disaffected young people returning to America from World War II—people unable or unwilling to assimilate into mainstream American society—banded together to form the infamous outlaw motorcycle clubs. One such club, the Booze Fighters, became the model for Johnny's Black Rebels Motorcycle Club in the film *The Wild One*. Another of the postwar outlaw motorcycle clubs to gain some notoriety was the Hell's Angels.

CAUTION

Steer Clear

I have personal experience with some of the clubs listed in this chapter, while others I've just heard of or read about. Not all clubs will have your best interests at heart. Some groups may be more interested in collecting dues than offering anything of value to members. I haven't run across any that fit that description (all the groups I have experience with have been worthwhile), but like anything else in motorcycling, use your head when joining a club.

The Japanese invasion led to another development in the motorcycle club scene. With all those nice people out riding around on their Hondas, it was only natural that some would form clubs. Which they did, by the thousands. Today you'll find clubs devoted to every make of bike ever built, from ATK to Zundap, along with hundreds of clubs for specific models.

Today there's a motorcycle club for just about every segment of society. You'll find motorcycle clubs for members of different ethnic groups, motorcycle clubs for computer geeks, and motorcycle clubs for gay and lesbian riders. Along with the traditional outlaw motorcycle clubs, you'll find law-abiding clubs for police officers and firefighters. There are clubs for recovering alcoholics and clubs for people who like to get falling-down drunk.

Structured clubs allow motorcyclists to pool resources and achieve things individual bikers could not. In the early years of motorcycling, clubs often centered on competition. Racing clubs were able to maintain racetracks and organize events much more efficiently than individual motorcyclists. That's still the case today, and race-promoting organizations tend to maintain clublike atmospheres.

Types of Clubs

Categorizing clubs is as difficult as categorizing human beings, always a tricky and dangerous endeavor. When you divide people into groups, you end up placing people in the wrong category as often as you place them in the correct category. At best, that's confusing; at worst, it can be hazardous to your health. Placing members of the Bandidos Motorcycle Club into the same category as the Hell's Angels Motorcycle Club might seem logical to an outsider, but certain humorless members of the two groups might not find it amusing. With that in mind, I'll attempt to describe the general categories of motorcycle clubs. (Note that you'll find contact information for many of the clubs mentioned in this chapter in Appendix C.)

Off-Road and Trail-Riding Clubs

A major challenge faced by off-road riders is finding a place to ride. Very little land remains open to trail riders. Off-road and trail-riding clubs often maintain trail systems for members. Even clubs that don't maintain their own trail systems will be able to help you find public or private land where you can ride. Off-road clubs usually conduct organized rides for members and often organize competitive events.

Off-road clubs exist in most areas of the country. For example, the Panhandle Trail Riders Association (PANTRA) maintains a trail network that extends from Washington State to Montana, with trails across the Idaho panhandle for members to use.

Other off-road clubs focus on organizing competitive events. Without clubs such as the Polka Dots Motorcycle Club, for example, which puts on three races each year near Sacramento, California, few off-road events would take place.

Off-road clubs may have higher dues than some other types of clubs, but maintaining trails is an expensive business. If you like to ride off-road, membership dues in a good club can be the least expensive way to gain access to a good trail system.

Racing and Sportbike Clubs

Sportbike clubs are similar to off-road clubs in function, but tend to be less labor-intensive, because sportbike club rides usually take place on public roads, so there are no trails to maintain. Sportbike clubs often organize sport tours for members, and some clubs arrange access to regional racetracks. The only way many riders can afford access to a closed-course racetrack where they can practice high-performance riding is through a club that arranges the rental of track time.

Antique-Motorcycle Clubs

If you collect and restore antique motorcycles, you'll find membership in one of the many antique-motorcycle clubs around the country essential. When restoring a bike, you can search for years for just the right carburetor you need to get your bike running or for the exact fender or tail lamp for your specific model and year. By using the extensive network of experts found in antique-bike clubs, you can make that process considerably easier. And if you can't locate a part through contacts made in an antique-bike club, club members can probably help you find someone who can make the part for you.

> **Motorcycology**
>
> Make certain that you have mastered your riding skills before joining a club dedicated to sport riding. Such clubs tend to place a premium on safe riding and have little tolerance for motorcyclists who ride beyond their skills. Club members are experienced riders who don't appreciate some poorly skilled hotshot endangering their lives.

Many antique clubs are organized under the umbrella of the Antique Motorcycle Club of America (A.M.C.A.), a not-for-profit organization founded in 1954. Worldwide membership in the A.M.C.A. is now more than 7,500; many members attend A.M.C.A. national meets held around the country each year. The club also publishes its own magazine, which comes out four times annually.

Woody Carson, national director of the Antique Motorcycle Club of America, and his one-of-a-kind 1925 Indian Prince LX2.

(Photo © 1998 Darwin Holmstrom)

Make- or Model-Specific Clubs

Many clubs were formed by fans of a particular brand or model of motorcycle. Some of these clubs, such as the Norton Owners Club, are organized around a brand or model of motorcycle that is no longer produced and could be classified as antique clubs as easily as make-specific clubs. Other make-specific clubs, such as the Harley Owners Group (HOG), tend to have a heavy ratio of people who own new bikes in their ranks. New bikes need less technical support than older bikes, so clubs such as HOG serve more as social outlets than as practical sources of parts and information.

HOG, a factory-sponsored club with 300 affiliates worldwide and nearly 1 million members, is one of the best-known motorcycle clubs in the world. HOG has helped fuel Harley's spectacular comeback as much as technological improvements to the bikes themselves. HOG helped Harley-Davidson foster a tight-knit community among its customers that, in turn, helped foster customer loyalty that borders on fanaticism.

BMW owners form another tightly knit community of riders. And these folks take their riding seriously. Many Beemer owners put tens of thousands of miles on their bikes every year and often rack up more than 100,000 miles on their machines. Some owners have been known to put 200,000 miles, 300,000 miles, or even more on a single motorcycle. Serious motorcyclists like this deserve a serious club, and the BMW Motorcycle Owners of America (BMWMOA) is indeed a serious organization. It puts on some of the finest rallies in North America and produces a monthly magazine that rivals any motorcycle journal you'll find on the newsstands.

Similarly, American Honda's Honda Rider's Club of America is home to an enthusiastic group of—naturally—Honda riders of every stripe, be they motorcyclists, ATV riders, or captains of Honda's lineup of personal watercraft. The HRCA also has its own magazines, one each for motorcyclists and for ATV enthusiasts. What's more, Honda's club offers its own annual rally, but the HRCA sets itself apart by being an all-brands rally. That's right—no matter what you ride, you're welcome at the yearly blast in Knoxville, Tennessee.

Often clubs devoted to a single popular model will emerge, like the Shadow Club USA, a club for fans of Honda's Shadow cruisers. Sometimes clubs will organize around a particular type of engine used by a company, such as the *Airheads* Beemer Club, a club for owners of BMW motorcycles powered by air-cooled Boxer motors. This group was organized in response to the increasing complexity and cost that accompanied BMW's recent technological advances.

Cycle Babble

Older air-cooled BMW Boxer twins are called **Airheads,** while newer air-and-oil-cooled Beemers are called **Oilheads.** There are motorcycle clubs organized by and devoted to the interests of owners of Airheads and Oilheads.

Then there are make-specific clubs that could just as easily be categorized as sport-riding clubs, organizations like the Crazed Ducati Riders of Massachusetts. Some might argue that there is no difference between a Ducati rider and a sport rider. (Some might also argue that Crazed Ducati Riders is redundant, but that's another story.)

> **Cycle Babble**
>
> **Orphan bikes** are rare bikes that are no longer in production. Finding parts and accessories for such bikes can prove difficult.

The most useful make- or model-specific clubs are clubs devoted to *orphan bikes*—rare bikes that are no longer in production. Such clubs can be invaluable sources of parts and technical information.

A group that fits this category is the Turbo Motorcycle International Owners Association (TMIOA). The TMIOA was started in 1987 originally for owners of Honda's CX Turbo motorcycles, but in December 1988, it broadened its focus to include coverage of all the factory turbocharged motorcycles. Turbo bikes were built by all the Japanese manufacturers in the early 1980s, but they all suffered from mechanical problems, to some degree, and never became popular. Now these bikes are sought after by collectors, but parts availability is a serious problem, especially given the history of mechanical troubles in such bikes. Clubs devoted to turbo bikes can save a turbo owner a lot of time and money when it comes to keeping his or her bike on the road.

Touring Clubs

Joining a touring club is a great way to get travel tips and advice from motorcyclists who have actually been there (regardless of where "there" is). You'll learn things from members of touring clubs that you won't learn anywhere else, such as where to find good restaurants and hotels, how to find the best roads, the locations of speed traps, and roads to avoid.

> **Motorcycology**
>
> When getting traveling advice from another rider who belongs to a touring-oriented club, take that rider's riding habits and personality into account when deciding whether to act on that advice. Some touring riders might consider a ride down the Alaska Highway a nice weekend jaunt.

Sometimes touring-oriented clubs center on a particular model of touring bike, such as Honda's Gold Wing or Yamaha's Venture. One such group, the Gold Wing Road Riders Association (GWRRA), is the world's largest club devoted to a single model of motorcycle. GWRRA members organize some of the most extravagant club gatherings in the United States.

Locale-Specific Clubs

Often clubs form with no common denominator other than location. Motorcyclists just want to get together with other people from their area who ride, regardless of what they ride or how they ride. Such clubs can provide you with information on riding in an area you won't find anywhere else, an especially valuable service for new riders. The WetLeather motorcycle club, for example, exists so members can get together and discuss the challenges faced by motorcyclists in the Pacific Northwest.

Female Motorcyclist Clubs

Women have been riding motorcycles as long as men, although never in as great numbers. And women have had their own motorcycle clubs almost as long as men. Organizations such as the Motor Maids have long been a part of the motorcycling scene.

But in recent years, the number of women who ride has grown, and now more women ride their own motorcycles than ever before. As more women enter the sport, the number and variety of women's motorcycle clubs has grown.

One of the largest women's groups is Women On Wheels (WOW). When WOW was founded in 1982, women who rode their own bikes were still exceptions, oddities in the motorcycling community. WOW provided an outlet for these women, a place where they could get together with other female riders. Today there are WOW chapters all across the United States.

In the past few years, more specialized women's motorcycling clubs have emerged, such as the Ebony Queens Motorcycle Club, a club for African American women.

Age-Specific Clubs

A trend that has gained momentum as the baby boomers age is the rise of age-specific clubs, organizations composed of motorcyclists who have reached a certain age. For example, the Retreads Motorcycle Club consists of riders who are at least 40 years old.

Lately, a few clubs composed of riders under a certain age have sprouted. In Oregon, for example, there's an organization called the Mudrats, a club for people 15 years old and younger who like to ride dirtbikes and all-terrain vehicles.

Motorcycology

Many of the clubs for riders of a certain age won't exclude you if you are too young to join. They may accept you into the group, although not as a full member. It may be worth the effort for you to find such a group because older riders generally have more experience and can teach newer riders a great deal.

A group of Retreads kicking back at a local watering hole after a long ride.

(Photo © 1998 Darwin Holmstrom)

Spiritually Oriented Clubs

During the past 20 years, Christian motorcycling clubs have multiplied prolifically. The Christian Motorcyclists Association (CMA), one of the largest of these organizations, can be found at rallies and events around the United States.

Christian motorcyclist groups do a great deal to promote a positive image of motorcycling to the general public. If you are so inclined, joining such a club would be an ideal way to combine your spirituality and passion for motorcycling.

Christians aren't the only group to combine their spiritual beliefs with motorcycling. There are Taoist and Buddhist motorcycle clubs, and there are pagan motorcycle clubs. There is even one group, the Bavarian Illuminati Motorcycle Club, that quotes the Western mystic Aleister Crowley in its club bylaws. The club has very little of what could be called structure, but members do receive a suggested reading list that includes *The Illuminatus! Trilogy*, by Robert Anton Wilson, and *Heart of Darkness*, by Joseph Conrad, as well as an eclectic collection of books on motorcycling and mysticism.

Activity-Oriented Clubs

A variety of clubs combine other interests with motorcycling. Sometimes these clubs combine motorcycle-related interests. If you're interested in motorcycling and camping, for example, you can join the International Brotherhood of Motorcycle Campers, a group dedicated to riders who camp out rather than stay in motels when they tour on their motorcycles.

Other clubs combine motorcycling with unrelated interests, such as the Motorcycling Amateur Radio Club (MARC), composed of motorcyclists who are also ham radio operators.

Motorcycle Moments

A man who lived in the town where I attended college once mounted a small refrigerator on the back of his motorcycle and rode the bike like that for an entire summer. Years later, I met the guy and asked him about the fridge. It turned out he was a member of the Motorcycling Amateur Radio Club, and he mounted his ham radio in the fridge to protect it from the elements. He gave up that system because the weight disrupted his motorcycle's handling, and now he tows his radio in a special trailer.

Motorcyclists who have access to a computer can even join virtual motorcycle clubs, organizations such as Cyber-Bikers On The Web. These are clubs for people who love to ride but also like to surf the Internet.

Socially Active Clubs

Many motorcycle groups form to support certain causes and hold poker runs and other events to raise funds for charity. One such group, Friends of Children with Cerebral Palsy, located in Regina, Saskatchewan (Canada), organizes an annual Ride for Dreams to raise money to help children with Cerebral Palsy.

Another club that raises a lot of money for a specific charity is the Women's Motorcyclist Foundation (WMF). In 1996, the WMF organized the National Pony Express Tour, a 14,537-mile motorcycle relay around the perimeter of the United States, to raise awareness of breast cancer and to raise research funds for the Susan G. Koman Foundation in Dallas, Texas. Female motorcyclists who participated in the ride (and their supporters) raised $317,000.

Profession-Related Clubs

Often motorcyclists in certain professions form motorcycle clubs with other members of their profession. One of the most famous clubs of this type is the Blue Knights, a club composed of law-enforcement officials. Chapters of the Blue Knights are located in all 50 states, as well as 12 other countries.

Creative Clubs

People are getting more creative when forming motorcycle clubs. Often these are just groups dedicated to having fun, such as the Good Vibrations Cycle Riders, located in Florida. Good Vibrations holds no meetings, collects no dues, and has just one bylaw in its charter: have fun.

Other groups solely devoted to having fun have appeared around the country. The Hell's Rice Burners Motorcycle Club from the Delaware area was formed for people who ride ratty old Japanese bikes. Ideally, members should pay no more than $25 when they buy their bikes. Little is known of the ominous Death's Head Motorcycle Club, located deep in Appalachia, except that members have a proclivity for body modification, such as piercing, tattooing, scarification (making shallow cuts in the skin), and branding.

There are clubs for curmudgeon motorcyclists, and there are clubs for vampires who ride, such as the Santa Cruz Vampires Motorcycle and Scooter Club. There is even a club for riders who don't like to bathe. Biker Scum is an organization dedicated to the pursuit of happiness through riding and the neglect of personal hygiene. Believe it or not, this club is quite popular. Originally formed in central Texas, the club now has chapters in Pennsylvania; Virginia; California; Indiana; Ontario, Canada; and Okinawa, Japan.

The American Motorcyclist Association

No single group plays a more influential role in motorcycling in the United States than the American Motorcyclist Association (AMA), a 220,000-member organization founded in 1924.

The world's largest motorsports-sanctioning body, the AMA oversees more than 80 national-level racing events all over the United States. These events encompass the entire motorcycle-racing spectrum and include events as diverse as the Superbike races at Daytona, Supercross and Arenacross racing, dirt-track racing, and hill climbing. The AMA's Member Activities Department coordinates thousands of amateur races across the country, with dozens of competition classes for everyone from grade-school kids to senior riders. Through its 1,200 chartered clubs, the AMA oversees more than 3,700 road-riding and competition events each year. If there's motorcycle racing taking place in the United States, the AMA is probably involved.

Motorcycology

There is no more effective way to protect your rights as a motorcyclist than to join the AMA. Write to:

American Motorcyclist Association
13515 Yarmouth Dr.
Pickering, Ohio 43147

You can call the AMA at 1-800-AMA-JOIN (1-800-262-5646), or e-mail it at ama@ama-cycle.org.

Perhaps even more important than its promotion of racing is the work of the AMA Government Relations Department, which works harder than any single organization to make riders aware of bad laws and antimotorcycling discrimination at the local, state, federal, and corporate levels. You'd be amazed at some of the antimotorcycle legislation proposed at all levels of government, as well as the discrimination to be found in the workplace. Fortunately for all of us, during its 80 years of existence, the AMA has developed successful methods for dealing with discrimination against motorcyclists. Even if you join no other motorcycle organization, I highly recommend joining the AMA.

Finding a Club

One of the best ways to locate a club in your area is to contact the AMA and get a list of AMA-chartered clubs in your area.

If you know of a local place (such as a bar, café, or motorcycle shop) where motorcyclists hang out, you can ask if the folks there know of any local clubs. The Internet is also a terrific resource for finding motorcycle clubs, especially some of the more off-the-wall organizations.

You can also check Appendix C for contact information for some of the national motorcycle groups that may be able to put you in touch with local groups in your area.

After you've found a club, look into it before joining. Attend a couple of meetings and visit with members. Perhaps you might even go for a ride with them. If you enjoy the time you spend with members, chances are, you'll enjoy being a member.

Joining a club may not be a necessity for enjoying the sport of motorcycling—motorcycling is, in the end, a solitary activity—but it can greatly enhance the experience. The enthusiasm club members have for riding is infectious and can motivate you to explore new areas of the sport. And if you live in a climate where you can't ride for long periods of time each year, meeting with your motorcycle club can help you make it through the long winter months.

The Least You Need to Know

- Club memberships can be practical as well as fun.
- Clubs can be great sources of hard-to-locate parts and information.
- Many clubs do a great deal of work supporting causes other than motorcycling, such as breast cancer research.
- Joining the AMA is the best way you can ensure the future of motorcycling.

Chapter 20

The Open Road: Touring and Rallies

In This Chapter

- Preparing your bike for a trip
- Planning your trip
- Packing gear on your bike safely
- Learning about motorcycle rallies around the country

Ever since I started riding motorcycles, I've felt a powerful desire to explore new places on a bike. As soon as I was old enough to get my motorcycle endorsement, I began taking serious motorcycle tours.

I enjoy all aspects of riding, from commuting to work to trail riding, but I enjoy touring on a bike most of all. I find nothing more thrilling than cresting a hill and seeing a new expanse of world open up before me. Whether I'm exploring the Sand Hill region of Nebraska, the High Desert in Southern California, the lush Ozark Mountains of Arkansas, or the wheat fields of Minnesota, I never get bored when I'm traveling on a bike.

In this chapter, I'm going to share with you some of the tips I've learned over the course of my trips.

I'm also going to talk a bit about where to go on your motorcycle (as well as where not to go). And I'll discuss different motorcycle-related events you can attend, such as rallies.

Any Bike Is a Touring Bike

If you have a dependable motorcycle, you can travel on it. Ed Otto, a competitive long-distance rider, rode 11,000 miles on a Honda Helix scooter during the 1995 *Iron Butt Rally*, one of the most grueling long-distance motorcycle rallies in the world.

Cycle Babble

The **Iron Butt Rally** is arguably the most grueling long-distance motorcycle rally in the world. Participants ride around the perimeter of the United States, often including side trips that take them hundreds or even thousands of miles out of their way. Finishing the rally requires that you ride at least 11,000 miles in 11 days. Top-10 finishers often ride 12,000 to 13,000 miles in that time.

Of course, some motorcycles make better tourers than others. Selecting a bike to tour on is an individual choice. It doesn't matter how well a motorcycle works for other riders—what matters is how well it works for *you*. How well does your motorcycle fit you physically? Is it comfortable on day-long rides? How well do its power-delivery characteristics suit your riding style?

You also need to feel comfortable with the reliability of your bike. You don't want to get stranded in the middle of some unfamiliar urban area or isolated mountain road on a bike. Before you decide to take a bike on an extended trip, you should know its mechanical condition. If you do travel on a bike that has a tendency to break down, you should be familiar enough with the bike's mechanics to perform some basic repair work on the side of the road.

Honda's Helix scooter might not be the ideal mount for 1,000-mile-a-day rides, but at a more relaxed pace, it can make a fine traveling companion.

(Photo courtesy Vreeke and Associates)

Planning a Trip

I have a tendency to overplan trips, marking out each gas stop on my map, along with my estimated time of arrival. But some of my best motorcycle tours have been the least planned. I once went on a meandering two-week trip through Wyoming and Colorado with a friend who is perhaps the least-organized human being I've ever met.

Once I let go and gave control to a higher power (in this case, my buddy's disorganized ways), I had the most relaxing trip of my life. And I saw more of the country I rode through than I ever had before. I discovered that the most entertaining road is the road to nowhere.

Motorcycology

If it's at all possible, don't overplan your trips. For some riders, the best motorcycle tours are the kind on which you don't have to be anywhere at any given time. This gives you time to stop and really experience the unusual things you encounter along the way.

Touring Range and Fuel Stops

But even on the road to nowhere, you have to prepare at least a minimal amount. Motorcycles have small gas tanks and can travel only a short distance between fuel stops, at least when compared to cars. You need to plan your trip so that you know you'll be able to find fuel when you need it.

Some bikes have more touring range than others, depending on the size of their fuel tanks and what kind of gas mileage they get. For example, a bike with a 4.7-gallon tank that gets 36 miles per gallon on average can travel 169.2 miles before you have to start walking, while a bike with a 3.7-gallon tank that gets 54 miles per gallon on average can go almost 200 miles before refueling.

Motorcycology

Learn to predict whether a town will have an open gas station by checking its population. State road maps always list the names of all the towns in the state, along with their populations. A town with a population of 500 or more should have a gas station, but the station may be closed in the evenings and on Sunday. To find an open gas station after hours or on a Sunday, you'll need to find a town with a population of 1,000 or higher. Make sure you plan your course accordingly.

Touring and sport-touring motorcycles generally have big fuel tanks, but sometimes they burn so much gas that you really don't have that great a range. Cruisers tend to have smaller tanks, but some cruisers, especially the V-twins, use less fuel, so they can travel nearly as far. Some bikes with exceptionally small tanks, such as older Harley-Davidson Sportsters, can barely travel 100 miles before they start sucking air out of their tanks.

> CAUTION
>
> **Steer Clear**
>
> When traveling through isolated areas such as the American West, it's better to err on the side of caution when planning your fuel stops. It's better to refuel too often than to not refuel often enough.

Not only is having to constantly refuel your bike time-consuming and annoying, it can also be dangerous. In many areas in the United States, especially in the West and Southwest, you can easily ride 150 miles between gas stations. These are isolated areas, and if you were to run out of fuel in such a place, you would probably be eaten by buzzards before someone found you.

Even if you aren't going any place in particular, keep your bike's range in mind when deciding which roads to take.

Don't push your luck when it comes to refueling. If you are getting low on fuel and pass a gas station, refill your tank. If you decide to wait until the next town, you could find that the town has no gas station.

Keep in mind that your fuel mileage can vary, depending on conditions. If you are riding fast or have a heavy load, you can count on running out of fuel sooner than if you are traveling more slowly or carrying a lighter load.

Preparing Your Bike

Throughout this book, I've tried to stress the importance of properly maintaining your motorcycle. When traveling long distances on a bike, this is especially important. If your bike were to break down in an isolated mountain pass, you could freeze to death before someone found you. Making certain your bike is in good shape before you take a trip serves an economic purpose as well. Having a breakdown far from home can be much more expensive than having your bike fall apart while commuting to work. When you break down in an isolated area, you don't have the luxury of shopping around for the best prices. You also don't have the luxury of finding a mechanic you trust.

Your best bet is to get your bike in as good shape as possible before taking a trip. Study the procedures in Chapters 16 and 17. Make certain that you perform all routine maintenance. Here's a checklist of procedures you should always perform before an extended trip:

- Change the oil.
- Top off the electrolyte in the battery.
- Check your coolant.
- Tighten every bolt on your bike.
- Replace leaky fork seals, as well as worn bearings and bushings in the frame.
- Replace worn shocks and fork springs.
- Pay close attention to your tires. If there is the slightest possibility that your tires will wear out on your trip, replace them before you go.

What to Bring?

No matter what I tell you, you will probably overestimate the amount of clothing and gear you'll need when you take your first motorcycle trip. But here are my suggestions for all you need for a safe, comfortable ride.

The Clothes Make the Motorcyclist

On my first extended trip, which I took about 15 years ago, I brought a couple of different jackets (for riding in a variety of weather conditions), along with five or six complete changes of clothing, including some dressy clothes in case I wanted to go out to eat or on a date.

Now I bring a couple of pairs of jeans, a couple of turtlenecks, a couple of sweatshirts, and a couple of T-shirts. I may bring three T-shirts if the weather is hot or if I plan to be gone a week or more. And I bring pretty much every pair of underwear and socks I own. If I go out for a nice dinner, I wear my cleanest pair of jeans and the turtleneck with the fewest holes in it.

> **Motorcycology**
>
> When packing for a motorcycle trip, pack light. A lighter load will tax your motorcycle less and will not have such a pronounced effect on your bike's handling. Leave a little extra space for any souvenirs you might pick up.

Your best bet is to travel light on a bike. Bring only clothing you'll wear. And you'll always seem to wear less than you bring. As you become a more experienced motorcycle traveler, you'll find that you bring less clothing on each successive trip.

Tools You'll Use

Although I pack fewer clothes for each successive trip, I find that my list of must-bring gear grows each year. Every time I've needed an item I didn't have, I've included that item on following trips.

I always bring a small selection of extra tools, even when I'm on a new bike. The toolkits that come with most bikes will do in a pinch, but I always like to have an extra set of combination spanner wrenches, a couple of pliers (needle-nose pliers and channel-lock pliers), a ratchet, and a small selection of sockets. I also include a cigarette lighter, a small selection of nuts and bolts (including some for connecting my battery cables to my battery), some electrical connectors, a roll of wire, and a couple of rolls of tape (friction and duct tape).

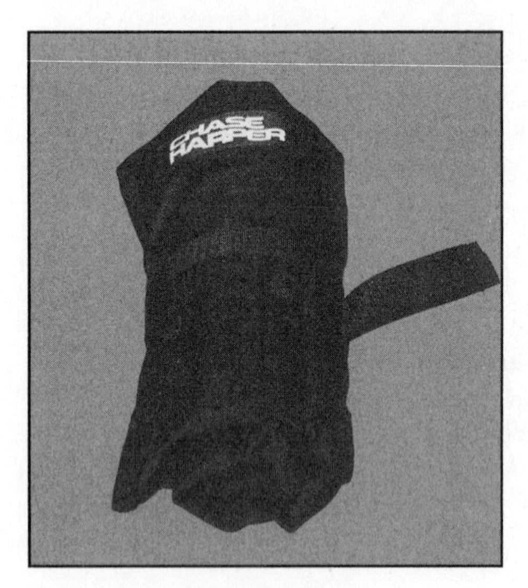

This tool pouch from Chase Harper provides an ideal way to pack your tools for a long motorcycle trip.

(Photo © 1998 Darwin Holmstrom)

Safety First: First Aid

I also carry a first-aid kit with me. I make certain that the kit includes the following items:

- A selection of bandages, including gauze bandages
- Adhesive tape

- An antibiotic of some sort
- Something for bee stings

This is a list of the absolute minimum amount of items a first-aid kit should include. If you can pack a more complete kit, you should do so, even if you need to leave something else behind to make room for it.

For the Scenic Routes: Photographic Equipment

I'm a photographer and always bring my camera equipment when I travel, which presents some challenges on a bike. The greatest of these challenges is weather protection. If you have watertight hard luggage, this is not as much of an issue, but riders with soft luggage will have to come up with a way to keep the rain off their camera equipment. Before a trip on which I'll be using soft luggage, I buy a box of the most durable garbage bags I can get (the kind for bagging leaves seems to be the toughest) and then double-wrap my cameras in these bags.

When your camera is packed away in your luggage, it can take too long to reach it, so I have a fanny-pack–type camera bag. If you want to keep your camera ready to use when you ride, I highly recommend this type of bag.

Motorcycology

Always buy a large box of heavy-duty garbage bags before going on a motorcycle trip. You'll be amazed at the uses you'll find for them. I place my clothes in them and then put the garbage bag in my saddlebags. Not only does this protect my clothes from getting wet, but it also makes it easier to pack and unpack my saddlebags. I also wrap my sleeping bag in garbage bags. If you've ever had to spend a night in a wet sleeping bag, you'll see the value of this practice.

Another option is to use small point-and-shoot cameras when you travel. You can keep these in your vest pockets or fairing pockets, where they'll stay dry and be ready when you need them.

If you pack your camera in your luggage, whether you have soft or hard luggage, be careful not to place it in a location where it will

Steer Clear

Make certain that your load is secure when packing a bike for a trip. If something falls off, it could get caught in your wheel or chain, causing you to lose traction and crash.

bounce around. Just the vibration from your bike can pound expensive cameras to pieces; if they bounce around in your trunk or against your shock absorbers while in your saddlebags, you could end up with very expensive paperweights instead of cameras.

Carrying your camera in a fanny pack or carrying a point-and-shoot camera in your vest pocket can eliminate much of this problem. If you transport your camera in your luggage, pack soft items, such as towels, clothing, or pillows, around it to absorb shocks and vibrations.

Protective Gear

I always wear a full-face helmet with a visor when traveling. Not only does a full-face helmet provide superior protection in an accident, but it also provides superior protection from the elements and superior comfort.

The most versatile piece of protective gear you can own is a waterproof riding suit like Aerostich's Darien jacket and pants (mentioned in Chapter 9). These suits eliminate the need for rain gear, freeing up a lot of luggage space, and they provide unmatched versatility. With all liners in place, such suits provide excellent cold-weather protection, yet with the liners removed and all vents opened, they are the best hot-weather gear you can buy. This is especially important when traveling in high mountains, where temperatures can vary by 60 or 70 degrees in just a few miles.

You Can Take It with You: Packing Your Bike

Once you've decided what to bring, you'll need to figure out how to bring it with you. Packing techniques are more important than you might think. If your gear falls off your bike, the best you can hope for is that you'll just lose a few items. A more likely outcome is that your gear will get caught in your wheels or chain, causing you to crash.

CAUTION

Steer Clear

When mounting soft luggage on your motorcycle, make certain that your luggage doesn't come into contact with your exhaust pipes, or you could lose your belongings in a fire.

Luggage

To provide enough carrying capacity for touring, you'll need to have some sort of luggage. Most bikes will accept soft saddlebags and a tankbag; these items are the easiest and most economical way to provide extra carrying capacity on your bike.

Some bikes won't accept soft luggage because of the shape of their tail pieces or because their exhaust pipes ride too high. This is especially problematic on sportbikes. Some bikes won't accept tankbags, either, because of the shape of their gas tanks. If this is a problem on your bike, there are tailpacks that strap onto the rider's portion of your seat. If you can't mount soft luggage and you don't have a passenger seat on your bike, you'll need to carry all your belongings in a backpack or choose a different bike for traveling.

A few companies, such as Givi, make hard luggage for many motorcycles. This luggage is expensive, and mounting it can prove quite a challenge, but the convenience of hard luggage makes it a worthwhile investment.

Soft luggage, such as this tankbag, tailpack, and saddlebags, all from Chase Harper, can convert just about any motorcycle into a tourer.

(Photo © 1998 Darwin Holmstrom)

If soft luggage won't fit on your motorcycle, you can carry your gear in a tailpack, such as this Supersport from Chase Harper.

(Photo courtesy of manufacturer)

Hard luggage, such as this Givi Wingrack system, can make a motorcycle significantly more useful.

(Photo courtesy of manufacturer)

In addition to soft luggage and a tankbag, I strap a duffel bag to the passenger seat of my bike. This provides all the carrying capacity I've ever needed.

Camping

If you choose to camp rather than stay in motels when you travel, you can save a lot of money, but you also need to bring a lot of extra gear. The bulkiest items you'll need to pack are your tent and sleeping bag. But if you use your head when packing, you can use these items to help make your load more secure. I'll tell you how to pack your camping gear in the next section.

Loading Up

Before attempting to pack your bike, go to your nearest bike shop and buy at least four bungee nets. Bungee nets are stretchy webs made of nylon ropes with metal hooks that attach to your bike. They are the most wonderful devices ever invented for motorcycle touring, especially if you camp out.

Use a pyramid design when packing a load on a bike—put the widest, stiffest pieces on the bottom, and put the narrower, spongier items toward the top. My own method is to lay my duffel bag crosswise on the passenger seat, so that the ends of the bag are resting on my saddlebags. Behind that, I lay my tent, also crosswise. I then place a bungee net over the two items, tightly securing it in the front and in the rear.

Steer Clear

Check your loads, including your soft luggage, frequently when traveling on a bike. The vibration from your bike can loosen hooks and straps. If you find a strap or a bungee hook that has worked its way loose, take the time to adjust it. The consequences of luggage flying loose can be deadly.

Then I lay my sleeping bag in the crotch created between the tent and the duffelbag. Often a single bungee net won't go all the way around my sleeping bag and still solidly attach to the bike, so I'll secure the bungee net in the front of the load and stretch it as far over the sleeping bag as it will go. Then I'll hook the rear of the bungee net to the hooks of the bungee net holding the tent and duffel bag in place. If the top net won't reach the hooks of the bottom net, I'll hook it to a place on the bottom net where the nylon cord is doubled up. Next, I firmly attach another bungee net to a secure point behind the load and hook it to the front of the bungee net covering the sleeping bag, again trying to attach it to the hooks on the other net. The fourth bungee net is a spare, since they sometimes stretch or break.

First, attach the widest and stiffest items at the base of your load.

(Photo © 1998 Darwin Holmstrom)

Different-size loads require variations on this theme. If you're traveling two-up, you'll need more carrying capacity. Unless you are riding an ultimate-behemoth touring bike or you're pulling a trailer (neither of which I recommend until you're an experienced rider), you should probably consider not camping when traveling two-up.

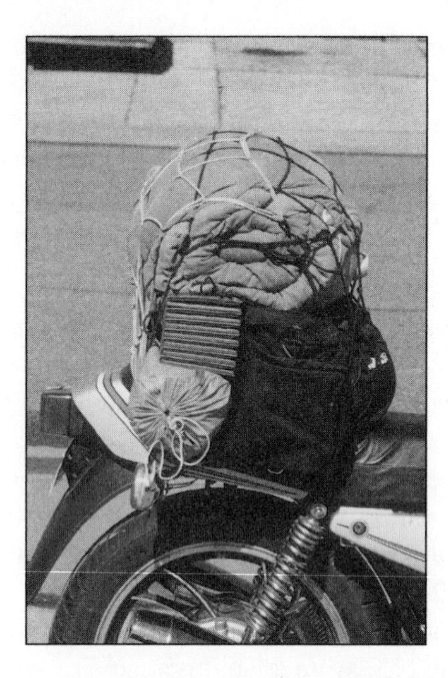

Next, attach narrower, softer items.

(Photo © 1998 Darwin Holmstrom)

Using a luggage rack also requires you to alter your methods of packing. A luggage rack can increase your carrying capacity and provide you with more secure points to attach bungee nets, but make certain that the rack is mounted securely, and don't overload the rack.

You may have to make adjustments to the method described here, but if you structure the load so that it is solid and securely attached to the bike, using a pyramid method to keep your center of gravity as low as possible, you should be fine. Check your load frequently (including the straps attaching your soft luggage to your bike); if anything starts to loosen, take the time to adjust and tighten it.

Pacing Yourself

Traveling on a motorcycle drains you physically much more than traveling in a car. It's important that you receive proper nutrition and rest when riding.

Unfortunately, fine dining isn't easy on the road. Road food is notoriously unhealthy and doesn't provide the kind of energy you need for touring. Try to eat as many carbohydrates as you can. Have pancakes instead of an omelet for breakfast. (And eat all your toast.) Have salads for dinner instead of steaks.

Most important, make certain that you drink enough water. If you drink just soda or coffee, the caffeine in those drinks actually depletes your body's supply of water. Get in the habit of buying a bottle of water each time you stop for gas instead of buying a can of soda. Onboard water systems are increasing in popularity. Aerostich Darien jackets even have a special pocket to hold CamelBak water systems. When riding long distances, exhaustion can creep up on you, diminishing your riding skills. You may not even be aware it is happening. This is especially problematic on hot days and can cause otherwise safe riders to make mistakes. As I've said repeatedly, you can't afford to make mistakes on a bike.

You need to be aware of your mental and physical condition. When you feel yourself getting tired, stop. Find a rest area and stretch your legs. Pull into a convenience store or gas station, buy some juice and a bag of peanuts, find a shady spot in the parking lot, and sit down for a bit. If you are out in the middle of nowhere, find a crossing or turnout where you can park your bike, and then find a shady spot to lean against a tree, or lie down in the grass and watch some clouds go by. Take a nap, if you feel like it. It may slow down your schedule, but if you continue riding when you're exhausted, you might never get where you're going.

Motorcycle Madness: Rallies

So now that your bike's all dressed up, you probably want someplace to go. Just about any place makes a good destination for a motorcycle tour—a visit to friends, to relatives, or just to nowhere in particular.

If you have no particular destination in mind, you might want to attend a motorcycle rally. Rallies make a logical destination for a bike trip. While the trip is its own reward on a bike tour, rallies are hard to beat, as far as destinations go.

The types of rallies you'll find are almost as varied as the types of clubs I discussed in Chapter 19. There are rallies for cruiser fans, rallies for tourers, rallies for sportbike riders, and rallies for antique bikes. There are Norton rallies, Moto Guzzi rallies, Ducati rallies, and BMW rallies.

Whatever your interests are, you can find a rally where you'll meet hundreds, or even thousands (in some cases, hundreds of thousands) of like-minded riders. Rallies are places where you can go and revel in all aspects of motorcycle culture.

Major Rallies

Motorcycle rallies have distinct personalities. Some are mild-mannered and relaxed, while others are obnoxious and just plain rude. Most fall somewhere in between. The biggest, loudest, rudest rally of all is Bike Week at Daytona.

Bike Week: Daytona

Held during the first week of March each year in Daytona, Florida, Daytona Bike Week is the wildest party in the United States.

Daytona began as a racing-oriented event, and racing still plays an important role in the rally. The American Historic Racing Motorcycle Association (AHRMA) helps sponsor and organize some of the best historic racing in the country at Daytona, along with a variety of antique-bike shows and contests.

> **Steer Clear**
>
> If you find events such as a bikini pull offensive, you'll probably want to avoid Daytona Bike Week.

Antiques and classics aren't the only motorcycles raced at Daytona. You can catch dirt-track racing, Motocross racing, and drag racing, along with the Daytona 200 Superbike race, the rally's main event.

But it's the variety of other activities that gives Daytona its unique character. All kinds of motorcycle-related events take place during Bike Week, like the American Motorcycle Institute's Brute Horsepower Shoot-Out Dyno contest, Spider's Show of World's Most Unusual Motorcycles, the Annual Alligator Road Tour, Side Car and Trike Day, the Classic and Modern Japanese Bike Rally, the European Bike Day and Show, flea markets, swap meets, and the Rat's Hole Custom Chopper Show.

The nonmotorcycling activities are what really make Daytona infamous. Many of these are not family-oriented activities. In addition to the ever-present live bands, free beer, and wet T-shirt contests, you'll be able to take in the Ugliest Old Lady contest, the Biggest Beer Belly contest, egg wrestling, the Slippery When Wet Oil Wrestling contest, his and hers tattoo contests, a celebrity bra auction, and Jesse the World Famous Human Bomb, who can blow himself up at least three times during the rally.

But Daytona is not all racing and debauchery. The American Diabetes Association sponsors a charity ride, the Real Ride For The Cure, and the American Red Cross holds a blood drive each year.

Daytona is not a destination for the easily offended, nor is it a place for anyone with a low tolerance for loud Harley-Davidsons. But if you're looking for an adventure on the wild side, you might want to check out Bike Week.

Sturgis Rally & Races

Sturgis is somewhat tamer than Daytona, generally attracting an older crowd, but calling it a family event is a bit of a stretch. Held the first full week of August each year in Sturgis, South Dakota, the Sturgis Rally & Races is a Midwestern version of Daytona Bike Week.

As in Daytona, racing was the original purpose for the gathering at Sturgis, but over the years, the spectacle of the rally began to eclipse the racing. There is still a lot of racing at Sturgis, sponsored by the AMA and the Jackpine Gypsies Motorcycle Club—everything from hill climbing to vintage racing to Grand National Dirt Track racing. That alone makes the rally worth attending.

Main Street in Sturgis, South Dakota, becomes a sea of chrome, leather, and denim during the annual Rally & Races, held each August.

(Photo © 1998 Darwin Holmstrom)

But also like Daytona, it's all the other events taking place that give Sturgis its character. Main Street during the rally becomes a sea of black leather and denim, swirling around the vendor booths lining the sidewalk.

One of the best things about the rally at Sturgis is riding in the Black Hills of South Dakota. The roads in the Black Hills offer terrific riding any time of the year, but during Bike Week, you'll be sharing those roads almost exclusively with other motorcyclists.

Sturgis gained a reputation in the 1970s as a wild party spot for outlaw bikers, but the wild days are history. Like the motorcycling public in general, Sturgis is becoming more mature.

Americade

For people who prefer not to spend their vacations being part of the world's biggest freak shows, there are other, more mature rallies that dispense with the tattoo contests and bikini pulls. The largest of these is the Americade Motorcycle Rally.

Americade was first held in May 1983 and takes place the first week of June each year at Lake George, a resort community in upstate New York. By 1986, total attendance had reached nearly 10,000 riders, making Americade the largest touring rally in the world. Approximately 40,000 riders attended the rally in recent years. Statistics collected by the folks running the rally show that the average attendees are likely to be married, 40 to 60 years old, and riding a touring motorcycle, although the rally attracts riders of all stripes, persuasions, and ages.

Other Rallies

As motorcycles become more popular, appealing to more diverse and ever larger numbers of riders, motorcycle rallies multiply and become more diverse. There are rallies scheduled at certain times of the year, such as Biketoberfest. There are rallies devoted to all brands, such as the Honda Hoot. There are even cultural motorcycle rallies like the Roundup, which began as a rally for African American riders but now encompasses any rider who just wants to have a good time. This is my personal favorite rally.

Most motorcycle clubs (like those mentioned in Chapter 19) hold national rallies. Women On Wheels holds its International Ride-In each summer at various locations around the country. The Christian Motorcyclists Association holds several rallies each year. The International Retreads has a big get-together each summer, as do the Harley Owners Group, the BMW Motorcycle Owners Association of America, the Moto Guzzi National Owners Club, and just about every other group you can imagine.

The American Motorcyclist Association holds its Vintage Motorcycle Days (VMD) at the Mid-Ohio Sports Car Course in Lexington, Ohio, each July, and this event provides some of the most spectacular vintage racing in the country.

One of the more entertaining events held each year is the Davis Rally, held in New Hampton, Iowa, every September. This rally offers much the same experience as

Americade, with a bit more elbow room: only about 4,000 motorcyclists attend each year, rather than 40,000. Another small rally that provides big entertainment is the Sportbike Rally in Parry Sound, Ontario. This is a great place for Yanks to go and see Canadians take on the sport.

One of the great things about all rallies is that you get to meet interesting people, many of whom you encounter again and again over the years. While the motorcycle community is growing, it's still a relatively small group, and sooner or later, you'll meet just about everybody, from Willie G. Davidson to Dennis Rodman. If you attend some rallies, you might even bump into me—I'll be the bald guy talking about motorcycles.

The Least You Need to Know

- Any dependable bike that you are comfortable riding can be a touring bike.
- While it's fun to be spontaneous when traveling on a bike, you should at least plan where you'll make your next fuel stop.
- Make certain that your bike is in top running condition before you take a trip, and don't take off on questionable tires.
- Sloppy packing on a motorcycle can lead to your gear falling off and getting caught in your wheels, causing you to crash.
- Attending rallies is a great way to meet other members of the motorcycling community.

Chapter 21

Speed Racer: Motorcycle Road Racing

In This Chapter

- The influence of racing on the sport of motorcycling
- The different types and classes of racing
- MotoGP/GP racing and other racing events
- Why Grand National Dirt Track is considered the American form of racing

Motorcycle road racing is as old and varied as motorcycling itself. Given the historical importance of racing and the impact it has had on street riders, a surprising number of motorcyclists have not discovered how exciting racing can be for spectators and competitors alike.

Racing provides drama as intense as any work of fiction. Take great American racer Kenny Roberts's first two Grand Prix (GP) seasons, for example. After defying all odds and becoming the first American to win a Grand Prix World Championship in his rookie season, Roberts broke his back during practice six weeks before the start of his second season.

It looked like the end of the line for the young racer, but fans were amazed to see Roberts back on the track by the second race of the year. The season that followed provided a tale as suspenseful as anything Hitchcock could have whipped up. The championship was not decided until the final race. Roberts's ultimate win after such a devastating accident has to rank as one of the all-time greatest triumphs in motor-sports history.

That's an extreme example, but incredible displays of human spirit are everyday occurrences on the racetrack.

In this chapter, I'm going to give you an overview of some of the more popular forms of road racing. I'll tell you a bit of history about the sport and about the people and organizations that make racing possible.

A Brief History of Motorcycle Road Racing

Motorcycle competition has been around as long as motorcycles themselves. Whether that takes the form of two sportbike riders trying to see who's faster on a twisty road, or two Harley owners trying to see who can glue more chrome "Live to Ride, Ride to Live" badges to their machines, competition will always be a part of motorcycling.

While cosmetic competitions pose nothing more than aesthetic threats, it soon became apparent that racing motorcycles on public roads posed a hazard to both riders and nonriders alike. By the turn of the century, promoters and racers were already working to organize racing, whether that racing took place on racetracks (as it tended to do in the United States) or on closed sections of public roads (as it often did in Europe).

Fédération Internationale de Motocyclisme (FIM)

As motorcycle racing grew in popularity, the need for organization grew. This was especially true in Europe, where motorcycle racing became a matter of national pride among fans from competing countries. In 1904, the Fédération Internationale des Clubs Motocyclistes (FICM) was created to develop and oversee international motorcycle racing, as well as to promote motorcycling in general.

In 1949, the FICM became the Fédération Internationale de Motocyclisme (FIM). Originally headquartered in England, the FIM transferred to Switzerland in 1959.

The FIM is now the primary sanctioning body for world-championship motorcycle-racing events, and it oversees both the MotoGP/Grand Prix Championship series and the World Superbike series. The FIM also sanctions a variety of other types of motorcycle racing, including everything from motocross to sidecar racing.

The American Motorcyclist Association and Racing

Since its formation in 1924, the American Motorcyclist Association (AMA) has maintained a presence in almost all aspects of professional motorcycle racing in the United States, including road racing, motocross, speedway, enduro, and observed trials.

Since the early 1970s, the AMA has been the American affiliate of the FIM. The AMA participates in the FIM's management and rules-making process, and has hosted many world-championship motorcycle-racing events. The AMA has also been heavily involved in amateur motorcycle racing. It runs the world's largest amateur motorcycle-racing program.

Types of Racing

As I said in Chapter 3, one bike served all purposes in the early years of the sport. You could buy a 500-cc BSA Gold Star Thumper, ride it to church on Sunday morning, make some quick alterations after church, and race it Sunday afternoon. And you could race it in any type of race you chose, whether it was a dirt-track race, an off-road scramble, or an international Grand Prix event.

Motorcycology

Because MotoGP bikes aren't based on production bikes, their designers aren't hampered in any way by designing around international pollution regulations. As a result, designers have used two-stroke engines almost exclusively. However, rule changes in 2002 converted MotoGP's premier class to four-stroke engines. In the 250-cc and 125-cc classes, though, powerplants are still two-strokes for now.

Those days are long gone. Every type of race bike is a highly specialized machine.

In modern professional road racing, bikes are generally divided into three main categories: Supersport, Superbike, and MotoGP/Grand Prix.

Supersport motorcycles are based on street-legal *production motorcycles*, with only minor modifications permitted. Superbikes are also based on street-legal production motorcycles, although extensive modifications are allowed. MotoGP/Grand Prix motorcycles are pure racing bikes designed solely for racetrack use.

Cycle Babble

Production motorcycles are the bikes manufacturers produce to sell to the general public, rather than bikes built specifically for racers.

In the United States, dirt-track racing is also popular. This type of racing takes place on oval tracks with dirt surfaces. The bikes raced in dirt track racing are purpose-built racing bikes, like those used in MotoGP/Grand Prix racing, but they bear some resemblance to street-going motorcycles.

The late Joey Dunlop crosses Ballaugh Bridge on a Honda NSR 500V during the Isle of Man TT.

(Photo © 1998 Brian J. Nelson)

FIM World Championship Grand Prix Series

The World Championship Grand Prix series is the most prestigious motorcycle-racing series in the world—the pinnacle of FIM racing. The bikes in the top class are the highest-performing machines on the face of the planet. Getting a ride on a Grand Prix bike requires years of dedication and superhuman riding skills. Unlike Superbike and Supersport hardware, which are based on street-going motorcycles, Grand Prix race bikes have nothing at all in common with any motorcycle you can buy. These machines are purpose-built racers wholly unsuited for public consumption and are so challenging to ride that only a select few professional road racers are ever able to master them.

And up until 2002, GP's most respected class, 500, was as exclusively two-stroke as the 250 and 125 classes remain. In 2002, though, the 500 class became the MotoGP class, and that year also saw a development year for 990-cc four-strokes, which have since become the only types of engines allowed. MotoGP race-bike designers had much the same freedom to create as their forebears did. Allowable 990-cc four-stroke engines include three-cylinders (130 kg overall motorcycle weight), four-cylinders (140 kg), and five-cylinders (150 kg). Although modern orthodoxy guarantees that the majority of entrants have four cylinders, the most successful yet has been Honda's V-5-powered RC211V, with two back-to-back world championships.

Grand National Dirt Track: American Racing

In the United States, many early races were held on horse-racing tracks at county fairgrounds around the country.

After World War II, this type of racing began to take the form we know today, and in 1954, the AMA established the Grand National Dirt Track series. Today that series is the oldest and most traditional racing program the AMA sanctions, and dirt-track racing has developed a distinctly American personality.

Although the series now consists only of dirt-track events, until 1986, several road-race nationals were included. As machines became more specialized, it became obvious that machines built for dirt-track racing were not suitable for use on paved courses, and machines built for paved courses certainly weren't suitable for use in the dirt. In 1986, the AMA divided dirt track and road racing into two distinct AMA championship series.

Over the years, a number of manufacturers have had success in the Grand National series, including Triumph, BSA, Yamaha, and Honda, but it is in this environment that Harley-Davidsons are in their element. Harleys have captured more Grand National Championships than any other make.

Anyone who rides their machines sideways at over 100 mph on dirt tracks has to have absolute faith in their abilities. Seeing the superhuman feats dirt-track racers perform week after week out on racetracks across America will humble even the most arrogant street squid.

Dirt-track racers make this look easy, but if you've ever tried sliding a motorcycle sideways through a turn at 100 mph on a rutted dirt road, you'll know it's anything but.

(Photo © 1998 Darwin Holmstrom)

Production-Based Motorcycle Racing

By the early 1970s, it was clear that the escalating cost of racing motorcycles was going to make it increasingly difficult for people to take up the sport. To try to keep racing affordable, clubs organized new series based on production motorcycles.

Such series proved popular with fans, and now some production-based series can cost nearly as much to get into as Grand Prix racing. Fortunately, new series are formed every year, many with rules specifically designed to keep costs down.

Superbike Racing

Superbike racing motorcycles are based on production Streetbikes, but with extensive modifications both to the powertrain and to the chassis. Because of this, Superbike racing is much more expensive to get into than Supersport racing.

Superbike racing is also one of the most popular forms of racing with fans. Although Superbikes have been extensively modified and are capable of near-Grand-Prix levels of performance, they still look like the bikes you or I can buy. Because of that, fans identify with these bikes.

Motorcycle Moments

When I started riding, I was more interested in dirtbikes than Streetbikes. I might have remained a dirt rider had I not discovered Superbike racing. In particular, I owe my interest in Streetbikes to two men and one bike: Phil Schilling, Cook Neilson, and their "California Hot Rod," the highly modified Ducati 750SS that Neilson rode to victory in the 1977 Daytona Superbike race. Following the exploits of Neilson and Schilling, the Hot Rod, to my eye the most beautiful motorcycle of all time, motivated me to move from the dirt to the street.

World Superbike Racing (SBK)

Although the World Superbike Racing series has been around only since 1988, it has quickly become one of the top international racing series in the world. The original idea was to provide the highest-quality four-stroke racing possible, while at the same time keeping the appearance of the racing bikes as close as possible to the Streetbikes on which they were based.

It worked. Motorcycle manufacturers realized the sales boost that success in such a series would give them, and they jumped in with both boots on, either fielding factory teams or giving full support to independent teams.

And unlike International Championship Grand Prix racing, you won't have to go to Brazil to see a race live. The U.S. round of the series is held each summer at the Laguna Seca racetrack in Monterey, California.

However, with the success of four-stroke MotoGP racing, World Superbike has seen its significance severely undercut. In fact, with several factories choosing to abandon SBK in favor of MotoGP, the former has seen a steady bleeding off of resources—development, sponsorship, riders, and dollars—to MotoGP, so much that some question whether World Superbike is even relevant anymore.

AMA Superbike Racing

No such dilemma seems to affect AMA Superbike racing. Although it was the prototype for SBK, AMA Superbike is thriving, whereas the other appears to be on the wane. That's because fans in the United States still care passionately about being able to buy on Monday the production basis of what their heroes win with on Sunday.

And the AMA has tried to make that connection even tighter. For a variety of reasons reflecting marketplace realities, the AMA shook up its road-racing classes for 2003. Superbike, for instance, which previously emphasized four-cylinder 750 machines and

Cycle Babble

When you **overbore** your engine, you drill out the cylinders—the holes in which the pistons move up and down. You then put oversize pistons in the holes, thereby increasing your engine capacity.

then liter-size V-twins, now has established parity in displacement for both engine configurations. Superbike now allows 900-cc to 1000-cc four-stroke engines, with no limit (based on what's available to the public) in terms of cylinder count.

AMA rules for Superbikes allow some factory racing equipment (motorcycles or parts designed specifically for racing motorcycles). Aftermarket and factory high-performance parts are allowed virtually without limit. You can *overbore* 750 engines (drill out the cylinders to increase engine displacement) up to 1 mm. There are no limitations for tires.

AMA Superstock and Supersport Racing

Superstock and Supersport class racing motorcycles are lightly modified street motorcycles, originally as delivered to the dealer from the manufacturer for use on public roads. Since 2003, the AMA has allowed Superstock engines to displace 750-cc to 1000-cc four-stroke four-cylinder engines. Supersport engine regulations remain almost unchanged, permitting a 600-cc engine of two or four cylinders. Limited-production motorcycles are not allowed in AMA Supersport classes.

For AMA Supersport and Superstock classes, the following items must be completely stock, identical to the equipment on a bike you can walk into a dealership and buy:

- Frame and swingarm assembly
- Front forks (aftermarket springs and air caps are allowed)
- Wheels

Motorcycology

Because of the limited modifications allowed to the bikes, building a Supersport racer is one of the least expensive ways to get into motorcycle road racing in the United States at the national level.

- Gasoline and oil tanks
- Fenders and side covers
- Brakes (racing-type brake pads and stock-size aftermarket disc-brake rotors may be used)
- Stock carburetors, with the exception of internal jetting changes, which are allowed
- Seat

A few modifications are allowed. You can add a fork brace and steering damper, and you can replace suspension components to improve handling. Racing-only tires are not allowed, but to get around that, a variety of racing tires are now legal for street use. Airboxes and air-filter elements may be removed or replaced with aftermarket items. Original equipment fairings may be removed or replaced with replica fairings, as long as the aftermarket fairings are true copies of the original.

Overboring the engine up to 1 mm is allowed, and aftermarket racing exhaust systems are allowed. Ignition systems must remain stock, although timing may be adjusted or modified.

AMA Formula Xtreme Class

Formula Xtreme (FX) gives manufacturers virtual carte blanche to create the nastiest thing on two wheels. Rules allow almost unlimited modifications to motorcycles' chassis and engines, with displacements breaking down like this: 600-cc four-cylinder four-strokes, 750-cc twin-cylinder four-strokes, and 250-cc to 330-cc two-strokes.

Vintage Racing

Even more affordable than Supersport racing is vintage racing, sponsored by organizations such as the American Historic Racing Motorcycle Association (AHRMA). Because this type of racing is accessible for so many people, it becomes more popular every year, both with fans and with racers. Racers enjoy the chance to get out and race these classic machines, and fans love to watch the bikes in action. And the racing itself is as exciting as in any modern series.

Motorcycology

Although vintage racing can be one of the least expensive ways to get into racing, many people think it is also one of the most entertaining forms. Often people racing vintage bikes are former racers, people who have known and raced with one another for decades. Over that time, many close friendships have formed, and that bonding creates a positive and entertaining atmosphere at vintage racing events.

Finding parts for older machines that are out of production can be a problem, forcing racers to use altered and nonstandard parts. This makes it difficult for organizers to require the use of stock items, as they do in Supersport racing.

Most vintage racing series use some variation of the following classes:

- Lightweight classic vintage (up to 250 cc)
- Junior classic vintage (251 cc to 350 cc)
- Senior classic vintage (351 cc to 500 cc)
- 750 cc formula vintage
- Lightweight classic Superbike
- Open classic Superbike

To be eligible for most forms of vintage racing, you'll need to start with road-racing or street-going motorcycles manufactured before 1968 (although there are usually exceptions for certain bikes).

There are a few restrictions on how you can build a vintage racer. You have to use carburetors that are consistent with the period during which the bike was manufactured, and you can't use modern, box-section swingarms. You can use modern rims and treaded racing tires, but they have to be in the original size.

If you want to race something a bit more modern, you can build a bike for the Classic Superbike class. Motorcycles manufactured between 1973 and 1985 are eligible for this series, provided that they have air-cooled engines and twin-shock rear suspension. Generally, there are two classes in the series: Lightweight Classic Superbike (which includes bikes up to 550 cc) and Open Classic Superbike (bikes up to 1100 cc).

Other Racing Series

In addition to the main national series, you can become involved in several other types of racing. I've been able to include only a few examples, but if you start looking, you will find a lot more.

The Isle of Man Tourist Trophy (TT)

Although no longer a sanctioned race (the British Grand Prix moved to Silverstone in 1976 because the Isle of Man course was deemed too dangerous), the Isle of Man TT is arguably the world's most famous motorcycle road race. The Mountain Circuit, where the race has been held since 1911, is also one of the world's most dangerous race courses.

Back in the early years of motorsports, races were often held on public roads that were closed down for a race. England had a law against closing public roads for racing, so racing promoters worked with the government of the Isle of Man, a small hunk of land in the Irish Sea, to open a race course there. Automobile racing began at the Isle in 1904, and the first Tourist Trophy motorcycle race was held in 1907.

During the time the race has been held on the Mountain Circuit, a wicked-fast 37.7-mile route over public roads, speeds have risen a bit. In 1911, O. C. Godfrey won the Senior 500-cc TT on an Indian, with an average speed of 47.63 mph. The current lap record, held by David Jeffries, is 127.29 mph, set in 2002.

Except for being interrupted by a couple of world wars, first between 1914 and 1920, and again between 1939 and 1946, TT and other races have been held every year at the Isle of Man. From 1949 until 1976, the Isle of Man Mountain Circuit was part of the Grand Prix Motorcycle World Championships.

The Isle of Man TT is one of the last old-style races in the world, and as such, it is one of the world's deadliest races. There are no runoffs for riders to regain control on if they veer off course. Instead, riders will likely end up in trees, against a stone wall, or in a fence if they make the slightest mistake on the narrow, winding roads. Such obstacles prove much less forgiving than the hay bales lining most race courses. When averaged over the race's 90-odd-year history, at least a couple of riders have been killed per year.

Drag Racing

I have to admit that I used to have a prejudice against drag racing. I thought it seemed crude and silly compared to motorcycle road racing. I couldn't have been more wrong, as I found out when I finally attended a motorcycle drag race.

The first motorcycle drag race I attended was an All Harley Drag Racing Association (AHDRA) event, and it forever changed my view of the sport. Watching the drag racers straddle their freaky-looking machines as they rocketed down the quarter-mile track at speeds of over 150 mph made me realize that drag racing requires every bit as much skill as road racing—just different skills.

And the entertainment provided by drag racing at least equals that provided by other forms of racing. If you ever have an opportunity to see a motorcycle drag race, do so. You won't regret it.

The noise, the smell of burning nitro, and the sheer power of the drag-racing spectacle can only be compared to a religious epiphany or a Led Zeppelin concert.

(Photo © 1998 Darwin Holmstrom)

I urge you to discover the excitement of motorcycle racing for yourself, either as a fan or as a racer. Attend any motorcycle racing event you can, whether it's a club Supersport race, a vintage dirt-track race, or a hill climb. And when you find yourself unable to attend such events, call the publishers listed in Appendix C, order some of the excellent books available on the subject, and read about racing.

The Least You Need to Know

- The AMA is the primary sanctioning body for motorcycle racing in the United States, and it is involved in nearly all organized racing in the United States.
- Motorcycles racing in the MotoGP series are some of the most powerful machines on the face of the planet, producing around 400 horsepower per liter.
- Vintage racing is perhaps the least expensive way to get into motorcycle road racing.
- The Isle of Man TT is one of the oldest races in the world, providing fans with a view into the past.

Chapter 22

How to Become a Motorcycle Road Racer

In This Chapter

- Getting started in racing
- Getting your racing license
- Taking a racing course
- Preparing your bike for racing

I hope that many of you will become racing fans after reading Chapter 21, partly because I want more people to become interested in this exciting sport, but mostly because I want to share something that has brought me so much pleasure.

Some of you may want to become more than just racing fans; some of you may want to become racers. In this chapter, I'm going to tell you how you can become a motorcycle road racer. It's not as difficult as it might seem. While expensive, racing motorcycles is still much less expensive than racing automobiles. It requires more training and skill than automobile racing, but here you're in luck. In recent years, several quality road-racing schools have appeared—places where you can learn to race or just learn to be a better rider. And you can find racing classes in just about any region of the country.

How to Become a Racer

Racing is not as dangerous as it might seem. It's more dangerous than a lot of activities—crocheting, for example—but less dangerous than others. Many racers feel safer on the track than they do on the street, and, statistically, they have a point. On a racetrack, the flow of traffic is controlled; everyone moves in the same direction, at roughly the same speed. And on a track, you eliminate your No. 1 traffic hazard: the left-turning driver.

Actually, by riding on a track with nothing but similar racing motorcycles, you eliminate the danger of car and truck drivers completely, a safety advantage that you will learn to appreciate as soon as you begin riding on public highways. Racing a motorcycle is safer than you might think, and you can minimize what danger there is with proper preparation.

Track Days

One way to experience firsthand the thrill of riding a motorcycle on a racetrack is to attend a track day. These are events in which you pay a fee and are allowed to ride your motorcycle on a racetrack. Such events have long been popular in Europe and have been gaining popularity in the United States. Usually, you are required to make a few modifications to your motorcycle. For example, you will likely have to replace the coolant in your radiator with regular water because coolant is very slippery and very difficult to clean up if you crash.

Motorcycology

To be successful in motorcycle racing, you need to have good upper- and lower-body strength, and you need to be in good cardiovascular condition. The best riders work out on a regular basis and eat low-fat, high-carbohydrate diets.

Vehicular Chess

Motorcycle road racing is a physical activity. You need to be able to wrestle your machine from a hard left turn to a hard right turn in a heartbeat. You need to be in fairly good physical condition. But racing is also a mental activity. A good racer not only rides fast, but he or she also maneuvers for position on the track much like a master chess player controls the area of a chessboard.

Levels of Racing

One thing to keep in mind when you start racing is that you are not going to start at the top. Even if you have more than $1.5 million to drop on a Honda RC211V MotoGP bike, that won't buy your way into the MotoGP circuit. Without the skill, training, and experience to ride the bike, you'll be a danger to yourself and others.

But you wouldn't want to start out in such a rarefied atmosphere even if you could. What fun would it be to go out and constantly get humiliated by the finest racers on the planet? That's why there are classes for almost any rider.

The Central Roadracing Association, the club that conducts road racing in Minnesota, has a couple of classes that are ideal for beginners: the Ultralightweight class and the Lightweight class, which are two of their most popular classes. The racing is a bit slower than it is in the Supersport or Superbike classes, but, trust me: it's fast enough. Speeds of 90 to 100 mph may sound slow to a spectator used to seeing the speeds of over 170 mph attained by some World Superbike racers, but when you're out there riding around the track, it seems pretty darn fast.

And getting into such classes is much less expensive. You can build a competitive racer for under $2,000 if you do much of the work on it yourself.

Besides low cost, part of the reason these categories are so popular with beginners and experienced racers alike is that the racing is much more competitive at these levels. When you get to national-level Superbike racing, a handful of racers with huge budgets and full factory support dominate the sport. At the club level, everyone is more or less equal, and riding ability plays more of a role in succeeding than sophisticated equipment.

Club Racing

The most convenient way to get into road racing is to become involved in club racing. Although competing professionally at the national or international levels can be prohibitively expensive, most areas around the United States have racing clubs that provide relatively affordable amateur racing. There are dozens of such clubs around the country, but I'm going to focus on two: the American Federation of Motorcyclists (AFM), a California-based club that has been

Motorcycology

Most motorcycle road-racing clubs have categories and classes for just about every level of rider, from 17-year-old experts to 70-year-old novices. If you have the slightest desire to go racing, you can't use age or experience level as an excuse not to do so.

very influential in road racing across the country, and the Central Roadracing Association (CRA), a Minnesota-based club (the CRA is the only racing organization with which I have personal experience).

American Federation of Motorcyclists (AFM)

One example of a club that promotes road racing is the American Federation of Motorcyclists (AFM), a California-based organization that conducts seven to nine racing events each year at Infineon Raceway in Sonoma, California; the Thunderhill Park Raceway, near Willows, California; and the Buttonwillow Raceway Park, near Buttonwillow, California.

Central Roadracing Association (CRA)

The Central Roadracing Association (CRA), located in Minnesota, conducts club racing at Brainerd International Raceway (BIR). CRA events are wildly popular with racing fans across the upper Midwest, with events attracting fans from as far away as Montana and Colorado. Without the CRA, organized road racing would not exist in the region.

Racing Categories and Classes

Categories and classes may differ slightly from one racing organization to the next. You'll need to consult the rule books of the organization you are joining for specific details, but most more or less mirror the categories used by CRA.

CRA has three general motorcycle-competition classes: Supersport, Superbike, and Grand Prix. In addition, it conducts races for a variety of amateur classes, generally divided according to engine displacement: Ultralightweight, Lightweight, Middleweight, Heavyweight, Unlimited, and Lightweight Sportsman Superbike. These classes are be defined as follows:

- **Ultralightweight.** The smallest (and slowest) bikes run in this class, making it the best choice for a beginning racer. However, it is also popular with racers right up to the expert level because the racing is usually very competitive. The CRA also has an Ultralightweight Grand Prix class in which Honda RS125s and Yamaha TZ125s compete.
- **Lightweight.** This popular class is also great for beginners. Although the Lightweight class is dominated by more powerful motorcycles, a good rider on a Suzuki GS500 can be competitive. Older, air-cooled 600-cc motorcycles such as

Yamaha's FZ600 are also allowed. In the Lightweight Grand Prix class, early-model Honda RS250s and Yamaha TZ250s are allowed.

- **Middleweight.** The Middleweights, one of the CRA's most popular classes, feature all current 600-cc sportbikes. In 1997, the CRA began allowing Triumph's Speed Triple, Ducati's 900SS, and Harley-Davidson's 1200 Sportster to compete. In the Middleweight Grand Prix class, current-model Honda RS250s and Yamaha TZ250s compete.
- **Heavyweight.** Popular 750-cc sportbikes compete in this class, along with Ducati's 851/888/916 series and Honda VTR1000s and Suzuki TL1000Ss.
- **Unlimited.** This expert-only class (novice racers are not allowed on motorcycles larger than Heavyweight) has no displacement limits. Any motorcycle can compete, as can any MotoGP machine (but so far, no rider has been able to scrape together $1.5 million-plus to buy one).
- **Lightweight Sportsman Superbike.** This is a class for older Lightweight motorcycles. Except for Yamaha's FZR400 and Honda's Hawk 650, just about any Lightweight Superbike is allowed.
- **Middleweight Sportsman Superbike.** This is also a class for older 600-cc sportbikes, such as Honda's Hurricane 600, Suzuki's Katana 600, and Kawasaki's Ninja 600. Yamaha's FZR400 is also allowed. The Lightweight Sportsman and Middleweight Sportsman races are usually run together.

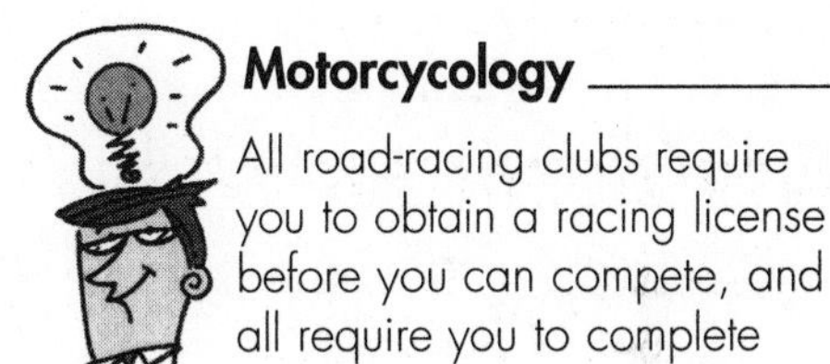

Motorcycology

All road-racing clubs require you to obtain a racing license before you can compete, and all require you to complete some form of rider course before you get a novice license.

Licensing

All clubs require you to purchase a racing license, which usually costs between $45 and $125. Some clubs will accept the licenses of certain other clubs, while some organizations will require you to go through the entire process from scratch before you can race in their club.

The licensing requirements vary from organization to organization (again, you'll need to check the rule books of any organization you are thinking of joining).

Racing Schools

To go racing, you are required to attend some sort of new rider's course. You can attend these through the clubs themselves, or you can attend one of the courses offered by various high-performance riding schools.

High-Performance Riding Schools

Schools specifically for people who want to learn to race, or who just want to ride better, have appeared across the country in recent years. Many of these schools take their classes on the road, offering high-performance riding courses at racetracks around the county. Completing a course from an accepted riding school qualifies you for a novice license in most clubs. Even if you don't race, attending a course offered by one of the following schools raises your riding abilities to new heights and makes you a much safer rider.

California Superbike School (CSS)

Founded by Keith Code, former racer and trainer of such legendary racers as Eddie Lawson, Wayne Rainy, Doug Chandler, and John Kocinski, the CSS is one of the oldest and most respected high-performance riding schools.

> **Motorcycology**
>
> Even if you don't want to race, attending a high-performance riding school will improve your riding skills immeasurably and, in doing so, make you a much safer rider.

Begun in 1980, this school set the standard for what a high-performance riding school should be. Courses are now offered at four levels: level 1 focuses on throttle control and cornering lines, level 2 focuses on overall awareness of your surroundings, level 3 concentrates on body positioning on the bike and the mental aspects of motorcycling, and level 4 focuses more tightly on the 15 specific riding techniques learned in previous levels.

For the beginner—and, in particular, for those who need structure in learning situations—the Code school is exactly the right course. You'll learn a huge amount from the first level and get rid of a host of bad habits. However, at the higher levels, it seems Code has less to teach, and there is, curiously, less track time.

Among instructor Keith Code's former pupils is racing champion John Kocinski, shown here aboard a Honda RC45 at the 1997 Laguna Seca World Superbike race.

(Photo © 1998 Brian J. Nelson)

Freddie Spencer's High-Performance Riding School

When I bought my first streetbike, Freddie Spencer was the hottest motorcycle racer in the world. During a 30-year racing career (1966–1995), the man learned a thing or two about riding. If you take this course, he'll share his secrets with you. Courses are offered at two levels: SR for street riders and SR Pro for those with racing aspirations. These courses are not cheap, but for 30 years' worth of Fast Freddie's experience, it's well worth the price.

CLASS Safety School

Begun by three-time AMA Superbike champion and English expatriate Reg Pridmore way back in 1978, CLASS offers almost three decades' worth of experience in training riders in the art of going fast safely. These one-day courses are offered at racetracks around the country, and it would be worth the price of admission just to hang out with Pridmore (by all accounts, one of the nicest people ever to be involved in racing) and his son, Jason, for a day. In many ways, CLASS is like self-directed study, with the instructors always there but rarely intrusive.

> **Motorcycology**
>
> While many racing clubs still require you to attend their own racing class, many will give you a discount for attending a racing school like CLASS.

Team Suzuki Endurance Advanced Riding School (TSEARS)

Held in concert with actual racing events at various tracks around the country, TSEARS courses not only teach you to race, but they also provide you with the intense atmosphere you will have to function in as a racer. Graduating from a TSEARS course will even earn you a novice racing license in a couple of national organizations.

STAR Motorcycle School

Jason Pridmore takes after his father, Reg Pridmore, in more ways than one. Like his father, Jason is a top-ranked national road racer. And like his father, Jason teaches a series of high-performance riding schools at various tracks around the country, the STAR Motorcycle School.

Kevin Schwantz Suzuki School

Kevin Schwantz, one of the few Americans ever to win a 500-cc World Grand Prix Championship title, has added his talents to the growing list of ex-racers teaching high-performance motorcycle-riding techniques for street or track use. Schwantz's school has received rave reviews from connoisseurs of such riding schools.

Motorcycology

If you attend a racing class offered by a racing club like the AFM, you need to provide your own motorcycle and racing gear.

Club Racing Classes

Most clubs offer their own racing classes that cost considerably less than those offered at the racing schools, but they still have a lot to offer both street riders and racers. The curriculum of such classes varies from club to club, but the courses offered by the AFM and CRA are fairly representative examples.

AFM Race School

To help new racers get started, the American Federation of Motorcyclists conducts the AFM Race School several times each year. This course is one of the most complete racing classes offered by a racing club. The AFM tries to make the courses fun, too, by holding races for new riders, complete with trophies, championship points, and contingency money.

Everyone has to pass the AFM Race School before they can compete in an AFM race, even if they have completed a professional course like CLASS, although the AFM does give a $25 discount if you can prove that you've completed a course in an accepted school during the previous 12 months. The AFM's philosophy is that while high-performance riding schools give you track experience, you'll need to learn many minor details before competing in real races. You'll need to learn about safety flags and bike preparation, as well as what to expect and what to do when racing with other people.

You need to provide your own bike and gear for AFM's Race School. To participate, you must have the following:

- A set of one-piece or zip-together leathers in excellent condition (no holes, rips, or tears)
- An undamaged full-face helmet with a 1995 or later Snell sticker inside that has not been damaged, or a BSI 6658-A or ECE 22-05 certification sticker
- Boots at least 8 inches high, and gloves in excellent condition
- A back protector (either built into the leathers or separate) that consists of impact-resistant plastic on the outside and foam on the inside, and that covers the spine from the shoulders to below the waist

These items are expensive, but you will need them if you want to race. Even if you don't race, such gear provides excellent protection on the street.

Preparing a Race Bike

As with just about everything in racing, the details of race-bike preparation vary from club to club, but most fairly closely follow the requirements set forth by the AFM. You can race just about any bike in the AFM, as long as it meets basic safety requirements and passes technical inspection. The AFM offers classes for bikes from 125 cc to over 1000 cc, and for bikes with little or no modifications to bikes built specifically for racing.

> **Motorcycology**
>
> The best way to learn about preparing a bike for racing is to visit the pit area of a racetrack during a race and talk with the racers. Most will be more than happy to offer you advice.

To prepare your bike for AFM racing, you'll need to remove some of the street equipment, such as turn signals, mirrors, the license plate and brackets, passenger footpegs, the sidestand, and the centerstand. Headlights and tail lights need be removed or taped over.

Cooling systems can't contain any antifreeze because spilling that slippery substance on a track poses a serious safety hazard. You'll need to install three number plates: one on each side and one on the front. Some bikes have an area on the fairing or seat that is large and flat enough to hold a number sticker. Novice number plates are yellow with the assigned AFM number in black. As a safety precaution, certain fasteners need to be safety wired or have locking devices.

The best way to learn how to set up your bike for racing is to obtain a rule book from the club you want to race with and study it. Then go to a race to browse through the pits, look at the bikes, and talk to people about how they set up their own bikes. I've found racers to be some of the nicest, friendliest people I've ever met, and I think you'll find them very helpful to talk to when getting started in motorcycle racing.

Buying Your First Racing Bike

When buying your first racing bike, follow the recommendations I outlined for buying your first streetbike. Choose a motorcycle that will allow you to get the most racing time and fun for the least money. Select a bike that isn't so large that it intimidates you or hinders your ability to learn. Bikes such as 250-cc twins (such as Kawasaki's Ninja 250), most thumpers, and 500-cc or 650-cc twins are good choices for beginners.

Motorcycology

Sometimes buying a bike that has already been built for racing is cheaper than preparing your own bike.

An alternative to preparing a race bike yourself is to buy a motorcycle that has already been converted into a racer. One of the best places to find such a machine is from road race–oriented want ads, like those found in the back of *Roadracing World.* You can also find race bikes for sale in the pit areas of racetracks when races are being held.

Attend a high-performance riding school and see if you are interested in becoming a racer. Even if you decide the sport is not for you, at the very least, you'll improve your riding ability immeasurably.

The Least You Need to Know

- Racing requires good mental and physical preparation on your part.
- There is a class of racing for riders of all ages and experience levels.
- All racing clubs require you to attend some sort of racing class and obtain a racing license.
- It can be cheaper to buy a race bike than it is to build one.

Appendix A

Biker's Buying Guide to New Bikes

Motorcyclist™ magazine runs an annual buyer's guide in its March issue that lists all street-legal motorcycles for sale for the following year, along with technical specifications, prices, and editors' comments. This guide alone makes subscribing to *Motorcyclist*™ worth the money. I've used this guide as a general template for this appendix, but I've modified the guide to be more useful for a new rider.

My recommendations vary somewhat from those of the *Motorcyclist*™ staff because I'm judging a bike using different criteria. The magazine publishes its guide for experienced motorcyclists, who look for different qualities in the machines than new riders would. My recommendations are geared more toward beginning riders, although experienced riders may also find them useful. I've evaluated each bike using the following criteria:

- **Ease of use.** Learning to ride is difficult enough without choosing a difficult motorcycle to learn on. In evaluating the bikes in this guide, I've placed a premium on power characteristics (because you will find smooth throttle control to be easier on bikes with a broad, smooth powerband) and on ease of handling.

  Note that ease of handling is not the same as outright handling prowess. When I discuss ease of handling, I'm talking about how maneuverable a bike is in the kind of situations in which you will ride. A bike might be the best-handling machine on the racetrack but be a real handful when you practice braking and swerving in the parking lot. Bikes that combine smooth power and easy handling earn my Best First Bike rating.

- **Versatility.** You probably aren't going to go out and buy several bikes right off the bat, so your first motorcycle should be capable of serving you in a variety of situations. It should also be a bike you can grow with rather than a machine you'll want to ditch midway through your first season of riding.
- **Ease of maintenance.** I don't have an unlimited expense account to maintain my fleet of bikes, so I perform most basic maintenance procedures myself and take ease of maintenance into account when I purchase a bike.
- **Fun.** Because the primary purpose of motorcycling is to have fun, selecting a bike based solely on its practicality would be foolish. I've also included style under the category of fun. I didn't feel that style warranted its own category because it relies so heavily on opinion, and my opinion of what looks stylish may vary from yours. If you like the way a bike looks, don't worry about what I or what anyone else thinks about it.

A lot of powerful, capable motorcycles function quite well as a first bike, provided that the rider exercises some discretion and maturity in applying the throttle. Thus, highly capable motorcycles such as Ducati's Monster 800S and Yamaha's FZ6, both top-notch sportbikes, have both earned Best First Bike ratings, as have some of the more manageable of the large-displacement cruisers. When someone sets his or her mind on a large-displacement cruiser, he or she usually buys such a bike, so I decided I might as well list the best choices in that category. To earn a Best First Bike rating, a large-displacement cruiser had to have a modest overall power output (for the most part, not a problem in this class) and have a claimed dry weight of well under 650 pounds (a bit more tricky).

This appendix lists virtually all street-legal motorcycles for sale in the United States, as well as all off-road and playbikes. I've excluded competition bikes such as motocross and trials motorcycles because such machines are meant for experienced riders. I've divided the appendix into five sections based on the system used by *Motorcyclist*™ magazine: Cruisers and Tourers; Sportbikes, Sport-Tourers, and Standards; Dual-Sports; Cross-Country and Enduro; and Playbikes. I describe each category in more detail at the beginning of each section. Within each category, I've organized the motorcycles alphabetically by manufacturer, and although no prices are listed, I've arranged the bikes from most expensive to least expensive.

Cruisers and Tourers

Since the advent of the touring cruiser (see Chapter 3), the line between touring bike and cruiser has blurred. With a couple of exceptions, most touring cruisers and touring bikes are too heavy and cumbersome for a novice rider, but the cruiser category provides ample examples of terrific first motorcycles. Often cruisers are on the heavy end of the motorcycle spectrum, but their low center of gravity (especially the V-twin-powered machines) can mask that weight, making them feel much lighter when moving. Also, the relaxed power output of most V-twin engines is ideal for newer riders trying to learn smooth throttle control. Generally, most motorcycles of 1000 cc or more are going to be too big, too heavy, and too powerful for novice riders. There are, of course, exceptions, and I've noted them.

BMW Cruisers and Tourers

BMW K1200LT

BMW had three LT models last year, but now there is only one. The 2004 LT has all the equipment of last year's midlevel Custom: cruise control, heated grips, an electrically operated windscreen, ABS, reverse gear, heated seats, and a stereo. Other options let you duplicate last year's top-level Exodus.

BMW R1150RT

I pucker up whenever I see an R1150RT because so many are ridden by cops; I instinctively roll off whenever I spot a white RT. Can't blame the bike—it's just fine. For 2004, the RT gets the two-spark engine, and a limited number are available in "Night Black," with AM/FM radio for a little more.

BMW R1200CL/Custom

BMW is knee-deep in the cruiser/tourer subsegment with the R1200CL. Based on the R1200C, the CL adds a handlebar-mounted fairing with quad headlights, revised ergonomics, and hard luggage. The Custom model piles on a radio, heated grips and seats, and cruise control. Both earn the two-spark engine for 2004.

BMW R1200C Phoenix

With a solo seat, two-tone paint, and a trick tinted windscreen, this is arguably the most custom of BMW's cruisers. Still, it includes BMW's Integral ABS and Telelever front and single-shock rear suspension—and two plugs per cylinder for 2004. The new colors are red/silver and cream/blue.

BMW R1200 Montauk

The Montauk is a new face in BMW's cruiser group. From the CL, it gains a big, fat front wheel, with a widened Telelever fork to hold it, wide bars, stacked headlights, a new windshield, and integral ABS. Underneath the gloss and glitter is BMW's 1170-cc eight-valve opposed-twin, now using twin-plug heads.

BMW R1200C Classic

BMW's original cruiser returns, with the new two-spark Boxer engine and BMW's lightened EVO brake system with integral ABS. It comes fully featured, with heated handgrips, a tall handlebar, a two-piece seat (pity the poor, aching passenger) and four color choices: black, metallic blue, metallic red, and silver.

Harley-Davidson Cruisers and Tourers

Harley-Davidson CVO Screamin' Eagle Electra Glide

The Screamin' Eagle version of the Electra Glide boasts a bored and stroked Twin Cam 88 (to 1690 cc, 103 cubic inches) tuned to Enraged Raptor specs. Custom touches abound, including three-spoke wheels, an AM/FM/CD stereo, and special instruments.

Harley-Davidson CVO Screamin' Eagle Softail Deuce

Harley's Custom Vehicle Operations (CVO) will create a limited number of this special Deuce model, with a 1550-cc Screamin' Eagle engine, slash-cut mufflers, a teardrop airbox, a low-profile seat with chrome inserts, a lowered suspension, and a 180-mm rear tire.

Harley-Davidson Ultra Classic Electra Glide

Compared with the Classic Electra Glide, the Ultra gets a CD player instead of cassette, a built-in intercom with helmet-mounted headset, and even cruise control. Under it all is the rubber-mounted Twin Cam 88 engine in fuel-injected form and the famous (if elderly) FLT chassis.

Harley-Davidson Road King Classic

Using The Motor Company's touring chassis—with a rubber-mounted Twin Cam 88 engine and belt drive—the Road King is the way to go for the long haul in classic style. Leather hard bags and whitewall tires distinguish the Classic from the hard-bagged Road King.

Harley-Davidson Road Glide

Harley's Road Glide is an unmistakably sleek and seemingly custom-built "semi-dresser" for those who want all-around utility with style. The fairing is tilted forward 4 degrees this year, with the windshield angled back. It has the same underpinnings as the other touring models holding an injected Twin Cam 88 V-twin.

Harley-Davidson Electra Glide Classic

The Classic Electra Glide gets a wider, more durable rear tire for 2004. Otherwise, it's the same luxurious tourer we've come to know and love, with a rubber-mounted, but not counterbalanced, 88-inch Twin Cam engine. The traditional bat-wing fairing houses full instruments and a stereo.

Harley-Davidson Heritage Softail Classic

This uses the same basic frame (with hidden dual rear dampers) and engine (rigid-mounted, counterbalanced Twin Cam 88) as the Deuce, but it takes a very different styling path. It's done up in a more historic motif, with a detachable windscreen and studded leather bags.

Harley-Davidson Road King Custom

"Custom" pretty much sums up this Road King: it comes with many of the custom touches owners apply to the basic models. The rear suspension is lowered, the windshield is replaced by a small chrome wind deflector, and leather bags with hidden mounts carry the freight.

The Wide Glide is light enough to function as a first bike, but there are better Big Twins for that job.

Harley-Davidson V-Rod A/B

Motorcyclist™'s 2002 Motorcycle of the Year now comes in colors: black, blue, red, gold/black, and teal/silver. The frame of the A model is now clear-coated (for extra protection) over a shinier silver finish. The B model has a blacked-out frame for a more sinister look. Like the silly-fast 'Rod needs help!

Harley-Davidson Softail Deuce

The Deuce combines the clean hidden-shock Softail chassis and the counterbalanced air-cooled, 45-degree, 88-inch V-twin. A stretched tank gives it a long, low look, and a disc rear wheel and 21-inch front wire wheel make the Deuce one of the most radical production bikes around.

Harley-Davidson Springer Softail

Nothing major to report here beyond a new handlebar and Badlander seat. Otherwise, it's business as usual with the Springer's retro front end—expected 21-inch spoke wheel in place—pushed along by the fine Twin Cam 88B engine. Electronic fuel injection is standard.

Harley-Davidson Road King

The Road King is the classic American touring machine, with hard saddlebags and cast wheels, plus an effort-saving cruise control. Rubber mounting quells the vibes from the balancer-free mill. A wider, 30 percent more durable rear tire is new for 2004. Options galore are available from the aftermarket and H-D.

Harley-Davidson Fat Boy

The Fat Boy's success means the wide look is definitely in—and has been for a long, long time. A porcine, 5-gallon tank; deep fenders; 16-inch disc wheels; fat fork tubes; and a big 7-inch headlight complete the scene. Underneath it all is the smooth, counterbalanced TC88B engine; injection is optional.

Harley-Davidson Dyna Wide Glide

Here's the deal: Dyna platform, meaning rubber-mounted 88-incher, wide-spread fork, and a skinny 21-inch front perched between. For 2004: a bigger, full-length-console tank, which is needed on any Hog with fuel injection. Carbureted models get the big tank, too, but the EFI will cost you $600.

Harley-Davidson Dyna Low Rider

Harley's trademark model gets a bigger fuel tank with a full-length console, plus redesigned ignition and electric panel covers. A low seat height (26.2 inches unladen, or 25.2 with a 180-pound rider) is made possible by a slammed suspension and a scooped saddle. You can get it with either a carburetor or EFI this year.

Harley-Davidson Softail Night Train

Think of it as a Softail in basic black. Even the engine is powder-coated in this elegant noncolor, and a drag bar on 6-inch risers gives it a cool, form-follows-function ambience. The 88 Twin Cam is counterbalanced, living under a tank with a new-for-2004 emblem. Oddly enough, you can get the Night Train in red now.

Harley-Davidson Electra Glide Standard

For the DIY crowd: Harley's basic touring rig comes with a bar-mounted fairing, hard saddlebags, and loads of potential. Because it's otherwise just like the other touring rigs, you can fit the Standard with a tail trunk, fairing lowers, plenty of chrome, and even EFI (for $600). A higher-mileage rear tire is new for 2004.

Harley-Davidson Dyna Super Glide Sport

A sporty air-cooled Harley cruiser? Why not? The Sport has a fully adjustable suspension and the responsive steering that comes from a comparatively tight 28-degree steering-head angle. EFI is available this year, delivering improved cooling and better throttle response.

Harley-Davidson Softail Standard

Everyone has to start somewhere. Nascent Harley types will do well to write a check for the Softail Standard. It's got the basics—a counterbalanced Twin Cam 88B engine, a hidden-shock rear suspension, and the right look at a price low enough to allow for your own customizing.

Harley-Davidson Dyna Super Glide

Maybe the Softail isn't your cup o' Joe. Budget-conscious cruiser types can latch on to the Super Glide, Harley's least-expensive Big Twin. It has the TC88 engine, a five-speed trans, and a belt drive. A bigger fuel tank and optional fuel injection are the main changes for 2004.

Harley-Davidson Sportster 1200 Roadster/Custom (Best First Bike)

The Sportster 1200 has a new rubber-mounted engine for 2004, cranking out 15 percent more power. There are two distinct models: the sportier Roadster, with a tach, dual front discs, a taller suspension, and a smaller fuel tank; and the Custom, with a 21-inch front wheel.

Harley-Davidson Sportster 883/883 Custom (Best First Bike)

The smallest, cheapest Harley gets the same basic changes as the 1200 this year: a rubber-mounted engine, more horsepower, a lower seat height, and, alas, quite a bit more weight. Choose the Custom, with a larger fuel tank and a lower dual seat, or the base 883, with a single seat and a small tank.

Honda Cruisers and Tourers

Honda Valkyrie Rune

This is what happens when you let the designers lock the studio door. Wicked, long, and low, the Gold Wing–based Rune will be built in extremely limited numbers. What do you get for your $25,500? A truly original, absolutely eye-catching cruiser that's utterly un-Honda.

Honda Gold Wing 1800

Not much new for Honda's huge (and hugely entertaining) maxi-tourer: handlebar switches are now illuminated, and there's a closable and adjustable windshield vent for extra summer air. As always, the silky flat-six pounds out the torque. ABS costs $1,000.

Honda VTX1800N

The new-for-2004 N-model VTX layers many of the styling touches of the Rune onto the classic VTX1800 V-twin chassis. It comes with cast wheels, slotted fender rails, straight-cut mufflers, and the new hidden-seam tank, of course. As with other VTXs, stock is just the start, with upgrades available from Honda.

Honda VTX1800 Retro/Spoke

Honda launched the VTX series with a drag-styled cruiser, but the heart of the market is in the "classically styled" iterations—hence the R (for *retro*) and S (for *spoke*) VTXs. Aside from the wheels, both versions are the same and feature a 52-degree, fuel-injected, 1795-cc V-twin.

Honda VTX1800C

The original street-rod-styled VTX1800C returns with no major changes—it even uses the old 4.5-gallon, see-the-seam tank. The potent 1795-cc, rubber-mounted V-twin returns unaltered, complete with two long-lasting iridium plugs per jug. Triple discs are linked for skill-independent braking performance.

Honda VTX1300S

The VTX1300S is distinguished by its classic cruiser styling, including floorboards and traditional spoked wheels. The engine is a 52-degree, liquid-cooled V-twin packed in a shorter, lighter, much more nimble chassis, compared with the big-guy 1800. In many ways, it's more for a whole lot less.

Honda VTX1300C

The street-rod-style C model is styled to resemble the original VTX1800. As with the Big Boy, the powertrain and basic chassis are the same as on the S version. The C gets its lighter, more aggressive look from smaller fenders, a slimmer saddle, footpegs instead of floorboards, and shorter mufflers.

Honda Shadow Sabre

Sharing its three-valve-per-cylinder engine with the Shadow Spirit, the hot-rod-styled Sabre is nonetheless the performance choice, thanks to its shorter gearing. Cast wheels with wide tires complete the aggressive look. Base models are black; black or purple flames cost $200 extra.

Honda Shadow Spirit (Best First Bike)

Turn back the clock, poof your hair, and reach for those big, clunky eyeglasses: the 1980s are here! Actually, in the Spirit, they never left. Despite cosmetic and technical improvements, the Spirit retains the same basic style and feel of those early Shadows. No changes for model-year 2004.

Honda Shadow Aero 750 (Best First Bike)

Now the only 750 in Honda's cruiser line, the Shadow Aero uses an upgraded version of last year's Shadow A.C.E. engine, but with a shaft drive. Done up in time-tested AmeriCruise style, the Aero should be just right for people careful of wallet or lacking in inseam.

Honda Shadow VLX/VLX Deluxe (Best First Bike)

Honda's entry-level cruiser gets no changes for 2004. It's what you expect: light, friendly, short, and newbie-friendly. Still only four gears in the box, but what do you want for $5,000? The Deluxe model gets you extra chrome on the engine and a choice of color that isn't black.

Honda Rebel

In the promotional materials for *Rebel Without a Cause*, James Dean's character is described as a "bad boy from a good family." Honda's little Rebel would love to be bad, but it's too cute to be anything but a worthy, if tiny, entry-level scootlet. It's popular with the Motorcycle Safety Foundation (MSF) for its ridiculously easy handling and anvil-like reliability.

Kawasaki Cruisers and Tourers

Kawasaki Vulcan 2000

Kawasaki calls this King of the Cruisers. If it's size alone that counts, it may have a point, with each cylinder displacing more than an entire ZX-10R. The pushrod, eight-valve, liquid-cooled engine is all new, but the machine's styling is a cool mix of retro and rocket. Belt drive is standard.

Kawasaki Vulcan 1500 Nomad

Kawasaki's flagship 1500 cruising tourer gets its motivation from the same basic liquid-cooled, counterbalanced, SOHC, 50-degree V-twin design used in all Vulcan 1500s and the 1600. The fuel-injected Nomad includes a large adjustable touring windshield and hard bags that open conveniently to the side.

Kawasaki Vulcan 1500 Mean Streak

Sometimes a name is an apt descriptor; sometimes it's wishful thinking. For the Mean Streak, it's a bit of both. Although it's outgunned by other power cruisers, the 1600 Streak can outrun almost any car. Think of it as a Golden Retriever of a motorcycle—willing to go anywhere you go, and do it with a big, sloppy grin.

Kawasaki Vulcan 1500 Drifter

The Drifter's deep fender skirts, solo saddle, long headlight, graceful shell, and wire-spoked wheels mimic the style of the most nostalgic V-twins (translation: Indians). But it's all modern Vulcan underneath, with the carbureted, 50-degree V-twin used in most Kawasaki cruisers.

Kawasaki Vulcan 1600 Classic FI

Kawasaki's 1500 was starting to seem a little outcubed, if you'll excuse the imagery. That's why the 1600 was launched last year, based on the V-twin familiar to Vulcan owners everywhere. It rides in a distinct chassis, with a longer wheelbase and smooth, elegant styling.

Kawasaki Vulcan 1500 Classic

This bike launched Kawasaki's successful 1500 series back in 1987, looking as Americans expected: a classic cruiser look, but with the performance and trouble-free technology for which the Japanese are so justifiably famous. Because it has been around so long, there's plenty of aftermarket stuff.

Kawasaki Vulcan 800 Drifter (Best First Bike)

The smaller sibling to the 1500 Drifter is a raging deal for an Indian-replica cruiser, and many people think the 800 looks even more like a classic Indian than its big brother. The 800 has much the same running gear as the 800 Classic, including 16-inch spoke wheels, a chain drive, and five speeds.

Kawasaki Vulcan 800 Classic (Best First Bike)

For the price, you might assume that this midcruiser is short on content. Kawasaki is feeling generous—something you can do when a model's been around approximately forever. The 800 Classic remains unchanged for 2004, with its the liquid-cooled, 805-cc V-twin, single-carb engine. Such a deal.

Kawasaki Vulcan 750 (Best First Bike)

Like your crazy aunt Edna, Kawasaki never, ever throws anything away. That explains why the tooling for bikes like the Vulcan 750 remains in use these many years. A highly competent cruiser chassis underpins unintentionally retro-1980s styling, all motivated by a shaft-drive, liquid-cooled V-twin.

Kawasaki Vulcan 800 (Best First Bike)

Are you as confused as I am? How many 800s does Kawasaki need to make, anyway? This budget version goes for the chopper look, with a 21-inch front wheel and bobbed rear end. The instruments live atop the 4-gallon fuel tank. The bike's fine, but I'm still confused (perhaps a permanent condition).

Kawasaki Vulcan 500 LTD (Best First Bike)

At one time, this bike was called the 454 LTD. (If you're old enough to remember Kawasaki's LTD cruisers, please sit down before you break a hip.) The spunky twin-cylinder cruiser pounds out pretty good power at a pretty good price and offers an unintimidating perch for smallies and newbies.

Kawasaki Eliminator 125

Just when you thought Kawasaki was actually going to eliminate one of its aging cruisers, it brings one back—and calls it the Eliminator, of all things. Actually, the Elim 125 just took a year off in 2003, to clear the public's palette, as it were. Its nearly subterranean seat height is just 26.9 inches. Eliminate on!

Moto Guzzi Cruisers and Tourers

Moto Guzzi California EV Touring

Guzzi's Touring version of the California EV adds a tall fork-mounted fairing plus lowers. Saddlebags and a top case are dealer-installed options. The air-cooled, two-valve-per-cylinder Goose engine is essentially unchanged, since about forever. The triple-disc brakes are linked.

Moto Guzzi California EV

The California EV is Guzzi's high-end semitouring cruiser, featuring a tall, pullback bar; chrome everywhere you look; and a passenger backrest/luggage rack—all standard. As with the Touring, saddlebags and a top box are options. Underneath, it's standard-issue Guzzi, circa 2004.

Moto Guzzi California Titanium

A small fairing, to split the wind at high speeds, is just the start of the Titanium's list of cool stuff. A lower bar and less chrome differentiate the Titanium from the mechanically identical Aluminum. The Titanium is painted, naturally, titanium gray. Sweet.

Moto Guzzi California Aluminum

Moto Guzzi is working through the list of lightweight structural metals, so here's the Aluminum, essentially the same bike as the Titanium without the wind protection. Like the Titanium, the Aluminum rides on 110/90-18 front and 140/80-17 rear tires on wire-spoke wheels.

Moto Guzzi Stone Touring

It's clear that the marketing folks at Guzzi are not current on American idioms. Let's hope they don't call their next bike the Slug. Regardless, Guzzi's Stone Touring is the traveling version of the Lake Como firm's simplest cruiser with fork-mounted windshield. Luggage is optional.

Moto Guzzi Stone

Guzzi's entry-level cruiser is by no means a stripper. The fuel-injected, air-cooled V-twin is the same as on the other cruisers, driving a five-speed gearbox and a shaft final drive. Guzzi cut costs by simplifying the Stone's detailing and content. Once upon a time, there was a Flint-colored Stone. Really.

Suzuki Cruisers and Tourers

Suzuki Marauder 1600

The new-for-Suzuki Marauder is actually (I'm going to whisper here) a not-so-new Kawasaki Mean Streak with a cosmetic makeover. Which is no bad thing, actually, since they're both pretty swell machines. There are slight bodywork differences and the engine is black, but the performance—and the price—are identical.

Suzuki Intruder 1500 LC

The long, low Intruder 1500 LC returns unaltered. And if you've ever been altered, you know that's a good thing. Derived from the old-as-time Intruder 1400 mill, the 1500 uses offset crankpins to reduce vibes. A big headlight, floorboards, and full fenders give it the "classic" look.

Suzuki Intruder 1400

Another candidate for the Methuselah Award, Suzuki's big Intruder is almost old enough to drink. (Better it than you, huh?) At one time, the bike's 1360-cc V-twin could outrun all the big twins, and it's still a peach today. Smooth, sleek styling, and ultraclean detailing are the Intruder's trademarks.

Suzuki Intruder Volusia (Best First Bike)

The Volusia, which returns without major changes for 2004, packs an 805-cc, liquid-cooled V-twin modified from the Intruder 800. Wrapped in classic, wide, roomy lines, the Volusia is a better traveling mount than the chopperesque Intruder, in my opinion. Colors other than black demand a $200 premium.

Suzuki Intruder 800 (Best First Bike)

First a 700, then a 750, and now an 800, the middle Intruder returns yet again for 2004—and without any changes. It was the first of the seemingly evergreen Intruder family, and its chopperlike profile cut quite a rakish figure in 1986. It's not the most comfortable bike on the planet, but for Sunday hops it's just fine, thank you.

Suzuki Marauder 800 (Best First Bike)

Alterations to the Marauder's Intruder 800-based engine soften top-end power and broaden midrange punch, which may seem backward, given the Marauder's cruiser-cum-streetfighter trappings. If you want your middle-of-the-road cruiser in an aggressive, hot-rod motif, plunk your money—and your butt—on down.

Suzuki LS650 Savage (Best First Bike)

You have to give Suzuki credit for staying the course with a 650-cc single, optimistically named Savage. The budget thumper gets little more than revised colors for 2004 and remains on the showroom floors to tempt newbies and shorties alike. It's got just enough cruiser style to avoid total wimpdom.

Triumph Cruisers and Tourers

Triumph Rocket III

Every time I saw this in spy photos, I thought it was a Photoshop hoax. But it's real, it's huge, and the word on the street is that it might be the fastest-ever production vehicle from 0 to 60 mph. At 2294 cc, it outsizes the new Vulcan 2000, and its unique inline-triple should make mincemeat out of competitors.

Triumph Bonneville Speedmaster

Take your basic Bonneville America; rejuggle the graphics; slap on a lower, straighter handlebar; and you've got the Speedmaster. Under the slightly altered exterior beats the heart of a Bonnie, with the 270-degree-crank, 790-cc, parallel-twin engine and five-speed box.

Triumph Thunderbird Sport

The Sport returns unchanged to Triumph's lineup; it's the only bike left using the original 855-cc, DOHC, liquid-cooled triple that put Triumph back on the map back in the 1990s. The T-Bird is actually right on the cusp of the standard/cruiser distinction, with its low handlebar, feet-back pegs, and tallish saddle.

Triumph Bonneville America

New for 2002, the Bonnie America gets no major changes for 2004. A longer, lower, mellowed-out, more cruiser-oriented version of the Bonneville, the America gets its own kind of Anglo/American retro styling and a thumpy-thump, 270-degree-crank engine. Triumph has bulked up on accessories, too.

Triumph Bonneville T100

The T100 is an upscale version of the Bonnie, with two-tone paint, standard kneepads on the tank, and new colors for 2003—Goodwood green and gold, and Sapphire blue and white. Otherwise, the T100 is a standard Bonnie, right down to the included faux oil-leak stain. (Just kidding.)

Triumph Bonneville

This may be the bike that best sums up the new Triumph. Totally modern yet unabashedly retro, the Bonneville trades on decades of goodwill and pathos yet is its own, highly capable machine. The sturdy parallel-twin feels just right, and its upright architecture makes it—like its ancestor—right for about any occasion.

Victory Cruisers and Tourers

Victory Arlen Ness Signature Series

Bet the other cruiser makers are kicking themselves for not signing Arlen and son to help put their styling on the map. This is a limited-edition version of the Vegas, festooned with all kinds of gleaming Ness-spec billet goodies. You could call it a Look Ness! Monster? Okay, don't.

Victory V92 Vegas

It's amazing what the input of the father-and-son team of Arlen and Cory Ness has done to upgrade Victory's street cred. Once known for dowdy cruisers, the other American streetbike company has rebounded big with the Vegas. An uprated Freedom engine makes it go—and go very well, thank you.

Victory V92TC Touring Cruiser

Returning basically unchanged, the V92TC is Victory's touring rig: it comes complete with a tall windscreen and hard saddlebags. Two years ago, all Victorys got a more powerful version of the original air/oil-cooled, four-valve-per-cylinder V-twin engine.

Victory Kingpin

The new Victory Kingpin starts with the same basic engine/chassis combo as the Vegas, but then it goes its own ruggedly independent way with deeper fenders; six-spoke, 18-inch cast wheels; and a fat 180-mm rear tire. An inverted fork pushes the look even farther into performance land. Victory is on the gas now.

Yamaha Cruisers and Tourers

Yamaha Royal Star Midnight Venture

This special Royal Star Venture adds a studded saddle and backrest, a chrome fork, and a blacked-out paint job that extends to the liquid-cooled, 1294-cc, 70-degree V-four engine. Electronics include a full audio system, cruise control, and an LCD dash display.

Yamaha Royal Star Venture

A Midnight Venture with less black and less chrome, the R/S Venture gives the same long-haul plushness from features that include a half fairing, hard luggage, floorboards, bucket seats, cruise control, and an audio system. Both Ventures carry the five-year Royal Star warranty, as you would expect.

Yamaha Road Star Silverado

All 2004 Road Stars get the punched-out 1670-cc engine, a raft of engine and drivetrain tweaks, new cast wheels, new brakes, a new handlebar, and a wider seat. The Silverado is the base touring model. The Midnight gets a chromed front end and other cosmetic touches.

Yamaha Road Star Warrior

The hot-rod Warrior already had the big motor last year, but in high-performance tune, with hotter cams, more open intake and exhaust, a two-into-one pipe—you get the idea. The W also has its own aluminum frame, aluminum swingarm, and three-spoke wheels.

Yamaha Road Star Midnight

This bad-boy Road Star gets the punched-out 1670-cc engine, a raft of engine and drive-train tweaks, and all kinds of stuff. The Midnight also receives added blackness, as in engine, tanks, fenders, and so on. The light at the end of this dark tunnel? The chromed front end, of course.

Yamaha Road Star

Even the base RS gets the punched-out 1670-cc engine, a list of engine and drive-train tweaks, new cast wheels, tubeless tires, and new brakes lifted right from the R1. The seat is wider and flatter, the drive belt is wider and lighter, and the handlebar is recurved for your pleasure.

Yamaha V-Max

Introduced nearly 20 years ago, the mighty V-Max survives for the same reason crocodiles have: it simply eats anything that gets in its way. If you were raised on V-twins, you owe it to yourself to ride, if not own, this roaring, raging V-four torque monster from the past. No changes for 2004—didn't need 'em.

Yamaha V-Star 1100 Silverado

The Silverado is the 1100 V-Star designed for the wide-open road, with an adjustable windshield, classic leather saddlebags, a passenger backrest, and studded seats. Under it all is the time-tested V-Star 1100 engine, an air-cooled 1063-cc engine, with its power transmitted through an exposed-shaft final drive.

Yamaha V-Star 1100 Classic (Best First Bike)

The Classic is essentially the Silverado touring version, but without the touring-specific shield, bags, and so on. Done up in more of a traditionally American motif, it's got deeper fenders, fat 16-inch tires on cast wheels, a covered fork, lower bars, and footboards. It has the same motivation from the air-cooled V-twin.

Yamaha V-Star 1100 Custom (Best First Bike)

The base model of the V-Star 1100 line, the Custom uses the same 1063-cc, two-valve-per-cylinder, SOHC engine; exposed-shaft final drive; steel frame suspension pieces; and triple-disc brakes as the others. The Custom differs with a lower, more narrow seat; a slimmer 18-inch spoked front wheel; and a junior-petite headlight.

Yamaha V-Star Silverado

If you don't need 1100 cc of air-cooled V-twin to feel manly (or womanly, for that matter), check out the touring version of the smallest V-Star. It's got an adjustable windshield and studded leather bags and seats—even a sissybar. Go ahead: say "sissybar" out loud.

Yamaha V-Star Classic (Best First Bike)

Big, poofy fenders, a low seat height, and a chrome bill that would choke a rap star—this must be the V-Star Classic. The 649-cc, air-cooled V-twin is surprisingly powerful, while the single-disc front brake does the job—just. This is supposedly one of Yamaha's very best sellers—as high-value bikes usually are.

Yamaha V-Star Custom (Best First Bike)

Psst. Here's the long, low chopper treatment applied to the likable and beginner-friendly V-Star platform. To prevent potential owner embarrassment, Yamaha does not broadcast the displacement in the smaller V-Star's moniker—only you know it's not a literbike. Hush up, will ya?

Yamaha Virago 250

What do beginners want? Just guessing, but maybe this: Yamaha's smallest Virago has good power, a low seat, and utterly manageable dimensions. It's relatively cheap, reliable as an end-of-year budget redo, and even cute … in a tiny terror sort of way.

Sportbikes, Sport-Tourers, and Standards

Most sportbikes make poor first bikes because they tend to be hard-edged and single-mindedly focused on riding fast. But many of you reading this book will eventually end up on sportbikes, and there is some logic in learning to ride on the type of bike you intend to ride later. Fortunately, there are some very good sportbikes that also make good tools for perfecting your riding skills. Foremost among these bikes is Suzuki's pair of SV650s: the naked SV650 and the more sporting SV650S, which features a more racy riding position and a small fairing. Other good choices in the sportbike category are Yamaha's marvelous FZ6, Kawasaki's enduring EX500 Ninja, and Ducati's stylish Supersport 800. One thing to keep in mind when considering a sportbike, however, is that most of these bikes have at least some plastic bodywork, and some bikes have extensive bodywork. That bodywork could be very expensive to replace if you have even the slightest tip-over. And you'll probably have at least a slight tip-over while learning to ride.

The sport-tourer category is something like the "Potpourri" category on the game show *Jeopardy:* it contains everything from gigantic touring bikes such as Honda's ST1300 to svelte sportbikes with luggage such as Aprilia's Futura. Most of these bikes are too bulky for a beginner, although some, such as Ducati's ST3, can do the job, if necessary. Others make flat-out terrific first bikes.

The standard category is even more of a mixed bag, but it provides the most versatile bikes for a beginner. Generally, these bikes are naked or without bodywork, although more examples are including a small fairing. Also, some naked bikes, such as Ducati's Monster 800S and the previously mentioned Suzuki SV650, make terrific sportbikes. I suggest not getting hung up on labels. Forget what other people think. Decide what type of bike most appeals to you, and go with it.

Aprilia Sportbikes, Sport-Tourers, and Standards

Aprilia RSV1000R Factory

Aprilia's fab Mille has been completely redesigned for 2004, making it lower, more comfortable, and easier to ride—not to mention faster. Its frame and suspension setup are designed to make sliding the rear more manageable. Standard on the top-line Factory model are Ohlins suspension and forged wheels.

Aprilia RSV Mille R

Don't be confused. Last year's top-o'-the-heap Mille was the R, and now that's the basic version. Still, it's a hottie, with new cylinder heads for more power, a stiffer and lighter frame, and rakish new bodywork. Showa/Boge suspension and four-pad conventional Brembos replace the Factory's high-spec stuff.

Aprilia RST1000 Futura

There are no major changes to Aprilia's sport-touring entry for 2004, and that's okay—they pretty much got it right the first time. It has the comfort and performance to rival the big sport tourers from Honda, Yamaha, and BMW—and it makes it all happen in a package that's between 100 and 200 pounds lighter. Maybe pasta is good for you after all.

Aprilia Tuono/Tuono Racing

Under the bare-bones bodywork, it's a 2003-spec Mille, but civilized with sit-up handlebars and a bikini nose fairing. The result is a fast, beautifully suspended, user-friendly, comfortable nudie-bike. The Racing version gets you Öhlins suspension and radial-mount brakes.

Aprilia SL1000 Falco

The Falco has been around a while, and, well, it's back again. Not that there's anything wrong with that: the kinder, gentler Aprilia sportbike gives you the wonderful Rotax 60-degree V of the legendary Mille, but in a sweet, aluminum-tube frame with a more moderate riding position. Falco or Tuono? Hmmmm.

Aprilia RS50

Size does matter—the smaller, the better. Essentially a screaming GP bike for the street, the RS50 makes your morning commute an all-out race just to stay ahead of the rumbling Hummers. I scream, you scream, the engine screams, we all scream—in revving, smoking, two-stroke delight.

BMW Sportbikes, Sport-Tourers, and Standards

BMW K1200GT

The K1200GT was a new model for 2003, so I understand why it hasn't changed much for '04. It's essentially a touring version of the venerable K1200RS, with a taller fairing upper and wind deflectors routing the air up and around. At more than 600 pounds, it's no racer, but it's a great all-weather mount.

BMW K1200RS

To call an almost 600-pound motorcycle a sportbike may be stretching the definition, but as BMWs go, the big, brawny K1200RS is the real sporting deal. The RS received a more friendly ergo package back in 2002, along with EVO brakes and standard Integral ABS.

BMW R1150RS

As the original Oilhead, the R-RS has an important place in BMW's lineup. Last year it grew to an 1130, with a six-speed to match most of the other Oilheads in the line, and it gained the new, more powerful EVO brakes. This year, it gets an extra spark plug for each cylinder.

BMW R1100S Boxer Cup Replika

Aren't those Germans cute, sticking to the Deutsche spelling of *replica?* An amalgam of standard R1100S and now-defunct R1100S Light parts, the Replika sports special paint, a wider rear rim, and a stiffer suspension. Only a handful will be made, half with ABS and half without.

BMW R1150R Edition 80

To celebrate its eightieth anniversary, BMW introduced the limited-edition R1150R Edition 80. Only 2,000 will be built, and only 200 of those will be making it to the States. Underneath the black-and-white San Quentin-Replika paint, the Edition 80 is a Rockster, and that's not bad.

BMW R1100S

The dramatic, David Robb–penned R1100S is essentially unchanged for 2004, with the exception of the two-spark heads: no more power, but better smoothness and flexibility. This is the last of the original-displacement Oilheads, but it packs the most peak horsepower. Heated handgrips and ABS are standard.

BMW R1150R Rockster

Still think BMWs are for retired museum curators? Look at this. Starting with the eminently functional R1150R, the Rockster adds slashing sci-fi graphics, plus a practical luggage platform behind the rider's saddle. This is not your eighth-grade physics teacher's BMW.

BMW R1150R

The R1150R Roadster uses a more classical chrome headlight and chrome trim where the more extreme models tend toward flat black. Underneath is the tractable and reliable Oilhead Boxer, ready to leap tall states in a single sitting. The seat height is low, but the enjoyment is not.

BMW F650CS

As ever, the CS is a cutesy urban scoot aimed at 20-somethings, 30-somethings, female-somethings, and newbie-somethings. The liquid-cooled thumper is pretty smooth, considering, and the bike's profile sets it apart.

Buell Sportbikes, Sport-Tourers, and Standards

Buell XB12R Firebolt

Take the Buell Firebolt XB9R, and give it some extra urge with the simple addition of a longer-stroke crank. What do you have? An all-American streetfighter, as before, but one with the cojones to back up its enraged-alien look. Buell trickery remains: a fuel-filled frame, an oil-filled swingarm, and clever engine isolation.

Buell XB12S Lightning

The Lightning incarnation of the XB12R concept looks a little rougher and feels a little meaner, but it has every bit of the original engineering, clean-sheet design, and knife-edge chassis dynamics. If you don't give a damn about how they do it in Hamamatsu, here's a little something from Wisconsin.

Buell XB9R Firebolt

A techno tour de force, the XB9R Firebolt represents Buell's attack on the entrenched sportbike orthodoxy. The fuel lives in the frame, the oil sloshes in the swingarm, and pushrods—each pushed by its own cam—pop big old two-to-a-cylinder poppets. It's not like anything else except another Buell.

Buell XB9S Lightning

I'm told that 40 parts differentiate the Lightning from the Firebolt, but it seems—and feels—like several dozen more. The standard tubular bar creates a compact (almost too compact) ergo package that makes an already tiny motorcycle seem absolutely miniscule. It has the same engine as XB9R Firebolt. No changes for 2004.

Buell Blast! (Best First Bike)

What does the Buell Blast! have to do to earn some respect? Um, I'll get back to you on that. Unchanged for 2004, the Blast looks built to a thin nickel (I'm too kind to say "cheap"), but it has proven to be nearly bulletproof in the hands of novice riders. You'll find modest performance here, but it's probably enough for the truly damp behind the ears.

Ducati Sportbikes, Sport-Tourers, and Standards

Ducati 999R

Here's yet another fiery red chunk of motolust for you. Ducati's lightweight, race-ready, all-red, monoposto 999R is on these pages simply to make you whine. Radial Brembo front brakes are the icing on this cinnamon-hot supermodel. If you're not a racer or exceedingly rich, you won't get one of these pumped-up, stunningly suspended superbikes. Life goes on—or does it?

Ducati 749R

Red frame, red fairing, single seat only. Oh, yes—it's the new 749R. Making an alleged 118 horsies at 10,250 rpm, the 749R's short-stroke Testastretta twin is Ducati's first with titanium valves. With ti con-rods for no extra charge, it's a bargain. Suspension? Öhlins. Cool factor? Priceless.

Ducati 999/999S

In Arrest-Me-Red or Screamin'-Yellow hues, Ducati's base-model 999 certainly doesn't *look* basic. Then there's the hotter S iteration: a single, adjustable seat or a dual saddle, and a race-ready, fully adjustable Öhlins suspension front and rear in place of the basic bike's Showa pieces. The S-spec engine is listed at 12 horsepower more than the basic 999—but both are fine, charismatic twins.

Ducati 749S

Based on Ducati's gnarliest superbike, the 999, Ducati's 749S uses a short-stroke version of the Testastretta engine in the big guy's basic chassis. Suspension is Showa front and rear, and the engine pumps out 110 horsepower, if you ask Ducati. You can get it in red or yellow in two-seat trim or with a nifty fore-and-aft adjustable solo version.

Ducati 749/Dark

The base 749 uses a Sachs, not a Showa, rear shock and loses the TiN coating on the fork legs. Horsepower is down to a Ducati-claimed 103, but the weight is down by a couple of pounds as well. In any case, you get all the essential swellness of this great-looking, free-revving midfielder, just at a price much less likely to cause a checkbook highside.

Ducati 998 FE/Matrix

Here's your last chance to own motorcycling's Mona Lisa. The red 998FE gets tricolor markings on its flanks and commemorative steering-head plaque. In between, there's a 136-horse Testastretta twin and Öhlins suspension. The 998 Matrix wears the same basic black livery from *The Matrix Reloaded*, but it won't make you ride like Trinity.

Ducati ST4s/ST4s ABS

Under the rakish new fairing, the 996-cc ST4S is essentially unchanged, but it gets better weather protection and a posterior-friendly saddle. The optional Bosch ABS has something I appreciate: an off switch. Colors include metallic dark gray, red, and yellow.

Ducati Monster S4R

New for 2004, the Monster S4R replaces the old S4 and combines the snorky, liquid-cooled, 113-horse desmoquattro engine of the 996 with a revised chassis featuring a new single-sided swingarm and high-exit exhausts. It even comes with Cobra Coupe/white-on-blue paint.

Ducati 1000DS Multistrada

Introduced as an early-release 2004 model, the radical Multistrada tosses the faux-adventure-tourer idea into a big Italian blender. More an upright sportbike than a dual-sport, the Multistrada is a truly wonderful do-anything sport utility bike (SUB).

Ducati ST3

The appearance of the ST3, with a new fairing and seat, represents the triumph of mind over macho, sanity over superego. The ST4S, with its desmoquattro engine, may be swell, but the new liquid-cooled, three-valve-per-cylinder ST3 mill might just work better over most roads.

Ducati SuperSport 1000DS

Ducati's new fuel-injected, 992-cc, dual-spark-plug engine was a big hit around the *Motorcyclist*™ offices; it may not be exciting on paper, but its great throttle response and meaty torque curve have made it a favorite no matter which chassis it comes in. The biggest SS gets an Öhlins shock, a Showa fork, and the expected Brembo triple discs.

Ducati Monster 1000S

The new 84-horse, air-cooled, 992-cc, dual-spark engine is the heart of this Italian nudie, and it's a sweetie: smooth, torquey, and wonderfully responsive right off the idle stop. The 1000S employs a Showa fork and Sachs shock, and the combination works just swimmingly. Colors are black, metallic gray, red, and yellow.

Ducati SuperSport 800

The SuperSport 620 is gone for 2004, making the significantly more worthy 800 the opening SS. This upgraded air-cooled engine pumps out just 10 horsepower less (75.4) than the 1000 Dual Spark, for a whopping $3,000. The midsize SS gets a Sachs shock, a Marzocchi fork, and the expected Brembo triple discs.

Ducati Monster 800S (Best First Bike)

Midrange Monsters, like their SuperSport stable mates, get the big-bore 802-cc desmodue engine, six-speed gearboxes, and triple Brembo discs. Unlike them, the Monster has a nonadjustable Showa as a fork; the rear end is held not so high by a Sachs shock. The Monster 800 can be had in the usual Ducati hues of black, red, and yellow.

Ducati Monster 620/620 Dark (Best First Bike)

Returning essentially unchanged, the Monster 620 keeps its fuel injection, adjustable shock, and twin Brembos up front. Intended as an entry-level Duck, the Monster 620 is appropriately light and low, with modest power. The Dark version is black and has but five speeds.

Honda Sportbikes, Sport-Tourers, and Standards

Honda ST1100

Honda's replacement for the long-running ST1100 is a better motorcycle in every regard. It's smooth, quick, amazingly light on its feet—and actually lighter than its predecessor, reversing a distressing trend. The ABS version gets an electrically adjusted windscreen in addition to the no-skid stoppers.

Honda RC51

The all-race, all-the-time RC51 was substantially revised for 2003—making it a better streetbike—but it has one added feature for 2004: Nicky Hayden's actual signature, right there on the tank. Is this Nicky's payback for his coveted MotoGP ride, having to sign all these RCs? Well, he's young and has the energy.

Honda CBR1000RR

Honda finally made a raceable literbike that actually displaces a liter: the all-new CBR1000RR. Like the CBR600R, it's designed using tricks from the all-conquering RC211V MotoGP bike, including a Unit-Pro Link suspension. Can it challenge the King of the Class, the GSX-R1000? Can't wait to find out.

Honda Interceptor

Redesigned for 2002, the Interceptor is back for '04 with one noteworthy change: asphalt joins red on the palette. The Interceptor remains one of the great do-it-all motorcycles, ready to machine-gun apexes on Sunday and traverse Texas on Tuesday.

Honda Super Hawk

The Super Hawk lives on in 2004, with no new features except for a black-with-gold-wheels color scheme. (Rumors of a replacement have stilled to nothing.) Not that there's anything wrong with the VTR keepin' on: the S-Hawk has long been lauded for its torque-monster V-twin engine, moderate ergonomics, and middle-of-the-road suspension.

Honda CBR600RR

Honda grabbed the brass ring with this deadly serious SuperSport 600 last year, so there was no reason to change a thing for 2004. New paint options are candy blue and a black/silver two-tone. Like the hot new CBR1000R, this puppy was modeled after Rossi's RC211V MotoGP bike, and it has the power, handling, and overall swellness that this so clearly implies.

Honda CBR600F4i

Europe got two models of this CBR, a hot Sport version (our F4i) and a regular model with a centerstand and a soft, single-piece seat. That bike is here for '04 as our F4i. Mechanically unchanged, the CBR is a fine and logical step down from the RR and should be a great all-arounder. It looks like a barracuda set loose in Hef's grotto, if you ask me.

Honda 919

Honda's designed-in-Europe naked bike receives an adjustable fork (preload and rebound damping) for 2004, plus a couple of new colors: silver and something called Matt Uranium. Wasn't he George's neighbor on *The Jetsons?* Powered by a repurposed CBR900RR engine, the 919 has power and agility in its favor.

Honda 599

The 919's little brother makes its first appearance here in the States for 2004, though it's been on the streets of Europe for years as the Hornet 600. Our 599 uses a carbureted, CBR600F3-based inline-four tuned for midrange and a steel-spine chassis. Colors: asphalt (matte black) or screaming yellow.

Honda Nighthawk

Will the last Nighthawk please stand up? With the demise of the Nighthawk 450 (long ago) and the 750 (this year), here you go: Honda's bottom-rung semisporty 'sickle. A favorite of vertically challenged riders, MSF instructors, and extraurban commuters, the son of Twinstar represents minimalist transportation.

Kawasaki Sportbikes, Sport-Tourers, and Standards

Kawasaki Ninja ZX-10R

Kawasaki rolls out an all-new ZX-10R that's tiny for a literbike, with less frontal area than most 600s. Its all-new engine is much more compact and lighter, and makes a ton more power; its exhaust is real titanium, and its aluminum frame arches up and over the engine to make the ZX-10R as narrow as possible. Zounds!

Kawasaki Ninja ZX-12R

You'd think with the top-speed wars over, Kawasaki would let the ZX-12R molder. No way. For 2004, the big Zed gets new twin-throttle fuel injection for better responses to the helm, and trick radial-mount front brakes. (Maybe they got a package deal.) Choose from blue or silver this year; green takes a holiday.

Kawasaki ZZR1200

Kawasaki's revived ZX-11 stormed the sport-touring ranks as the bigger, faster ZZR1200 back in 2002, and for '04 the only news is paint: silver is the only choice. GIVI-built hard luggage firmly establishes the ZZR1200R's sport-touring credentials. Packing 145 rear-wheel horses doesn't hurt, either.

Kawasaki Z1000

Mollify the old-schoolers with the Eddie Lawson–esque ZRX1200R, and you've got room in the model line to do this: a wicked, angular, new-age naked that takes obvious aim at Yamaha's standard-setting standard, the FZ1. A 1.8-mm overbore on the ZX-9R engine gives 953 cc, and you get dual-throttle injection as well as a trick four-muffler exhaust. Wheelies, anyone?

Kawasaki Concours

Industry insiders predicted that the Concours, which dates back to the 1980s, would bow out with the '02 arrival of the ZZR1200. In '04, they're still wrong. Although there's nothing new to note, the fact that the original Japanese sport-tourer is still around is saying a lot. Concours owners are, I'm told, a loyal bunch. Color: black with gray lowers.

Kawasaki Ninja ZX-6R/6RR

Kawasaki's old ZX-6R was loved for its all-around goodness. Well, screw that. The new 636-cc Six is deadly serious, especially the race-ready RR version, which is sized at an honest 599 cc to be eligible for racing; the RR sports a close-ratio trans and an adjustable swingarm pivot. New stuff for the RR in '04: new cams, bigger intake valves, and other tweaks.

Kawasaki ZRX1200R

There's no denying the appeal of the ZRX1200R, particularly to those who remember when, back in the day, Kawasaki roadrace pilots had to hang on to their bilious-green, old-school, tube-frame superbikes for dear life. You won't find anything really new this year, save for a color combo: lime green is gone (sniff), replaced by silver with black or red with silver.

Kawasaki ZZR600

What's in a name? Not a lot, really. The 2004 ZZR600 is really '02's ZX-6E, but now wearing the European model designation. This former top-ranked 600 seems a bit old-fashioned these days, but it still packs great power and offers what can only be called a middleweight sport-touring profile.

Kawasaki Ninja 500R

With the GS500 hiatus last year, you had to wonder whether a blue-and-white Ninja 500R with a Katana badge would show up in Suzuki dealers. Alas, the Ninja remains the living legend, a feisty parallel-twin econobike that has real performance, if not extreme sophistication. One of these days, it'll get updated—but not today.

Kawasaki Ninja 250R

Back in the day, we all expected the high-revving, hard-charging Ninja 250 to revive the stagnant 250 class, but, well, it's only one bike after all. It's still selling in modest numbers to smaller riders and the few (but vocal) supporters of the quarter-liter sportbike class. Fast? Not really. Fun? Absolutely.

Moto Guzzi Sportbikes, Sport-Tourers, and Standards

Moto Guzzi MGS01 Corsa/Serie

Guzzi is rocketing—okay, rumbling—into the twenty-first century with its MGS01 models. The Corsa is a racetrack-only machine, with a rousing 1225 cc of overhead cam, four-valve goodness. The Serie is the street version, with the displacement pulled back to 992 cc.

Moto Guzzi V11 Coppa Italia

This commemorative Gooz was produced to celebrate the Italian Naked Bike Championship in 2003. The design is classic, proudly exposing the latest 90-degree V-twin, with its added crossover pipe and increased compression. Brembo Gold Series brakes, plus an Öhlins suspension and steering damper are all good.

Moto Guzzi V11 Le Mans/Rosso Corsa/Nero Corsa

Moto Guzzi's top-ranked sportbike for 2004 is the half-faired V11 Le Mans. Three versions are offered: the standard Le Mans and two up-spec versions, the Rosso Corsa and Nero Corsa. (Black or red, get it?) Both high-end bikes have an Öhlins suspension but share the 1064-cc V-twin and six-speed with the base Le Mans.

Moto Guzzi V11 Café Sport

This version of the V11 is styled, appropriately enough, in a café motif but with a refreshingly high handlebar and a relaxed riding position. Under the tank is the now-standard latest-gen longitudinal V-twin, complete with crossover pipe and higher 9.8:1 compression ratio. Plus, there are lots of carbon fiber bits.

Moto Guzzi V11 Ballabio

Descended indirectly from Guzzi's infamous 850 and 1000 Le Mans twins, the latest V11 claims 91 horses at 7800 rpm and comes with a practical half-fairing in red or black. Named after an Italian hillclimb, the Ballabio earns a Marzocchi fork and a Sachs shock. A small bikini fairing breaks the wind.

Moto Guzzi V11 Sport Naked

Guzzi's latest-gen 90-degree V-twin provides 91 horses' worth of oomph, breathing through a Marelli injection system and sending power, as always, through a shaft final drive. If you like your riding done naked and Italian, this just might peg your excitement meter.

Moto Guzzi Breva V1100 I.E.

Considering Moto Guzzi's penchant for making lots of models out of not so many different pieces, the Breva 1100 seemed all but inevitable. It's the same modern styling treatment of the Breva 750, but it uses a thoroughly updated driveline.

Moto Guzzi Breva V750 I.E.

Moto Guzzi cribs from its past for this entry-level model, the Breva. Based on the old V75 pushrod V-twin, the Breva's air-cooled, transverse power plant gets fuel injection and a five-speed transmission plus fresh styling, a newbie-friendly 31.1-inch-high seat, and naked simplicity. What's not to like?

MV Sportbikes, Sport-Tourers, and Standards

MV Agusta F4 Brutale Oro/Strada

For years, we were promised the Brutale, and now it's finally here. It's a compact, frenetic piece of Italian motodesire, with amazing looks, a high-revving engine, and a suspension equally at home on the track as it is on the street. Hear the sound of an F1 grid every time you downshift.

MV Agusta F4 SPR/Strada EVO3

MV's stunning superbike comes in the basic Strada format (whose engine is now on Evolution 3, hence the EVO3 moniker) and up-spec, ready-to-track-day SPR. With uprated suspension and a solo-only saddle, the SPR must be the dream bike for all well-heeled go-fasters.

MZ Sportbikes, Sport-Tourers, and Standards

MZ 1000S

We're gonna get it—the MZ 1000S, that is. This radical semisporty model from our German friends could possibly vault the company into the big time. The engine is a neat counterbalanced, four-valve-per-cylinder parallel twin, the styling is crisp, and the riding position apparently is quite livable. Prost!

MZ Baghira Black Panther/Street Moto

This Yamaha-powered SuperMotard-style thumper looks like a bad boy, but don't be misled. It's actually a comfortable motorcycle upon which you will certainly not see yourself coming and going. Black Panther is, um, black. No changes for the 2004 models.

MZ RT125/RT125 SM

One more (okay, small) reason to be thankful the Berlin Wall is down: the traditionally styled naked version (RT125) pairs up with the SuperMotard-wannabe RT125 SM. Both are powered by a liquid-cooled 124-cc single, ride on teeny-tiny tires, and promise the beginning rider an easy time.

Suzuki Sportbikes, Sport-Tourers, and Standards

Suzuki GSX1300R Hayabusa

This is pretty much as good as real-world high-performance travel gets. With the speed war fading in memory, Suzuki is happy to let the 'Busa live out a quiet life—if you can call 9-second quarter-miles quiet—so there are no changes worth noting on the 2004 bike. It's still way smooth, amazingly civil, surprisingly comfortable, and blindingly fast.

Suzuki GSX-R1000

Celebrated as the king of literbikes for a couple of years now—and for a darn good reason—the GSX-R1000 packs mondo power, super-stable chassis, and a racing heritage second to none. It was freshened last year with a new fairing, a black frame, and radial-mount brakes, so no major changes appear this year. Honda, Kawasaki, and Yamaha are desperate to catch up.

Suzuki GSX-R750

Even though the 1000-cc Superbike rules are threatening to make 750s an endangered species, Suzuki is still working hard on keeping the GSX-R750 on top, with an all-new, lighter engine for 2004. The pistons are lighter, the ports are bigger, the valves are titanium—you get the picture. It was great; now it's greater. Get one before it's too late, 750 fans.

Suzuki GSX-R600

Nothing ever stands still in the 600 class, and the all-new GSX-R600 is proof. The new engine has refinements just about everywhere, from cylinders integrated with the cases to friction-fighting tweaks, to titanium valves. The chassis is also new, with radial brakes and a plethora of let's-go-faster improvements. It should be amazing.

Suzuki SV1000/S

Identical except for the fairings and handlebars, the new SV1000 and SV1000S represent Suzuki's giving in to the marketplace. Since the SV650 bowed in 1999, riders have been crying for a full-liter version. Here it is, with a TL1000S-based engine, injection, and angular styling. It's Ducati fun at a, well, Suzuki price.

Suzuki Bandit 1200S

Stir in new colors (blue and gray this year) and a stainless-steel muffler, and you've got the major news for the big Bandit this year. A perennial favorite for its GSX-R1100–based air/oil-cooled engine, simple styling, and honest personality, the Bandit is available in the half-faired S version only this year.

Suzuki Katana 750

The Katana is designed for riders who want a livable, comfortable, fully faired sportbike but can't afford to buy (or insure) a GSX-R. No matter that its air/oil-cooled engine has its roots in the mid-1980s—it works, and works well. For 2004, the muffler is now stainless steel, and California models get a catalyzer.

Suzuki Katana 600

The 600 Katana survives for the same reason sharks have been around for millions of years: the design just works. Katana's combination of comfort, reliability, and affordability is often just right. It gets new colors (blue and yellow) and a stainless muffler for 2004.

Suzuki SV650/S

Suzuki's compelling little V-twin got an overhaul for 2003, gaining fuel injection and a new aluminum frame, and I'm glad to report that it's even more bitchin' than before. The '04 models have a slightly lower seat height, making this perennial favorite even more appealing to the vertically challenged.

Suzuki GS500F

Wearing its new GSX-R–esque fairing and bodywork, the little air-cooled twin that could still can—especially if you're new to this sportbike thing and maybe strapped for cash. A buck under $5,000 buys you proven power in a friendly chassis with a fresh face for 2004. Rookie canyon commandos on a budget have a steadfast companion here.

Suzuki GZ250

Getting into this whole cruising thing shouldn't be an exercise in intimidation, and with a GZ250, it isn't. Suzuki's bantamweight boulevardier makes sure it's fun. The bone-simple air-cooled single makes accessible power, while a low seat keeps the street accessible to short legs. Maybe most important is an accessible price tag.

Triumph Sportbikes, Sport-Tourers, and Standards

Triumph Sprint ST

No major changes for the Sprint ST sport-tourer: it's still pretty fast, pretty comfortable, and remarkably versatile. The suspension is a little on the down-market side, but if you're the kind of rider who'd rather ride than fine-tune your low-speed compression damping, you might not ever notice. Bags standard.

Triumph Daytona 955i

The 2004 Daytona 955i gets an exterior makeover, with a sleeker, more aerodynamic upper fairing, reshaped mirrors, revised air intakes, and a trim new seat cowl. Underneath it all is the same swell near-liter triple, with a lovely snarl and rumble all its own. With a $1,700 drop from '03 pricing, it's cheap, too!

Triumph Speed Triple

To the cognoscenti, the Speed Triple may be the best Triumph made. Fast, furious, excitable, and outlandish, it's also easy to live with and halfway comfortable. Now it's also a raging deal, with almost $2,000 chiseled out of the price. It's a thoroughly naughty naked, with a torque-stomping triple and a hoolign's attitude.

Triumph Daytona 600

If you thought Triumph's first 600-class sportbike was too little, too late—a really nice Honda CBR600F4i, in other words—this angular, more aggressive Daytona 600, introduced last year, may be your cuppa. Lighter, better developed, and more powerful than before, the distinctive little Daytona carries the high hopes.

Triumph Thruxton 900

Brits used to modify their Bonnies compulsively. Now Triumph does it for them—and us—with the Thruxton. The engine grows to 865 cc, with hotter cams, new carburetors, and megaphone-style pipes. Other tweaks include drop handlebars, rear-set footpegs, revised fork and shocks, and bigger front brakes.

Triumph Speed Four

Virtually identical to the now-departed TT600, the Speed Four nonetheless manages to be its own bike. Nakedized in the fashion of Triumph's own Speed Triple, the Four is serious middleweight fun, and it rides with the kind of vigor many so-called performance nakeds would do well to emulate. You'll like the new, lower price.

Yamaha Sportbikes, Sport-Tourers, and Standards

Yamaha FJR1300/FJR1300 ABS

The FJR is essentially two bikes in one: a highly capable and comfortable sport-tourer, with a wonderfully powerful, sweet-handling high-speed GT bike thrown in for free. The 2004 model brings stiffer suspension, bigger brakes, a taller windscreen, and optional ABS.

Yamaha YZF-R1

Table stakes in the literbike wars have been raised again. The 2004 R1 is essentially all-new, from its 180-claimed horsepower to its forward-tilted engine, over-the-top aluminum frame, radial front brakes, and titanium, under-the-seat exhaust. If you need proof that Yamaha is hitting its stride, here you go.

Yamaha FZ1

Motorcyclist™ named the FZ1 the best naked bike last year, and even though it's unchanged for 2004, I see nothing that would cause me to change my mind. With its R1-derived engine, sit-up riding position, and all-around goodness, the FZ1 doesn't stay parked in the garage for long. The '04 colors are candy blue and gray/black for $100 more.

Yamaha YZF-R6

Great things were expected of Yamaha's new R6, and it certainly delivered, winning the 2003 AMA 600 SuperSport championship right out of the box. Changes for '04 are minimal: remapped fuel injection, a new fuel-injection pump system, and a gently tweaked exhaust. In other words, it's still light and powerful. Colors are candy blue and silver.

Yamaha YZF600R

Nothing more than new colors (blue or silver) are up for Yamaha's middleweight pride of 1998. The vastly underrated YZF600R is an ideal midrange (or even entry-level) mount that's far more capable and comfortable than many other B-level 600s. Don't let the low-spec steel frame and sub-90-horsepower output put you off: it was great then … and still a treat.

Yamaha FZ6

It was only a matter of time before Yamaha brought the sweetness of the FZ1 to the middleweight class. The specs are up there, with a retuned version of the R6's screaming 600; a lightweight, rigid aluminum frame; and a half-fairing that actually protects you from the wind. All that, and at a price that neatly undercuts much of the competition.

Dual-Sports

There was a time when most riders started out with dirtbikes, moved up to dual-sports, and then graduated to streetbikes. These days, new riders often go straight for the big-inch cruiser or sportbike of their choice, ignoring the fact that they often haven't mastered the skills needed to ride such equipment. In this day and age of land closures, finding places to ride a dirtbike has become increasingly difficult, but the dual-sport category is booming. With the exception of the ultimate-behemoth class of giant trail bikes coming from Europe, just about any of these motorcycles can be a terrific first bike.

Aprilia Dual-Sports

Aprilia Caponord

The Caponord is back essentially unchanged for 2004. It's a big, tall adventure tourer, in the mold of the BMW R1150GS. These puppies are all the rage in Europe, where people love one motorcycle to do just about everything—think an SUV that loves to wheelie. This one is not for the short of inseam.

BMW Dual-Sports

BMW R1150GS Adventure

The GS is not just a motorcycle—it's a way of life. The two-spark engine is new, as it is on all BMW Boxers. The more adventurous Adventure features more suspension travel, big aluminum side cases, engine guards, and other Sahara-ready goodies. The upscale GS also has a shorter first gear for tiptoeing through the tules, and ABS II.

BMW R1150GS

Good roads, bad roads, or no roads; BMW's omnivorous GS has been taking travelers farther off the beaten tracks for more than two decades now. Although unchanged from last year, this one can still take you to work today and to Tierra del Fuego tomorrow. Heated grips are standard, as are Partial Integral/EVO brakes with ABS and an adjustable windshield.

Honda Dual-Sports

Honda XR650L (Best First Bike)

Compared to current, liquid-cooled dirt four-strokes, the air-cooled XR650L is big, fat, and old. The only problem is, it works wonderfully—the perfect motorcycle for people who want to ride everywhere and see everything. A legend from Baja to Bangor, it may be responsible for the popularity of dual-sport riding today.

Kawasaki Dual-Sports

Kawasaki KLR650 (Best First Bike)

Kawasaki's big DP single is a little more street-oriented than the Honda XR650L, with a liquid-cooled engine and better wind protection at the cost of a little extra weight. It's a combat tourer, it's a canyon carver, it's an off-road plonker, it's a Baja blaster. And it even comes in red, confusing the heck out of all the Honda riders at Mike's Sky Rancho.

Kawasaki KLR250 (Best First Bike)

High-tech yet compellingly friendly, the KLR250 is the kind of kinder, gentler dirtbike you see strapped to the back of adventure-bound motor homes. It'll go almost anywhere—it just won't do it particularly fast. Four valves and two counterbalancers make power and smoothness, respectively. No changes of note for 2004.

KTM Dual-Sports

KTM 950 Adventure S

This street version of KTM's big rally racer is more fun than a bathtub full of Jell-O. The engine is wonderful: compact and torquey. The chassis reminds me just how good a streetbike can be. The S version is 1.4 inches taller, with new rally graphics.

KTM 950 Adventure

Aside from less suspension travel and a lower seat, KTM's basic Adventure twin is anything but. It's actually more accessible if you're not as tall as an NBA center. Available in orange, silver, or black for '04, it carries nearly 6 gallons of fuel for the 90-horse V-twin, and it's better behaved off-road than you'd expect a 500-pound dual-sport to be.

Suzuki Dual-Sports

Suzuki DL1000 V-STROM

If you like the idea of a go-anywhere Big Twin but know you'll ride most of your miles on pavement, the big V-STROM is about right. It's lower than the Europeans and works as well, or better, on the dirt roads you're liable to travel. With optional bags, it can do it all.

Suzuki DL650 V-STROM

I love the SV650 streetbike, and this adventure-tourer version should be extra wonderful as well. With a compact yet semiprotective fairing, complete with adjustable windshield, it should make a swell middleweight sport-tourer. Less weight and a lower seat should make it even better than the 1000 on fire roads.

Suzuki DR-Z400S

More a dirtbike that you can take on the street, the DR-Z400S is the dual-sport for serious dirt people. The engine makes enough power for almost any off-road need, and the chassis and true long-travel suspension are easily up to the occasional enduro. Lights, license plate, action!

Suzuki DR650SE (Best First Bike)

Roost mightily on local trails, horrify the Starbucks barista with actual dirt on your face, and then ride to work all week. Powered by a steadfast electric-start 644-cc single, Suzuki's DR650SE acts like a garage full of motorcycles for less than $5,000. Vertically challenged types can lower the seat 1.6 inches.

Suzuki DR200SE

This is what Stinky Pete, the prospector from *Toy Story*, would have ridden out to his claim in the desert. Not tall, loud, or exciting, the DR200E is nonetheless perfect for small, beginning, or more casual riders. Nothing new for 2004, but what would you change?

Triumph Dual-Sports

Triumph Tiger

Unchanged for 2004, the Tiger is Triumph's shot at an adventure tourer. The injected, liquid-cooled 955, stolen from the gnarly Speed Triple, seems a little out of place in this twin-saturated segment, but you can't argue with its extra power out on the highway.

Yamaha Dual-Sports

Yamaha XT225

If the XT225 were a person, it'd be old enough to date. Why is it still around? Because it's exactly what many casual dual-purpose riders want: a relatively low, relatively lightweight machine with just enough power to make life interesting. Call this the Hugginator.

Yamaha TW200

Okay, the TW may not look all that butch. But it foments a kind of silly fun all its own, with those big, floaty tires bouncing over the dunes like high-speed basketballs. Think of it not as a motorcycle, but as a street-legal ATV that lost a wheel a few years back.

Cross-Country and Enduro

For those lucky enough to have access to off-road riding trails, there is still no better way to start riding than to do it in the dirt. But the off-road class of motorcycles is bewilderingly complex, containing everything from overgrown two-stroke, trials bikes to tame, off-road trailbikes, to full-boat motocross race bikes with lights. When choosing a first bike in this category, you must choose a bike you can manage, or you will never develop your off-road riding skills. Master those skills, and you will be a much better rider on the street, too.

ATK Cross-Country and Enduro

ATK 125 Enduro

If you want to float like a butterfly and sting like a bee, there are easier ways than boxing, such as driving ATK's slick 125 Enduro, a USA-made two-stoke equipped to challenge just about any trail, from Utah slick rock to the slick mud and roots of New England. The Rotax engine is counterbalanced to keep the vibes down even at higher revs. The hard part: keeping your heart rate down.

ATK 620/700 Intimidator

That's right, a whopping 685 cc (or 616 cc, for the slightly less insane) of earth-moving, horizon-seeking two-stroke power. The engines are built by Maico, the German company that made too much seem just right with the legendary Maico 501 of the 1970s. If you, like Scottie, always need more power, Cap'n, ATK might just have the wild-haired weapon for you.

Beta Cross-Country and Enduro

Beta RR50 Enduro/Enduro Aluminum

Better known for its extensive line of trailbikes and mini racers, Beta is bringing its full-size (21-inch front/18-inch rear wheel), 49-cc enduro to America for 2004. Two versions—one with a steel frame, one with a lighter, stiffer aluminum frame—are available, and an 80-cc engine kit is optional. Mo' hotta, mo' Beta.

Gas Gas Cross-Country and Enduro

Gas Gas EC125/EC200/EC250/EC300

Gas Gas sounds like the sound-effects track from a Jim Carrey movie, but there's nothing tasteless about these Italian enduro machines. Trick stuff abounds: the standard fork on these Gas Gassers is a 45-mm Marzocchi, but for an extra $750, you can get an even more wonderful Öhlins fork to match the standard Öhlins shock. I've got your Gas Gas right here, buddy.

Gas Gas FSE450

If you want to "gas" it, this just might be the bike for you. The FSE450 has all the neat touches found on other modern four-stroke enduros: liquid cooling, a four-valve head, electric start, and a generally top-shelf component suite. The stock fork is a 45-mm Marzocchi, but an extra $750 gets you a trick 46-mm inverted Öhlins to match the already swell Öhlins shock.

Honda Cross-Country and Enduro

Honda XR650R

This big dog is the king of the "B for B" category: built for Baja. If the road is long, fast, and eye-watering, this liquid-cooled aluminum-chassis bomber is just about perfect. And if the stock 649-cc power plant isn't enough, your dealer can slip you a kit to crank out even more fire-road–shredding torque. ¿Un mas cerveza, señor?

Honda XR400R

With its seamless balance of power, handling, and weight, there's a reason the XR400R is America's most popular 400-class trail machine. A fully adjustable 43-mm Showa cartridge fork and Pro-Link/Showa rear end soak up the bumps, and the reliable-as-a-hammer, air-cooled, dry-sump motor keeps the XR400R churning and burning.

Honda XR250R

Smaller riders—or fans of tight, technical trails—just might find the XR250R perfect. Lighter, smaller, yet nearly as sophisticated as the XR400R, it's also one of the great values in off-road motorcycling. With its air-cooled SOHC engine, right-side-up fork, and mild-mannered disposition, it may not be cutting edge—but if you want comfort as well as speed, it may be just right.

Husaberg Cross-Country and Enduro

Husaberg FE450e/FE550e/FE650e

Husaberg's earth-moving four-strokes come in three tasty enduro versions, from the semisane FE450e all the way to the thoroughly excessive FE650e. Whether you choose mild or wild, you get the same high-quality bits: a lightweight, chrome-moly frame, WP suspension, electric start, Brembo brakes—the works. Do good things (and strong drink) come from Sweden? Absolutely!

Husqvarna Cross-Country and Enduro

Husqvarna TE250/TE450/TE510

Anders Eriksson nabbed his seventh World Enduro Championship on the TE450 four-stroke: if you want to win, consider one of these high-tech strokers. They use titanium valves and exhaust pipes, plus a trick F-1-style rocker-arm and an engine that pumps out strong, smooth power. Lightweight electric starting also means all your energy goes into the race.

Husqvarna WR250/WR125

Two-stroke enduro bikes are the ultimate in lightweight, agile off-roaders, and Husqvarna's WR duo comes complete with superb credentials, including an amazing 67 World Championship titles. For 2004, both WRs benefit from the same updates as the CR 'crossers, including an improved exhaust system, intake porting changes, and a more direct path from airbox to carb.

Kawasaki Cross-Country and Enduro

Kawasaki KLX300R

What does the "R" stand for in Team Green's KLX300R? I could be mistaken, but it just might stand for off-road legend Larry Roeseler, the man who made the KLX300 so justifiably famous. Serious power comes from the four-stroke power plant, while a KX-inspired chassis—featuring Uni-Trak suspension and an inverted fork—calms, bumps, and whoops.

Kawasaki KDX220R/KDX200 (Best First Bike)

Here's a pair of race- or play-ready dirtbikes separated only by 18 cc of displacement. The big-brother 220 uses a 2-mm-smaller carb and revised porting to keep the power delivery smooth and manageable. Both bikes possess KX-like perimeter frames, plush suspension, and lightweight disc brakes—ready to rip in the woods or on the trail.

KTM Cross-Country and Enduro

KTM 525 EXC/MXC RFS and 450 EXC/MXC RFS

In KTM-speak, EXC models have lights, digital speedo/odos, and wide-ratio gearboxes—and MXC models don't. These Austrian superthumpers all come standard with six-speed transmissions and are equipped with lightweight electric starting—you push their buttons, and they push yours! They can also be had in a G-version, meaning they're California green-sticker legal.

KTM 400/250 EXC RFS

Based on the Austrian company's legendary chassis design and equipped with the latest in top-drawer WP suspension components, the 400/250 EXC Racing Four-Strokes (RFS) are high-revving enduro/woods/trail machines that can satisfy beginning and pro racers alike. They're also available in a green-stickie/California-legal "G" model.

KTM 250 EXC

This classic two-stroke, pro-spec enduro racer features a full complement of top-shelf components, including a high-quality, totally adjustable WP suspension; front and rear revised (and very orange) bodywork; exhaust-system tweaks; a revised clutch master cylinder; and the overall high degree of design and performance for which KTM is known.

KTM 300 MXC

Think of KTM's 300 MXC as a 250 with open-class-type grunt, and it makes perfect sense. As with other KTM MXC models, the 300 is designed to be a desert/Grand Prix/track machine, with a close-ratio tranny and no annoying lights or speedo. It's a heck of an off-road performer, on track or trail, and like all KTMs, it fairly bristles with the latest WP componentry.

KTM 200 EXC

Despite the fact that there's not always an "official" category for 200-cc machines, KTM's 193-cc 200 EXC remains highly popular. That shouldn't surprise you, really; not only does it offer 125-like handling and maneuverability, but it's also plenty quick, thanks to KTM's tried-and-true two-stroke engineering.

Suzuki Cross-Country and Enduro

Suzuki DR-Z400E

The kickstart-only DR-Z400 is gone for 2004—looks like nearly everybody prefers the E-model's electric starter. And why not? The E's push-button spinner added just a little weight for a whole lot of trailside convenience. Back for '04 is the same powerful four-stroke, liquid-cooled engine, the same chrome-moly frame, and the same high-end, long-travel suspension.

Suzuki DR-Z250 (Best First Bike)

Suzuki's DR-Z250 is what's known in the motorcycle world as a "gapper": a bike that bridges the gap between big-guy off-road thumpers and smaller, less-serious playbikes. The electric-start DR-Z does this by offering serious off-road performance in a smaller, lower, more user-friendly package, one perfect for everyone from full-size novices to height-challenged vets.

Yamaha Cross-Country and Enduro

Yamaha WR450F

Based on the fabulous YZ450F, the WR450F is Yamaha's take on the open-class desert or enduro machine. Powered by the YZ's liquid-cooled, titanium-valve 449-cc four-stroke, the WR adds an electric starter; a wide-ratio transmission; a slightly plusher, revised-for-2004 suspension; an 18-inch rear wheel; and a headlight/taillight assembly. Brrrraaap!

Yamaha WR250F

As it does with the WR450F, Yamaha offers a desert/enduro version of its five-valve YZ250F—the quick-revving, highly maneuverable WR250F. The 2004 WR features electric starting (yeah!), a new 46-mm fork with revised damping and antistick coating, lightweight new aluminum brake pistons, and a high-grip seat cover. BooYaa!

Playbikes

The playbikes category is odd because what some companies consider playbikes, others might consider to be full-fledged race bikes. Some of the off-road bikes in the cross-country and enduro categories are really just for playing off-road, although some of the bikes in the playbike category are mildly detuned race bikes. With a very few exceptions, the bikes in this class are minibikes and are best suited for very young novices.

Honda Playbikes

Honda CRF230F (Best First Bike)

New last year, the CRF230F replaced the venerable XR200R in Honda's lineup as a midsize, easy-to-ride recreational machine that still performs eagerly enough to keep more experienced riders happy. The looks are great, the air-cooled four-stroke engine is flexible and dead reliable, and comfy ergos and plush suspension keep the ride stress-free.

Honda CRF150F (Best First Bike)

The CRF150F is another one of Honda's low-stress, recreational off-roaders—it offers the same type of all-around, easy-to-ride performance as the CRF230F, but in a smaller, even-more-manageable package. Positioned halfway between the 230F and the old-as-time-itself XR100R, the CRF150F has a low-maintenance nature and race-inspired body and graphics that are sure to please.

Kawasaki Playbikes

Kawasaki KLX125L/KLX125

A pair of affordable, entry-level recreational dirtbikes, these two differ only in wheel size: the taller L-model rides on a 19-inch front and a 16-inch rear wheel, while the standard model uses a 17/14-inch combination for a lower seat height and more handling ease. Both are powered by a reliable four-stroke engine—and both come back for 2004 $100 cheaper than last year.

Kawasaki KLX110

All-new for 2002, the KLX110 comes back as an entry-level recreational dirtbike that's not only easy to ride, but simple to take care of as well. Motivated by an air-cooled four-stroke engine with a three-speed transmission and automatic clutch, the smallest KLX offers big KX styling, knobby tires, a low-to-the-ground seat—and a $100 price reduction from last year.

Kawasaki KDX50

New last year, the KDX50 is the beginner bike Kawasaki-owning parents were waiting for. Powered by a simple and durable two-stroke engine, the KDX shows that its small size is perfect for the little ones. To help calm nervous parents' nerves, the bike offers a throttle limiter to keep things from getting out of control.

Suzuki Playbikes

Suzuki DR-Z125L/DR-Z125

New last year, these versatile playbikes thrive anywhere there's dirt. Powered by a dependable single-cylinder four-stroke engine, these first-timer mounts show their main difference in wheel size: The L-model uses a 19/16 (front/rear) combo, while the standard version uses smaller, 17/14-inch hoops for more inseam-challenged confidence. It's $100 cheaper for 2004.

Suzuki DR-Z110

Also back for 2004 is the smallest DR-Z model, the 110. Easy-to-use four-stroke power and a semiautomatic centrifugal clutch take the guesswork out of takeoffs, while a super-low seat height of just 25.6 inches makes this a perfect beginner bike. Maybe the best part is that it looks like its larger DR-Z brothers.

Suzuki JR80

Let's say that your son (or daughter) is just starting out on the dirt and is at least nine years old but is a touch too big for Suzuki's JR50—what to do? Try the JR80, a beginner bike that's one step more advanced than the littlest JR. A low seat height makes it easy to ride, while its two-stroke engine offers simplicity and ease of maintenance.

Suzuki JR50

A long-time favorite of moms and dads, not to mention kids, the JR50 is arguably one of the best kid-spec dirtbikes available. Light in weight, small in stature, and loaded with such safety conveniences as a throttle limiter, the JR50 is a near-bulletproof yellow zonker that'll teach your kids right and give them plenty of smiles in the process.

Yamaha Playbikes

Yamaha TT-R250 (Best First Bike)

Artfully balancing on the fence between playbike and serious off-road machine, Yamaha's TT-R250 offers that sometimes-elusive combination of laid-back fun and adrenaline-inspiring performance. A reliable, air-cooled, electric-start four-stroke offers easy-to-use power, while quality suspension bits and YZ-inspired graphics and bodywork make the bike plenty capable.

Yamaha TT-R225 (Best First Bike)

Sometimes a manufacturer's own words do the job perfectly: "Designed for both new and casual off-road riders … the TT-R225 is tailor-made for fun." A low seat height and electric starter further this mission, as do the reliable four-stroke engine and rugged frame. "Perfect for novice, women, and recreational riders"—I agree.

Yamaha TT-R125E/TT-R125L/TT-R125LE

Playbikes that share basic chassis and engine platforms are nothing new, and Yamaha's TT-R125E, TT-R125L, and TT-R125LE do the job surprisingly well. The differences: E-models feature electric start, and the L-versions use a 19-inch front and 16-inch rear and slightly more rear travel, while the standard TT-RE runs smaller (17/14-inch) hoops.

Yamaha TT-R90

Yamaha's smallest four-stroke is the TT-R90, and it's one of those entry-level dirtbikes that generates miles of smiles for newer and younger riders. Power comes from a reliable 89-cc four-stroke with electric start, a three-speed transmission, and an automatic clutch. Its low seat height means newbies can easily touch the ground as well.

Yamaha PW80

Think of the PW80 as Yamaha's perfect second bike. It's only slightly larger than the legendary PW50 starter bike and includes a 79-cc two-stroke engine; a three-speed transmission with automatic clutch; a throttle limiter; a trick, single-shock rear suspension; and handy grab-handles so it's easy for moms and dads to load. Nice.

Yamaha PW50

Many people regard the PW50 as the "perfect" beginner bike—and a lot of them are giggling kids. Weighing just 82 pounds and carrying its seat just 19 inches above the dirt, Yamaha's Pee-Dub offers no-shifting power and, like the PW80, a throttle limiter. Oil injection and shaft drive help keep maintenance chores simple.

Appendix B

Biker's Buying Guide to Used Bikes

Appendix A listed just about every new streetbike sold in the United States, some of which can honestly be called bargains. But as you may have noted, even the so-called bargains will require you to lay out some serious cash before you can park one in your garage.

If the price of a new bike is beyond your means, you needn't worry much; the used-bike market can help get you on two wheels.

While some motorcyclists trash their machines, most keep them in fairly good condition. Many of the used bikes you'll find will be in nearly the same shape as a new bike.

In Chapter 7, I told you how to make certain a used bike is in sound mechanical shape. In this appendix, I list some used bikes that will make exceptional first motorcycles.

Because used-bike prices vary according to a variety of factors, from the condition of the bike to locale, I'm not including prices in this guide. Generally, bikes that cost more new tend to cost more used. Just as a new BMW costs more than a new Kawasaki, a used BMW will cost more than a used Kawasaki.

As with the "Biker's Buying Guide to New Bikes" in Appendix A, I've listed the used bikes alphabetically, by make. I've included only bikes manufactured since 1982. However, some good, dependable motorcycles were manufactured before that time, and if you find one that runs well and is in good shape, you shouldn't pass it up just because it's older. But be aware that you will have more mechanical trouble with older bikes than with newer bikes. In addition, technological advances from the early 1980s to the present make motorcycles manufactured since then safer and more practical.

For more information, the *AMA Official Motorcycle Value Guide* is one of the best sources we've found for accurate used-bike prices. Published monthly, the guide goes for $74 for a year's subscription, and individual copies can be purchased for $16.95 by calling Black Book National Auto Research at 1-800- 972-5312, or visit www.blackbookusa.com on the web. The services of *Kelly Blue Book* can also be a big help. You can find out the typical problems of any given model and determine the bike's current value. Go to www.kbb.com on the Internet.

Aprilia

Aprilia has been selling motorcycles in the United States for a few years now. Although there aren't a ton of used Aprilias on the market, there are a few. More recent models are better.

Aprilia Pegaso

Aprilia's Pegaso makes a terrific first bike, whether you buy it new or used. While it presents itself as some sort of dual-sport, this one works best on the street. Although few injected versions have been imported into the United States, I recommend going with the simpler carbureted version, which will be much smoother and easier for a novice to ride.

BMW

Like new BMWs, used Beemers tend to cost more than most other bikes, but they are well worth the extra money. The care with which these bikes are built means they tend to last longer than most other motorcycles.

BMW R1150R/R1100R/R850R

BMW's least expensive Oilhead bike, the R model (available in 850-cc, 1100-cc, and 1150-cc versions), makes a terrific first bike, the kind we like to recommend. That is because it is a competent machine that will serve riders well long after they graduate from being novices to experienced riders.

R80GS/R100GS

These big Beemer dual-sports, the original leviathans of the trailbike world, might be a bit of a handful for a new rider, but their torquey, tractable engines and overall balance make them much easier to ride than other bikes of similar engine displacement. These are expensive motorcycles, but they tend to last a long time.

R80/R80ST

This is a street-only version of the original R80GS dual-sport. The R80s are even easier for an inexperienced rider to learn on than the GS series because they have lower seats—a factor that seems to make new riders feel more secure. The R80s are relative bargains, too. These are some of the few used Beemers you'll find priced less than $3,000.

K75/K75S/K75C

These bikes use three-cylinder versions of BMW's unique flat, four-cylinder engine. They are rather large bikes for a beginner, but as with the R80 and R100 boxer twins, their power-delivery characteristics make them easy to ride. Also like the Boxers, they tend to cost more than most other used bikes.

BMW F650

We heartily recommend the original carbureted version of BMW's F650 as a first bike. In fact, we recommend it as a second, third, or forty-fifth bike because it is that good. Built on the same assembly line as Aprilia's Pegaso, this bike differs from the Aprilia in having a four-valve head rather than Aprilia's five-valve head, but BMW's version puts out even more power than the Aprilia, so apparently it gets on just fine without that extra valve.

Honda

Honda is another manufacturer that makes motorcycles of exceptional quality. You'll find a lot of nice used Hondas out there.

NX650

Back in the late 1980s, Honda decided to produce a dual-sport that didn't look like one—or like anything else the motorcycling world had seen before. The result was the unique NX650, a streetbike based on Honda's XL600R dual-sport. Honda created a rather interesting and useful street thumper, one that will cost you less than half of what the cheapest new 650 single will cost you.

XL350R/XL500R/XL600R/XR650L

These bikes are rather crude compared to the newer XR650R dual-sports, but in their day, they were the nicest trailbikes around. The dual-carburetion system of the XL600R can cause the power delivery to seem a bit abrupt, making that bike more difficult for a novice to master than some other thumpers. Considering that used XLs will cost you only between $750 and $1,500, you can probably learn to live with it.

XL600V Transalp

This V-twin dual-sport, which was imported into the United States only in 1989 and 1990, is one of the best all-around motorcycles produced those years and is very easy for a beginning rider to master. This model is very popular in Europe.

VTR250 Interceptor

While only a 250, this little V-twin sportbike is capable of freeway riding. It is also a fun, good-handling little bugger—and pretty, too.

CB650SC/CB700SC Nighthawks

If you're looking for a good inline-four-cylinder Japanese motorcycle, I highly recommend Honda's original Nighthawk series. In fact, I (and many motorcyclists) prefer them to the newer 750 Nighthawks simply because they have shaft drives, while the newer Nighthawks have chains. Even with shaft drives, they are some of the best-handling motorcycles of their day. Some riders take issue with their 16-inch front wheels, which make these bikes seem a bit twitchy in some circumstances, although many novices prefer the maneuverability those same wheels provide.

CB750 Nighthawk

While the newer Nighthawk hasn't won me over quite like the older version, it is still a fantastic all-around motorcycle, and a clean used example represents an even better value than a new one.

FT500/VT500 Ascots

These are two very different bikes. The FT uses an air-cooled, single-cylinder engine derived from the XL500 dual-sport, while the VT uses a liquid-cooled V-twin lifted from the 500 Shadow. Both make excellent first bikes.

NT 650 Hawk GT

These little V-twin sportbikes have become more popular since Honda stopped importing them to the United States. They are more fun on a twisty road than just about any motorcycle I've ever ridden, and one of my greatest regrets is not buying one. The only drawback is that they're a bit cramped for riders over 6 feet tall.

VF500C V30 Magna/VF500F Interceptor

Both these bikes use different versions of the same engine. The Magna surrounds the engine with one of history's most elegant little cruisers, while the Interceptor is the finest-handling motorcycle built in the mid-1980s.

VT500/VT600/VT700/VT750/VT800/VT1100 Shadows

The Shadow cruiser line contains some of the most reliable motorcycles manufactured in the past couple of decades. I especially recommend the 1986–1987 VT700 Shadows, which combine striking looks and genuine comfort with the low maintenance of a shaft drive and hydraulically adjusted valves. In my opinion, this model makes a better all-around motorcycle than any of the new midsize cruisers. The 1988 VT800 looks much the same as the VT700, but it comes with only a four-speed transmission, detracting from its versatility.

Kawasaki

Because Kawasaki has a reputation as a high-performance company, many Kawasaki motorcycles will have seen hard use. But they are rugged bikes that can withstand a lot of abuse.

KLR600/KLR650/KL650-B2 Tengai/KLX650

Not much has changed in the KLR line since the 600 first appeared in 1984, which is a good thing because it's such a good basic motorcycle. The Tengai is a funky rally-style version (one of the most unique-looking dual-sports to come out of Japan), and the KLX is a more off-road-worthy machine. All make fine first bikes.

EL250 Eliminator

This nifty little power cruiser shares its engine with the EX250 Ninja, meaning that it is a snappy bike. These motorcycles are easy to ride, plenty fast, and, with their small bikini fairings, just about the cutest bikes ever made.

EX250 Ninja

This is the same bike as the 250 Ninja that Kawasaki sells today, and it hasn't changed much since its introduction in 1986, except for graphics. If the new bike is a best buy, the used version is even better.

EN450 454 LTD/EN500 Vulcan 500

These ancestors to the Vulcan 500 LTD are fast little cruisers, but many people question their styling. If you don't mind the way they look, they are useful bikes.

EX500/500 Ninja

Kawasaki has made incremental improvements to its 500 Ninja over its long production run, but the original is still a very good bike. A 1987 model will cost about far less than what you'll pay for a new model.

KZ550/KZ550 LTD/KZ550 GPz/KZ550 Spectre

Kawasaki's 550 four-cylinder bike was impressive when it first appeared, and it's still an impressive bike. Reliable as a claw hammer, the 550 still has enough power to get you into serious trouble with legal authorities. The best of the bunch is the GPz, which practically created the current 600-cc sportbike class.

ZR550 Zephyr

Although the Zephyr is a very good bike, it isn't noticeably better than its predecessor, the KZ550—and it costs more. Still, if you can find a deal on a ZR550 Zephyr, you'll have a great motorcycle.

VN700/750 Vulcan

If you can get past the styling of this one, you'll find a great motorcycle underneath.

Vulcan 800/Vulcan 800 Classic/Vulcan 800 Drifter

Kawasaki's 800-cc Vulcans make great first bikes. Their hardtail-look rear ends, created by hiding the shocks, give them a low center of gravity that allows for easy handling at parking-lot speeds and stability at freeway speeds. The standard Vulcan 800 looks like a 1970s-era chopper, the Vulcan 800 Classic re-creates the look of a 1950s-era touring bike, and the Vulcan 800 Drifter recalls the classic streamlined Indians of the 1940s.

ZL600 Eliminator

This is a fun, easy-to-ride power cruiser. Its main drawback is a too-small fuel tank that can barely go 100 miles between fill-ups.

Suzuki

Suzuki has built some unique, often highly functional motorcycles, but throughout the company's history designers have occasionally created bikes that the buying public has not warmed up to. One such bike, the rotary-engine RE5, almost bankrupted the company. On the other hand, when Suzuki designers get the look of a bike right, they create some of the prettiest machines on the road.

DR350S/SE/DR650S/SE

Basically, these are the same as later versions of Suzuki's dual-sports, at lower prices.

GS500E

Everything I said about this bike in Appendix A goes for the used version, except the price. These bikes have been popular ultralight racers, so if you buy a used GS500E, make certain that it hasn't been raced.

GS550E/ES/L/M/GS650G/GL/GS650M Katana

Any of Suzuki's air-cooled four-cylinder 550s and 650s make excellent, dependable bikes, but these are older, so expect them to need small repairs more frequently than newer motorcycles. The switch gear and electrical components are the items most likely to need some attention.

GSF400 Bandit

Some people consider the smallest Bandit, built between 1991 and 1993, one of the best-handling motorcycles ever made. You have to rev the snot out of its little four-cylinder engine, but when you do, it goes like stink.

GSX600F/GSX750F Katanas

These are high-performance sportbikes that require a rider with self control, but they are such good all-around motorcycles that if you think you can trust yourself, you might want to consider buying one.

VX800, Intruder, VZ800 Marauder

These capable motorcycles might be a bit much for most new riders, but those who feel comfortable with bikes of this size will find them best buys.

Yamaha

Yamahas are rugged, well-constructed bikes, although the fit and finish aren't always up to Honda's standards. Don't be surprised to find chrome plating peeling off older Yamahas.

XT350/XT550/XT600

These bikes trace their roots back to the original big Japanese thumper, the XT500 of the 1970s. Although it was a very nice dual-sport, it wasn't competitive with the other thumpers from Japan and was discontinued in 1995.

XJ550 Seca/Maxim/XJ650 Seca/Maxim/XJ700 Maxim

Yamaha's first four-cylinder midsize engine series, which powers all these bikes, set new standards for performance when introduced in 1981 and has proven rugged and dependable over the years. The same basic engine design was still used in the 1998 Seca II.

FJ600

Although it was considered a sportbike in its day, the FJ seems like a standard now. With its frame-mounted half-fairing and sporty riding position, this bike is still striking. If you can find a clean example, buy it.

YX600 Radian

The successor to the FJ600 had all that bike's mechanical virtues but lacked the FJ's style. It's still a good bike, though.

XJ600S Seca II

If a new Seca II costing $5,300 was a best buy, then buying an older version of the exact same machine for $3,000 less should earn the buyer a place in the bargain-hunter's hall of fame.

Appendix C

Resources

Throughout this book, I've discussed what a wonderful community of people you will meet when you become a motorcyclist. This appendix tells you how to get in touch with that community. I list the addresses of some major clubs and organizations, and I also tell you where you can find all the books, videotapes, accessories, and other paraphernalia you'll want and need.

Motorcycle Safety Foundation (MSF)

The Motorcycle Safety Foundation is a national nonprofit organization sponsored by the U.S. distributors of BMW, Ducati, Honda, Kawasaki, Suzuki, and Yamaha motorcycles. I've tried to stress the value of taking a Motorcycle Safety Foundation RiderCourse, but in case I haven't made myself perfectly clear, taking such a course can save your life. No other action you can take will help you have a safer motorcycling career. To find a RiderCourse near you, contact:

Motorcycle Safety Foundation
2 Jenner St., Suite 150
Irvine, CA 92718–3812
1-800-446-9227
www.msf-usa.org

American Motorcyclist Association (AMA)

Taking an MSF RiderCourse is the most important thing you can do to help make you a safer rider. Joining the AMA is the most important thing you can do to safeguard your rights as a motorcyclist. Contact the AMA today at:

American Motorcyclist Association
13515 Yarmouth Dr.
Pickerington, OH 43147
1-800-AMA-JOIN
www.ama-cycle.org

Clubs and Organizations

As I said in Chapter 19, joining a club can be your best way to get in touch with your local motorcycling community. The following list gives you the names and addresses of just a few of the thousands of clubs available.

Biker Scum

Biker Scum is a motorcycle group dedicated to the pursuit of happiness through riding and the neglect of personal hygiene. Their goal is to form a worldwide network of riders, connected via the Internet, who assist other motorcyclists when planning trips, specifically by giving them advice on local roads and brew pubs. So far, they have chapters in Pennsylvania; Texas; Virginia; California; Indiana; Ontario, Canada; and Okinawa, Japan. To contact Biker Scum, send e-mail to:

http://drlubell.home.mindspring.com/bscum.html

Blue Knights

The Blue Knights is a club specifically for law-enforcement officials, with chapters located in all 50 states. To find the chapter nearest you, contact:

Blue Knights International Law Enforcement Motorcycle Club, Inc.
International Headquarters
38 Alden St.
Bangor, ME 04401
1-800-BKI-LEMC (prospective members only)

BMW Motorcycle Owners of America (BMWMOA)

BMWMOA has chapters across the country and puts on some of the best rallies you'll find anywhere. Plus, it puts out an excellent monthly magazine. You can contact its national headquarters at:

BMW Motorcycle Owners of America
PO Box 3982
Ballwin, MO 63022
636-394-7277
www.bmwmoa.org

Christian Motorcyclists Association (CMA)

As I said in Chapter 1, motorcycling is a spiritual activity—so much so that some people like to formally combine it with their religion. If you would like to do the same, a great way to do so is by joining the CMA. These folks put on some terrific events and have chapters all across the country. Contact them at:

Christian Motorcyclists Association
PO Box 9
Highway 71 South
Hatfield, AR 71945
870-389-6196
www.cmausa.org

Gold Wing Road Riders Association (GWRRA)

GWRRA is the largest club in the world devoted to a single motorcycle: the Honda Gold Wing. Membership is open to owners of the ultimate behemoth, as well as Honda Valkyries. You can contact GWRRA at:

GWRRA International Headquarters
21423 N. 11th Ave.
Phoenix, AZ 85027
www.gwrra.org

Motor Maids

Motor Maids is not only one of the oldest clubs for female motorcyclists; it's one of the oldest motorcycle clubs, period. Some of the women still riding with Motor Maids were dispatch motorcyclists in World War II. Contact them at:

Motor Maids
PO Box 157
Erie, MI 48133
www.motormaids.org

Retreads Motorcycle Club International, Inc.

Retreads Motorcycle Club International boasts a membership of 5,000 motorcyclists, and all of them have at least two things in common: they have reached the age of 40, and they love to ride motorcycles. If you are interested in locating a club near you, just go to the club's home page:

http://retreads.org

Turbo Motorcycle International Owners Association (TMIOA)

The TMIOA is a club for owners of all the factory turbo-charged motorcycles. You can contact them at:

Turbo Motorcycle International Owners Association
PO Box 1653
Albrightsville, PA 18210
http://turbomotorcycles.org

Women On Wheels (WOW)

I've spent some time with members of this motorcycle club for women and have found them to be some of the most enjoyable motorcyclists I've ever ridden with. If you are a female motorcyclist, I highly recommend joining your local chapter of WOW. To find your nearest chapter, contact Women On Wheels at:

WOW International Headquarters
PO Box 14180
St. Paul, MN 55114
1-800-322-1969
www.womenonwheels.org

Ronnie Cramer's Motorcycle Web Index—Clubs/Organizations

This site has the most complete listing I've found of motorcycle clubs and organizations. If there is a club—or even a type of club—you're looking for, you should be able to find it here. Check out Ronnie Cramer's Motorcycle Web:

www.sepnet.com/cycle

Books and Videotapes

You can learn anything you've ever wanted to know about motorcycles and motorcycling by reading one of the tens of thousands of books available on the subject.

Whitehorse Press

Whitehorse Press publishes and distributes nothing but motorcycle books. It's owned and operated by Dan and Judy Kennedy, both of whom are devoted motorcyclists as well as publishers, and that devotion to the sport shows in their books. Whitehorse publishes many excellent books on motorcycling, and its catalog contains one of the most complete selections of motorcycle-related books and products you'll find anywhere. To obtain the latest catalog, contact them at:

Whitehorse Press
107 E. Conway Road
Center Conway, NH 03813-4012
1-800-531-1133
www.whitehorsepress.com

Motorbooks International

Motorbooks International publishes and distributes books on all aspects of vehicular culture, from antique tractors to airplanes. It also produces and distributes an incredibly diverse collection of motorcycle books. You can order a catalog at:

Motorbooks International
PO Box 1
Osceola, WI 54020-0001
1-800-826-6600
www.motorbooks.com

Web Pages

You can find literally hundreds of motorcycle-related web pages on the Internet. My favorites are the ones that update their content on a daily basis. The great thing about these webzines is that they have absolutely up-to-the-minute news. Within minutes of the finish of a national or international race, you can log on to one of the racing-oriented sites such as www.speedtv.com and get the latest points standings. If a racer is injured, you can monitor his condition by checking the Internet. When a company releases a new model of motorcycle, you don't have to wait months to see it on the cover of a magazine because it is instantaneously broadcast over the Internet.

While there is a nearly infinite number of motorcycle-related web pages on the Internet, I just want to list a few of my personal favorites, along with their addresses. Again, this is my subjective listing, so do your own research because you may find magazines that you like far better than the ones listed here.

AMA Superbike: www.superbikeplanet.com

American Motorcycle: www.americanmotor.com

MotoGP: http://motogp.tiscali.com/en/motogp/index.htm

Motoworld.com: www.motoworld.com

Motorcycle Daily: www.motorcycledaily.com

Motor Cycle News: www.motorcyclenews.com

Motorcycle Online: www.motorcycle.com

Motorcycle World: www.motorcycleworld.com

Roadracing World: http://venus.13x.com/roadracingworld/

Speed Channel: www.speedtv.com

Motorcyclist, *Motorcycle Cruiser*, and others: www.primedia.com/divisions/enthusiastmedia

Mailing Lists

To find mailing lists related to your particular motorcycling interests, start searching around on the Internet. There you will find the home pages of such lists, along with instructions on joining the group.

Suggested Reading

The following list includes some of the most important books you can read when starting out as a motorcyclist. Everyone has their own preferences and individual tastes, so any suggested reading list has to be somewhat subjective. But whatever your tastes, you will find the following books useful:

Harley-Davidson Evolution Motorcycles
Greg Field
Motorbooks International, hardbound, 2001, 192 pages
This book covers Harley history from The Motor Company's precipitous decline and near bankruptcy in the late 1970s and first half of the 1980s to its resurrection and eventual return to the No. 1 position in the American market. Author Greg Field has done a fantastic job researching company history and the history of the Evolution engine family, the series of engines that powered Harley's remarkable comeback. This is one of my favorite motorcycle books.

Harley-Davidson in the 1960s
Allan Girdler and Jeff Hackett
Motorbooks International, softbound, 2001, 96 pages
Author Allan Girdler and photographer Jeff Hackett document the history of the most important American motorcycle company of all time during the tumultuous 1960s. This was a time when the monolithic corporation AMF bought out the original families that had run Harley Davidson since the company's inception just after the turn of the century.

A Century of Indian
Ed Youngblood
Motorbooks International, hardbound, 2001, 156 pages
This beautifully photographed book tells the story of Indian motorcycles through the "Century of Indian" exhibit at the Motorcycle Hall of Fame Museum. Youngblood developed the book in conjunction with his work developing the exhibit and penned the informative yet entertaining text that accompanies the photography.

Honda Gold Wing
Darwin Holmstrom
Whitehorse Press, softbound, 2001, 96 pages
The story of the Gold Wing is, in many ways, the story of American motorcycling, making this a worthy read for anyone interested in the sport. Besides, I wrote it. Hey, if you've gotten this far, you can't hate my writing. Yes, this is a shameless plug.

How to Set Up Your Motorcycle Workshop: Designing, Tooling, and Stocking
Charles G. Masi
Whitehorse Press, softbound, 1996, 160 pages
This book can save you a lot of headaches (as well as a lot of aches in other places) when doing your own motorcycle maintenance. Masi even manages to make the subject entertaining, with his offbeat sense of humor.

Against the Wind—A Rider's Account of the Incredible Iron Butt Rally
Ron Ayres
Whitehorse Press, softbound, 1997, 240 pages
This book gives you an inside look at what it is like to compete in one of the most demanding motorcycle endurance events in the world. Ayres's storytelling skills make what is already a fascinating story even more fun to read.

Pictorial History of Japanese Motorcycles
Cornelis Vanderheuvel
Elmar/Bay View Books, hardbound, 1997, 168 pages
(distributed by Classic Motorbooks)
This book does an excellent job of chronicling the evolution of the Japanese motorcycle industry—an evolution that helped make motorcycling accessible to most of the people riding today. More than 375 color illustrations are included.

One Man Caravan
Robert Edison Fulton Jr.
Whitehorse Press, softbound, 1996, 288 pages
In this book, Fulton chronicles his 17-month around-the-world motorcycle trip, which he began in 1932. In this fascinating story, Fulton gives the reader an idea of what it was like to tour on a motorcycle in the days before electric starters and gas stations on every corner.

Motorcycle Owner's Manual: A Practical Guide to Keeping Your Motorcycle in Top Condition
Hugo Wilson
DK Publishing, softbound, 1997, 112 pages
(distributed by Whitehorse Press)
This book won't replace a good repair manual specifically for your bike, as the author himself admits, but it serves as an excellent additional source of information. General procedures are explained much more clearly than in most manuals, and the photos are easier to follow.

The Motorcycle Safety Foundation's Guide to Motorcycling Excellence: Skills, Knowledge, and Strategies for Riding Right
Motorcycle Safety Foundation

Whitehorse Press, softbound, 1995, 176 pages
If you can't take a RiderCourse, at least buy the Motorcycle Safety Foundation's book, which is a collection of its instructional material. If I discovered that any idea, technique, or practice I discussed in this book differed from MSF practice, I deferred to them—these folks know what they're doing, and they know how to save lives.

World Superbikes: The First Ten Years
Julian Ryder, photographs by Kel Edge
Haynes Publishing, softbound, 1997, 160 pages
(distributed by Classic Motorbooks)
When World Superbike racing first began in 1988, journalist Julian Ryder left the Grand Prix circuit to cover the new series. He's been doing so ever since, and now he's written a book chronicling the first decade of the immensely popular series. His in-depth knowledge of the racers and the sport in general make this a gripping book, and Edge's photography is superb.

Ducati Story: Racing and Production Models 1945 to the Present Day
Ian Falloon
Patrick Stephens Limited, hardbound, 1996, 160 pages
(distributed by Classic Motorbooks)
During the past decade, many books have been written about Ducati. This is one of the best of those books. *Ducati Story* is a case study in how to build the finest high-performance motorcycles in the world and how *not* to conduct a business. Motorcyclists and business types alike should find this a fascinating book.

Zen and the Art of Motorcycle Maintenance: An Inquiry into Values
Robert M. Persig
Bantam Books, softbound, 1974, 380 pages
(distributed by Whitehorse Press)
I try to reread Persig's motorcycle classic at least once a year, and each time, it is like reading a different book. It may prove a tough read for those without a philosophical bent, but it is worth the effort.

Hell's Angels: A Strange and Terrible Saga
Dr. Hunter S. Thompson
Ballantine Books, softbound, 1967, 276 pages
(distributed by Whitehorse Press)
Hunter S. Thompson may be more famous for his excessive lifestyle than for his writing, but long after everyone has forgotten about his excesses, his writing will live on. His command of the English language rivals that of any author, living or dead, and when he chooses to write about motorcycles, so much the better.

Recommended Viewing

Street Smarts: The Advanced Course in Urban Survival video series
Produced by Paul Winters and David West, distributed by Whitehorse Press
Nothing compares to taking an MSF RiderCourse, but if you choose not to do so, at least buy these three videos—they may save your life. Much of the material presented in the videos is covered in a RiderCourse, and while you won't benefit from individual instruction and instructor feedback, you'll at least be able to see how it's done. Ideally, you should take a RiderCourse and buy these videos. Considering what's at stake, the relatively low cost of these videos represents one of the best investments you can make.

Parts and Accessories

In the long run, you're better off buying as many motorcycle supplies as you can from your local dealers, but often you won't be able to find what you want locally, and you'll have to look elsewhere. The following list provides you with names, addresses, and phone numbers where you can find just about anything you need.

Aerostich

To get one of Aerostich's fantastic riding suits, you're going to have to go directly to the source and give owner Andy Goldfine a call. Even if you're not in the market for a riding suit, you should contact him and get a copy of the Aerostich catalog, which contains the most useful collection of quality riding accessories you'll find anywhere. It is also the most entertaining catalog you'll ever read.

Aero Design
8 S. 18th Ave. West
Duluth, MN 55806-2148
1-800-222-1994
www.aerostich.com

Chaparral Motorsports

Chaparral has one of the widest selections of gear and accessories for both on- and off-road riding you'll find anywhere. Contact them at:

Chaparral Motorsports
555 S. H St.
San Bernardino, CA 92410
1-800-841-2960
www.chaparral-racing.com

Dennis Kirk, Inc.

Dennis Kirk may not always have the lowest prices on all items, but they have an incredibly wide selection and they get your stuff to you fast. Besides, on some items, they will match the best price you can find elsewhere. Contact them at:

Dennis Kirk, Inc.
955 S. Field Ave.
Rush City, MN 55069
1-800-328-9280
www.denniskirk.com

Dynojet Research, Inc.

Many motorcycles come with their carburetion set too lean. Not only does this hinder performance, but it can cause your engine to run hot, especially if you install an aftermarket air filter. If your bike suffers from such problems, or if you just want to improve its overall performance, the helpful folks at Dynojet Research can set you up with just the carburetor jetting kit. Contact them at:

Dynojet Research, Inc.
2191 Mendenhall Dr.
North Las Vegas, NV 89081
1-800-992-4993 or 1-800-992-3525
www.dynojet.com

J&P Cycles

If you have a Harley-Davidson garbage wagon and want to chop it, if you have a basket-case Harley chopper and want to refurbish it, if you want to spiff up your Harley, or if you just want to build a complete motorcycle from spare parts, you'll find everything you need to do so in the J&P Cycles catalog. Contact them at:

J&P Cycles
PO Box 138
13225 Circle Dr.
Anamosa, IA 52205
1-800-397-4844
www.j-pcycles.com
jpcycles@netins.net

JC Whitney

If you're a careful shopper, you can get some killer buys on motorcycle accessories from JC Whitney. Although inexpensive, some of the items JC Whitney carries are of surprisingly high quality. You can contact them at:

JC Whitney
1 JC Whitney Way
LaSalle, IL 61301
1-800-603-4383
www.jcwhitney.com

National Cycle, Inc.

National Cycle builds some of the finest aftermarket windshields and fairings you can buy. I've owned six of them and have found them all to be of the highest quality. You can purchase products from any shop or catalog, but if you call the folks at National Cycle and order direct, they can help you select the windshield or accessory that best fulfills your needs. It is a tremendous opportunity for you to benefit from their experience. Contact National Cycle at:

National Cycle, Inc.
2200 S. Maywood Dr.
PO Box 158
Maywood, IL 60153
1-877-972-7336
www.nationalcycle.com

Sport Wheels

Ex-racer Denny Kannenberg owns more motorcycles than anybody—at least 10,000, at last count. He also owns the world's largest motorcycle-salvage operation, meaning that he has more used parts to sell than anyone else. And even though he's located in Jordan, Minnesota, he does business with motorcyclists across the country. If you ever need something—whether it is a part or a complete motorcycle—and can't find it, give Denny a call. You can contact Sport Wheels at:

1-800-821-5975
www.sportwheel.com

Tuners and Builders

As a new rider, you really don't need to make your motorcycle any faster than it is. I'm not trying to be a wet blanket; it's just that today's motorcycles are ultra-high-performance machines right out of the crate. If you do want more power, the following people can help you out.

Graves Motorsports, Inc.

Chuck Graves knows a thing or two about building fast bikes. In 1993, he won the Formula USA championship, and he's a four-time Willow Springs Formula One champion. Contact him at:

Graves Motorsports, Inc.
7645 Densmore Ave.
Van Nuys, CA 91406
818-902-1942
www.gravesports.com

Hahn Racecraft

Bill Hahn's claim to fame is building motorcycles for drag racing. For a price, he'll help you build what will without a doubt be the quickest motorcycle in town. Contact him at:

Hahn Racecraft
1981 D Wiesbrook Dr.
Oswego, IL 60543
630-801-1417
www.hahnracecraft.com

HyperCycle

If, for some reason, you want a flat-out AMA Superbike for the street, you should get a hold of the folks at HyperCycle. Contact them at:

HyperCycle
15941 Arminta St.
Van Nuys, CA 91406
1-877-486-3125
www.hypercycle.com

Mr. Turbo

Mr. Turbo builds turbo kits for a variety of motorcycles, from ZX11 Ninjas to Harley dressers. Contact them at:

Mr. Turbo
4014 Hopper Road
Houston, TX 77093
281-442-7113
www.mrturbo.com

Racing Clubs

The following is a list of clubs that can help you get started in motorcycle road racing.

American Federation of Motorcyclists
6167 Jarvis Ave. #333
Newark, CA 94560
510-796-7005
www.afmracing.org

American Historic Racing Motorcycle Association
PO Box 1648
Brighton, MN 48116
810-225-6085
www.ahrma.org

Central Motorcycle Roadracing Association
PO Box 123888
Ft. Worth, TX 76121-3888
1-817-377-1599
www.cmaracing.com

Central Roadracing Association Inc.
PO Box 5385
Hopkins, MN 55343
612-332-4070

Hallett Road Racing Association
www.hallettracing.com/comma.html

Mid-Atlantic Road Racing Club
PO Box 2292
Wheaton, MD 20915
703-494-9394
http://marrc.nova.org

Motorcycle Roadracing Association
PO Box 4187
Denver, CO 80204
303-530-5678
www.mra-racing.org

Northern California Mini Road Racing Association
PO Box 2791
Citrus Heights, CA 95611-2791
916-722-5517

Oregon Motorcycle Road Racing Association
www.omrra.com

Utah Sport Bike Association
www.utahsba.com

Washington Motorcycle Road Racing Association
www.wmrra.com

Western Eastern Roadracers' Association
www.wera.com

Willow Springs Motorcycle Club
PO Box 911
http://members.aol.com/racewsmc/

High-Performance Riding Schools

Besides taking the Experienced RiderCourse from the Motorcycle Safety Foundation, the best way to improve your riding skills (and your chances of having an injury-free riding career) is to take a course in high-performance riding. Whether you are going racing or you just want to hone your street-riding skills, taking a quality high-performance riding course can teach you things that can save your life. Usually these schools are expensive, but if they can make you a better (and safer) rider, they are worth the money.

Although most of these schools have their headquarters in the American Southwest, many conduct classes at different racetracks around the country, making it easier for riders to attend. Call or write for a schedule of class dates and locations.

CLASS Motorcycle Schools
320 E. Santa Maria St., Suite M
Santa Paula, CA 93060-3800
805-933-9936
www.classrides.com

DP Safety School
PO Box 1551
Morro Bay, CA 93443
805-772-8301
www.dpsafetyschool.com/main.html

Freddie Spencer's High Performance Riding School
7055 Speedway Blvd., Suite E106
Las Vegas, NV 89115
1-888-672-7219
www.fastfreddie.com

California Superbike School
940 San Fernando Road
Los Angeles, CA 90065
323-224-2734
www.superbikeschool.com/us/index.shtml

STAR Motorcycle School
www.starmotorcycle.com

Appendix D

Cycle Babble Glossary

ABS (Antilock Brake System) System that detects when a wheel is not turning and releases pressure to the brake on that wheel, preventing a skid.

aftermarket The sector of the market that sells parts and accessories other than original equipment manufacturers (OEMs).

Airheads A term for older, air-cooled BMW Boxer Twins.

ape hangers A term coined at the height of the custom-bike movement to describe tall handlebars that forced the rider to reach skyward to grasp the controls, making the rider adopt an apelike posture.

bagger A motorcycle equipped with saddlebags and other touring amenities.

belt-drive system A final-drive system that transmits the power to the rear wheel via a drive belt.

Big Twins The engines in the larger Harley-Davidson bikes.

bobbers The custom bikes American riders built after World War II. The owners cut off, or bobbed, much of the bodywork.

bottom end The bottom part of the engine, where the crankshaft and (usually) the transmission reside.

Boxer A two-cylinder engine with the pistons opposing each other, resembling fists flying away from each other.

brakes (disc and drum) Disc brakes use stationary calipers that squeeze pads against the discs that rotate with the wheel. Drum brakes use horseshoe-shape brake shoes that expand against the inner surface of the wheel hub.

café chop Converting a stock motorcycle into a café racer.

café racer Motorcycles modified to resemble racing motorcycles from the 1950s and '60s. They are called café racers because their owners supposedly raced from café to café in London, where the bikes first appeared in the 1960s.

cam A rod with eccentric lobes on it that opens the valves.

carbon fiber A high-tech material favored in many motorcycle applications because it is extremely strong and light. The distinctive look of carbon fiber has become trendy.

carburetor A device that mixes fuel with air to create the fuel charge burned in the combustion chamber.

cases The two clamshell-like halves in the bottom end of the engine, surrounded by a metal shell.

centerstand A stand that supports the motorcycle in an upright position.

centerstand tang A small lever attached to the centerstand.

chain-drive system A final-drive system that transmits the power to the rear wheel via a chain.

chassis The combined frame and suspension on a motorcycle.

chopper Once used to describe a custom motorcycle that had all superfluous parts chopped off in order to make the bike faster, a chopper today is a type of custom bike that usually has an extended fork, no rear suspension, and high handlebars.

clip-ons Handlebars that attach directly to the fork tubes, rather than to the top yoke, and hold the fork tubes together.

clutch A device that disengages power from the crankshaft to the transmission, allowing a rider to change gears.

combustion chamber The area at the top of the cylinder where the fuel charge burns and pushes the pistons down.

coming on the cam The term used when a four-stroke reaches its powerband.

coming on the pipe The term used when a two-stroke reaches its powerband.

connecting rods Rods that attach the crankshaft to the pistons via the eccentric journals. The rods' up-and-down movement is converted into a circular motion through the design of the journals.

constant-radius turn A turn with a steady, constant arc. In a decreasing-radius corner, the arc gets sharper as you progress through the curve, while in an increasing-radius corner, the arc becomes less sharp.

contact patch The area of your tire that actually contacts the road while you ride.

counterbalancer A weight inside an engine that cancels some of the engine's vibration.

countersteering The way you use the handlebar(s) to lean the bike into a turn. If you want to turn right, you push the handlebar(s) to the left, and vice versa.

cowling A piece of bodywork that covers the engine area.

crotch rocket A term some people use to refer to sportbikes.

crowns The tops of the pistons.

cycle The up-and-down motion of the piston. The terms *cycle* and *stroke* are used interchangeably when referring to engine types.

cylinder block The hunk of aluminum with holes bored through it, inside which the pistons move up and down.

cylinders The hollow shafts in the top end of an engine inside which internal combustion occurs.

decreasing-radius corner A turn in which the arc gets sharper as you progress through the curve.

dirtbike Bikes intended for off-road use that aren't legal to ride on public roads. Sometimes the term *pure-dirt* is used to distinguish a dirtbike from a dual-sport motorcycle.

discs The metal rotors the caliper presses the pads against to brake.

double-cradle frame A bike frame with two steel tubes circling the engine from the front and cradling it.

dresser A motorcycle set up for long-distance touring.

dual-sport Street-legal motorcycles with varying degrees of off-road capabilities. Also called dual-purpose motorcycles.

eccentric journals Used to attach the connecting rods to the crankshaft.

ergonomics The science used to design devices, systems, and physical conditions that conform to the human body. This is a prime consideration when designing a motorcycle.

Evolution (Evo) When Harley-Davidson began using aluminum to build its cylinder jugs, it called this new engine the Evolution.

fairings The devices mounted at the front of a motorcycle to protect the rider from the elements. These range from simple, Plexiglas shields to complex, encompassing body panels.

false neutral When you fail to engage gears and the transmission behaves as though it is in neutral, even though it isn't.

flat cylinders Cylinders arranged in a flat, opposing configuration, found in the flat-four- and flat-six-cylinder engines used in Honda's Gold Wings.

foot paddling The way an unskilled rider walks his or her motorcycle around at low speeds.

forks The metal tubes holding the front wheel to the rest of the motorcycle.

four-cylinder bike A motorcycle with four cylinders.

fuel-injection system System that mixes the fuel-air charges and forcibly injects them into the combustion chambers, unlike carburetors, which rely on the vacuum created by the engine to draw the charges into the combustion chambers.

garbage wagon A scornful term used by some outlaw bikers to describe touring bikes.

gearhead A person with a strong interest in all things mechanical; a motorcyclist.

gearset A set of gears within a bike's transmission.

high-siding Pitching a bike over away from the direction you are turning. This is the most dangerous kind of crash.

horsepower A measure of an engine's strength.

hydroplane When your tires start to float on top of water, causing them to lose contact with the road's surface.

increasing-radius corner A turn in which the arc becomes less sharp as you go through the curve.

inline-four An engine with four cylinders in a row.

inline-triple An engine with three cylinders placed in a row.

Iron Butt Rally The most grueling long-distance motorcycle rally in the world. The rally requires that you ride at least 11,000 miles in 11 days to finish.

Knucklehead A term for Harley-Davidson's first overhead-valve Big Twin, introduced in 1936.

L-twin engine A V-twin engine with its cylinders splayed apart at a 90-degree angle, which creates a smoother-running engine. These engines can be placed either transversely (crosswise) or longitudinally (lengthwise) in the motorcycle frame.

lane splitting Riding between lanes of traffic on a freeway.

laying the bike down A crash in which you slide down on one side of the bike.

leviathan Used to describe big, multicylinder dual-sports.

lugging the engine Letting the rpm fall below the engine's powerband.

manual transmission A device consisting of a set of gears (the gearset) that alter the final-drive ratio of a vehicle to enable an operator to get up to speed. Automatic transmissions do not have gearsets; they use a complex system of fluid and metal bands to vary the final-drive ratio of a vehicle.

naked bikes Bikes without any type of fairing.

Oilheads Newer, air-and-oil-cooled BMW Boxer engines.

open-class When referring to street-legal sportbikes, open-class designates motorcycles with engines that displace more than 800 cubic centimeters of volume.

original equipment manufacturers (OEM) The companies that build the bikes.

orphan bikes Rare bikes that are no longer in production.

Otto cycle Term sometimes used for the four-stroke engine, in honor of its inventor, Otto Benz.

overbore When you overbore your engine, you drill out the cylinders and then put oversize pistons in the holes, effectively increasing your engine capacity.

overhead-cam system A system in which the cam rides above the cylinder head. There are single-overhead-cam (SOHC) and double-overhead-cam (DOHC) designs.

Panhead A term for Harley-Davidson's second-generation overhead-valve Big Twin, introduced in 1948.

parallel-twin engine A two-cylinder engine with its cylinders placed side by side in an upright position.

pistons The slugs moving up and down within the cylinders.

powerband A certain rpm (revolutions per minute—how many times per minute an engine's crankshaft spins around) range in which an engine makes most of its power.

primary drive A drive system—via gears, chain, or belt—connecting the engine's crankshaft to its clutch, and from there to its transmission.

production motorcycles The bikes manufacturers produce to sell to the general public, rather than bikes built specifically for racers.

pushrod system System in which the cams are generally located below the cylinder heads and push on the rocker arms by moving long rods, called the pushrods.

radial When used to describe a tire, refers to the way the cords of a tire are constructed.

rain grooves Channels cut into a road's surface to help water run off the road during a rainstorm.

repair link A link in some motorcycle chains that can be disassembled for chain repair.

repli-racers Hard-edged sportbikes. These motorcycles are characterized by riding positions that tuck the rider into an extreme crouch, forcing him or her to practically lay down on the fuel tank.

revolutions per minute (rpm) The number of times the crankshaft spins around each minute. Often the term *revs* is used, especially in conversation.

riding two-up Carrying a passenger on your bike.

rocker arms Devices that work like upside-down teeter totters and push on the valve stems.

rubber-mounted Engines that use a system of rubber cushions and/or jointed engine mounts to isolate engine vibration from the rider.

shaft-drive system A final-drive system that transmits the power to the rear wheel via a drive shaft.

shaft jacking Shaky or bumpy motion created by the impact of acceleration and then fed back into the bike's frame.

Shovelhead A term for Harley's third-generation overhead-valve Big Twin engine, introduced in 1966.

sidecars Small carriages attached to the side of a motorcycle to provide extra carrying capacity.

sissybar The backrest put behind the passenger's portion of the saddle.

snicking The act of shifting a well-functioning transmission is often called snicking because that's the sound the action makes. A transmission that doesn't snick into gear is described as sloppy-shifting.

solid-mounted Engine that is bolted directly to the frame tubes.

splitting the cases The metal shell surrounding the bottom end is composed of two clamshell-like halves, called cases. Taking these apart to repair the motor is called splitting the cases. *See also* bottom end.

sport-tourer A motorcycle that combines the comfort and carrying capacity of a touring bike with the handling and power of a sportbike, with larger fairings and hard, lockable luggage.

sportbike A motorcycle designed for optimal speed and handling characteristics, often with extensive bodywork.

springer fork Springer forks use large, exposed springs to dampen the impact of road irregularities.

squid Someone who rides a sportbike on the street as if he or she were on a racetrack.

steering geometry The geometrical relationship between the motorcycle frame, the angle of the fork, and the position of the front tire.

streetfighter A bare-bones sportbike, stripped of all extraneous body work (also called a hooligan or naked bike).

stroke The up-and-down motion of the piston.

suspension The forks, shocks, and, to a degree, tires of a motorcycle. The springs, fluids, and air in and construction of the tires in these items support the motorcycle.

tappets Small metal slugs between the cam and the pushrod or rocker arm.

Telelever system The most successful alternate front suspension, made by BMW, which transfers the shock-absorption function of a hydraulic fork to a shock absorber located behind the steering head.

thumper Bikes with large-displacement, single-cylinder, four-stroke engines.

top end The upper part of the engine, which contains the pistons, cylinders, and valve gear, and the induction system, which consists of the apparatus that mixes an air-and-fuel charge and feeds it into the combustion chamber.

torque A twisting force and, in a motorcycle, a measure of the leverage the engine exerts on the rear wheel.

touring bike A bike equipped for longer rides with fairings and lockable saddlebags.

traction A tire's ability to grip the road.

travel The distance that suspension components—the forks and shocks—move when the bike rides over bumps.

twin-spar frame A bike frame with two steel or aluminum spars (flat beams) that pass around or over the engine.

two-up A term for carrying a passenger on your motorcycle.

two-stroke engine An engine whose power cycle consists of just two movements, or strokes: The piston moves down, drawing in the fuel-air charge, and then up, combusting the charge.

unitized transmission A transmission (often referred to as a unit transmission) that is an integral part of the engine's bottom end.

Universal Japanese Motorcycle (UJM) During the 1970s, the Japanese became so identified with the four-cylinder, standard-style motorcycle that this term was coined to describe them.

V-four An engine of four cylinders, arranged in a V-shape configuration, with two cylinders on each side of the V.

V-twin A two-cylinder engine with its cylinders placed in a V shape.

valve guides Metal tubes that house the valves.

valve train The system of valves that lets the fuel charges in and the exhaust gases out.

valves Devices consisting of metal stems with flat discs on one end that open and close to let fuel charges in and exhaust gases out.

Index

A

B

C

D

E

F

R

S

T

U

V

W-X

Y-Z